DAKOTA PHILOSOPHER

DAKOTA PHILOSOPHER

Charles Eastman and American Indian Thought

DAVID MARTÍNEZ

MINNESOTA HISTORICAL SOCIETY PRESS

www.mhspress.org

The Minnesota Historical Society Press is a member of the Association of American University Presses.

Manufactured in the United States of America

10 9 8 7 6 5 4 3 2 1

♾ The paper used in this publication meets the minimum require- ments of the American National Standard for Information Sciences— Permanence for Printed Library Materials, ANSI Z39.48-1984.

International Standard Book Number
ISBN 13: 978-0-87351-629-7 (paper)
ISBN 10: 0-87351-629-X (paper)

Library of Congress Cataloging-in-Publication Data
Martínez, David, 1963–
Dakota philosopher: Charles Eastman and American Indian thought / David Martínez.
    p.   cm.
Includes bibliographical references and index.
ISBN-13: 978-0-87351-629-7 (pbk.: alk. paper)
ISBN-10: 0-87351-629-X (pbk.: alk. paper)
    1. Eastman, Charles Alexander, 1858–1939.
    2. Santee Indians—Biography.
    3. Dakota philosophy.
    4. Dakota Indians—Religion.
    5. Dakota Indians—Social life and customs.
    6. American literature—Indian authors.
    7. Indians in literature.
    I. Title.
E99.S22E183 2009
299′.7852—dc22
2008023162

Frontispiece: Charles Eastman, 1906, courtesy Library of Congress

To my mom,

Marilyn T. Martínez,

Living proof that Indian women make the best mothers

CONTENTS

5
Exile From *Mnisota Makoce*
Eastman and the 1862 U.S.–Dakota War / *123*

Stranger in America
Eastman as Role Model

I am an Indian, and am well aware of the difficulties
I have to encounter to win the favorable notice of the white man
George Copway, *The Life of Kah-ge-ga-gah-bowh*

Being an Indian in the world is the loneliest kind of existence. At least, such is the case when one leaves behind the comfort and security of family and tribe for the wider world of modern societies, such as the metropolitan areas that now dominate the American landscape. Even before the Americans completed their colonization of the "frontier," Indians often found themselves as the proverbial—certainly ironic— stranger in a strange land. Charles A. Eastman's experience with the phenomenon of strangeness occurs throughout his classic 1916 auto- biography, *From the Deep Woods to Civilization.* On his way to the Santee Indian School, Eastman encountered a family of sod farmers, from whom he bargained some food and lodging for the night. Having never dined with a white family before, Eastman uneasily took his place at the table, stating, "I felt not unlike a young blue heron just leaving the nest to partake of his first meal on an unsafe, swinging branch. I was entirely uncertain of my perch."[1]

Then, after receiving news of his father's death while attending the Santee school, Eastman made the resounding commitment to continue following the path to education upon which his father had set him, which took him to Beloit College in Wisconsin in September 1876, where he saw evidence of the Mound Builder civilization on campus, the Rock River once so beloved to Black Hawk, and two male students who referred to him as "Sitting Bull's nephew." These incidences were followed by an account of Eastman's first recitation for a Professor Petti- bone. Although Eastman felt confident about his intellectual abilities, speaking in English was still his Achilles' heel. He was not only far from home but also in a completely different cultural universe. Yet, as Eastman tells it, he persevered and prevailed in the English-only, Anglo-American world where he found himself:

> I was now a stranger in a strange country, and deep in a strange life from which I could not retreat. I was like a deaf man with eyes continually on the alert for the expression of faces, and to find them in general friendly toward me was somewhat reassuring. In spite of some nerve-trying moments, I soon recovered my balance and set to work. I absorbed knowledge through every pore. The more I got, the larger my capacity grew, and my appetite increased in proportion. I discovered that my anticipations of this new life were nearly all wrong, and was suddenly confronted with problems entirely foreign to my experience. If I had been told to swim across a lake, or run with a message through an unknown country, I should have had some conception of the task; but the idea of each word as having an office and a place and a specific name, and standing in relation to other words like the bricks in a wall, was almost beyond my grasp. As for history and geography, to me they were legends and traditions, and I soon learned to appreciate the pure logic of mathematics. A recent letter from a Beloit schoolmate says, "You were the only boy who could beat me in algebra!"[2]

As many college students soon learn, the world became even stranger upon leaving campus. Eastman got a taste of this strangeness when he left Beloit for Knox College in Illinois, stopping to change trains in Chicago. It was here where, on the one hand, Eastman realized "the day of the Indian had passed forever," while, on the other, he "was cautioned against trusting strangers, and told that [he] must look out for pickpockets." Compared to the times he was stared at and asked awkward questions while in white society, Eastman's return to Indian Country—specifically, the Pine Ridge Agency in South Dakota—as a "'white doctor' who was also an Indian" was conspicuously less stressful. Although, as Eastman later learned, "there were many and diverse speculations abroad as to my success or failure in this new role . . . at the time I was unconscious of an audience." Life, however, was much more disorienting after Eastman and his new family were compelled to move from Pine Ridge in the wake of the Wounded Knee Massacre to St. Paul, Minnesota, where he attempted to start up a private practice, of which Eastman wrote: "Although a young couple in a strange city, we were cordially received socially, and while seriously handicapped by lack of means, we had determined to win out. I opened an office, hung out my sign, and waited for patients. It was the hardest work I had ever done!"[3]

Between ongoing financial concerns and a growing interest in community service on behalf of American Indians, Eastman's life never became very comfortable. This hardship, though, only added to his knowledge and wisdom as a popular writer and much-sought public speaker. Nonetheless, Eastman continues to be taunted by latter-day critics for his assimilationist tendencies, as if he were the Dakota equivalent to Dinesh D'Souza. Although Eastman was known to mingle with the Republicans of his day, he always advocated for the interests and well-being of American Indians. Indeed, it is important to consider the fact that he induced many in the Anglo-American community to listen when they most urgently needed to hear about the so-called "Indian problem" from an Indian perspective. Eastman was promoting Indian rights many years before the 1934 Wheeler-Howard Act and generations before the Red Power movement. Just as important, it should not be overlooked that Eastman, although college-educated, was never an academic in the sense that today's professors of American Indian Studies (and its variants in other programs and departments) are academics. Yet, as I will demonstrate in the following pages, Eastman, by virtue of his Indian ethic, his indigenous experiences, and his native eloquence, became a paragon of the American Indian intellectual, and his writing and political agenda still inform the contemporary Indian community.

What is plainly needed at this time is an analysis and appreciation of what Eastman accomplished as a writer and thinker. Too often he has been held up merely as a victim of assimilation—too much of a gentleman to shake the foundations of federal Indian policy. The Eastman I portray is vastly different. Referring once again to *From the Deep Woods to Civilization,* I was struck while teaching this book in a seminar on American Indian intellectuals by a brief passage in which Eastman struggled with his new life as a student at a nearby day school in Flandreau. His grandmother and father, both of whom he cherished and respected, were at opposite ends of opinion regarding the benefits of the white man's education. "I needed counsel," Eastman confesses, "and human counsel did not satisfy me." So, he went into the woods and sought the "Great Mystery." "When I came back," Eastman declared, "my heart was strong. I desired to follow the new trail to the end." Without making much ado of his experience, Eastman sought a vision, and what he received from the Great Mystery motivated his decision to go to school. With respect to this, I imagine—since one must treat a vision with circumspection—this vision continued to inspire Eastman throughout his career, in particular, as a writer and thinker. But what kind of writer would Eastman become? Was there a tradition from which he could partake? Why write in the first place?[4]

Long before Eastman ever considered drawing up the "sketches" that would later become *Indian Boyhood*, American Indians had been setting their thoughts, ideas, and opinions down on paper. What survives is an astounding record of writings that bear witness to what indigenous people endured as colonizing forces spread farther westward. In its wake were a host of injustices that plagued Indian communities, who typically were guilty of little more than being in the way of progress. Samson Occom, the father of the Indian literary tradition and an eighteenth-century Mohegan minister, wrestled with this reality and the concomitant role of the writer when he penned a special sermon for a condemned Indian brother. "The world is already full of books; and the people of GOD are abundantly furnished with excellent books upon divine subjects; and it seems that every subject has been written upon over and over again"—so wrote Occom in "A Sermon Preached at the Execution of Moses Paul, An Indian" in 1772, just a few short years before the Americans began their rebellion against the British crown. Thus begins a relationship between unfairly treated Indians and the outraged Indian writers who bear witness for them, which Eastman would be forced to engage at various points throughout his life, the 1862 U.S.-Dakota War and the 1890 Wounded Knee Massacre being but two of the most poignant times.[5]

With respect to poor Moses Paul, what was clearly a very somber occasion, in which the Mohegan minister took on the task of reminding his racially and socially mixed audience that they were "sinners," too, was also an important moment in American Indian intellectual history. For Occom's remarks about the world being full of books—and very scholarly ones, at that—meant that adding another volume to such a highbrow tradition, especially at this grave time, was inconsequential. Moses Paul, the condemned, was not in need of a theological treatise, but rather some words of solace.

On the other hand, the people gathered to watch an Indian man executed needed something else—a moral awakening to the realization that Moses Paul's ultimate crime was not killing a white man but *being an Indian*. This offense to white society Occom knew firsthand, as he was accused of profligacy by the committee of church elders that supported his ministry, even though he had the slightest income and the harshest conditions among his peers in the Presbyterian community.

Occom, however, did not forsake his commitment to Jesus or to leading a Christian life in the church, even as he witnessed case after case of hypocrisy among his white brethren. It was the whites, after all, as he and generations of Indian preachers and writers would point out, who introduced the scourge of rum and whiskey into Indian communities, in addition to stealing land and breaking treaties. At the same time, just as it was not the fault of the Great Mystery when an Indian person goes bad, so too was it the case that the Christian God is not to blame when a white person does wrong. Whatever the path one chooses to follow, it is up to that person to stay on its course. By the same token, one should not do things to try to corrupt another—and this was what Occom wanted to impress upon his listeners. The whites may not have forced the Indians to drink their liquors, but they were the ones who chose to bring them in and take advantage of their effects upon an unsuspecting tribe.

With this in mind, what appealed to Occom about Christianity was the simplicity of its message—do unto others as you would have them do unto you, love your neighbor, be poor in spirit. These kinds of virtues many an Indian person would say were already being practiced by Indian nations long before white settlers ever entered their midst. And with this simple message in his heart, Occom turned to the New Light movement within Protestantism, which sought to open up the church to people from all walks of life, not just an "elect" few. Moreover, the New Lights espoused preaching in more immediately accessible language, which even children and the unlettered could comprehend.

Such religious populism, if you will, would later inform the Great Awakening and the Second Great Awakening, not to mention the rise in Methodism across the frontier. The Americanization of these religious movements is reflected in the works of William Apess, Joseph Johnson, and George Copway, three very important Indian evangelists who sought Christian answers for their Indian brethren—answers which are not without controversy in today's Indian community but which were commonplace solutions proposed by earnest individuals greatly concerned with the future well-being of Indian people, as they witnessed what today's generation only reads about in books—the direct impact of war, disease, and forced removal.

Charles Eastman, in turn, would witness the tail end, but by no means less traumatic episodes of westward expansion. At the age of four, Eastman and his family, along with droves of other Dakotas, were sent into exile in the aftermath of the 1862 U.S.–Dakota War, which cost the Indians their homeland, many casualties on the battlefield, as well as thirty-eight men hung for alleged war crimes. Among those slated for execution but spared were Eastman's father and brothers.

Eastman's close acquaintance with travesty resumed after he acquired his medical degree from the Boston University Medical College, upon which he was assigned to the Pine Ridge Agency in fall of 1890. As soon as he arrived he was confronted with the growing unrest created by the Ghost Dance movement, which threatened to bring both divisiveness and violence into the community. Despite Eastman's erstwhile efforts at brokering an attitude of tolerance from the Indian agent, the young doctor had to stand by and wait for the dead and wounded to be brought in as the massacre ensued.

Although Eastman converted to Christianity long before he became a doctor, having taken up the faith sometime after his father's release from a federal prison in Iowa, where he was held for his participation in the 1862 war, Eastman did not become a writer until a few years after leaving Pine Ridge for St. Paul, Minnesota, in 1893. While he struggled to get his private practice off the ground, Eastman began some "sketches" for the sake of his young son, who came too late to know the free and independent life that Eastman enjoyed as a young Indian boy across the plains and woods of Manitoba, where many Dakotas stayed during their years of post-1862 exile.

Thus, with a youthful audience in mind Eastman's writing career got under way, the initial product, in 1902, being *Indian Boyhood,* the first volume of Eastman's autobiography, the subsequent part coming in 1916, *From the Deep Woods to Civilization*. In addition, Eastman published seven more books and several smaller pieces for a variety of venues, all oriented toward a wide audience of Indians and non-Indians alike, perhaps with some emphasis on reaching the latter more than the former. Moreover, what makes Eastman's books unique is that, while the world may be filled with books already, as Occom claimed, the world definitely did not have nearly enough books written by American Indians. Significantly, what Eastman maintained as a part of the burgeoning American Indian intellectual tradition is an appreciation for eloquence and clear statements, befitting the finest Native orators from Red Jacket to Chief Seattle. Eastman was less interested in dazzling his audience with analytical prowess and theoretical finesse and more with enlightening people about the history, culture, and religion of Indian people, which he did with the objective of promoting Indian rights.

Throughout all his writings, Eastman never fails to respect the Great Mystery that subtends all of Creation. Keeping this in mind, Eastman does not presume to have all the answers, and he willingly shared the public intellectual's stage with a range of Indian and non-Indian peers. Yet, for all his grace and unassuming character, one would be misguided to think of Eastman's writings as simple or easy to understand, in the sense of being able to comprehend their full meaning in a single read. On the contrary, Eastman is deceptively uncomplicated. I have been reading his work for years, and I am still surprised by what I see each time I open one of his books. Even books that were ostensibly for young readers bear the indigenous sophistication of the oral tradition, which consists of narratives that draw from a deep well of wisdom. Like a well-told parable or allegory, there are many layers to Eastman's stories, be they about animals or commissioners of Indian affairs.

As such, even though I am a Gila River Pima from Arizona living in the early twenty-first century, I find Eastman, a Santee Dakota from Minnesota who died in 1939, to be an inspiring role model, not only for myself but for all Indians pursuing their education in hopes of making a positive difference—for their nation and for Indian people in general. With respect to this ideal, the purpose of my book is to treat Eastman as an intellectual, which may sound trite until one considers that of all the images and stereotypes bestowed upon Indians, the label of *intellectual* never comes to mind. Why not? We are just as wise and knowledgeable as any other people. As a philosophy major in college, I could not help but be aware that Indians had answers too for all the profound questions on which philosophers from Plato to Kant and beyond have reflected throughout the centuries. We just did not answer in the same way that our white counterparts did in the ivory tower, which includes not privileging the western philosophical tradition. After all, if "citing" the major figures of the western philosophical canon is the premise for "doing philosophy," then is it really knowledge, insight, or wisdom that is being produced or is it simply the conceit of an ethnocentric view of the world? Indian people are not merely examples of the "state of nature," in spite of what Hobbes, Locke, and Rousseau may have to say about us; rather, we are ways of being on the earth, as determined by the Creator. Doing indigenous philosophy means remembering this fundamental truth. At the same time, Eastman's example demonstrates that living the life of the indigenous mind requires not disconnecting oneself from the world but, on the contrary, immersing oneself in the land and people.

It is time to say "thank you" to the many individuals who helped me along the way. Writing this book has been a wondrous learning experience. The most important lesson I have learned over the months and years I have devoted to this project is that every book is ultimately written by many hands. While I must bear, willingly, the responsibility for the content and argument set forth in these pages, I must also, gratefully, acknowledge the individuals who contributed in one way or another to the creation of this work.

To begin with, I would not have had the time or the resources to complete this book were it not for the generous support of the D'Arcy McNickle Center for American Indian History and the Newberry Library. In particular, I owe a huge debt of gratitude to the committee that awarded me the 2003–4 Consortium for Institutional Cooperation Faculty Fellowship, which made it possible for me to commit myself wholeheartedly to developing this project. Anyone who has had the pleasure of using the Newberry's expansive collections knows what a supreme privilege it is to have access to this one-of-a-kind material. Toward this end, I must extend a word of thanks to David E. Wilkins (Lumbee), who encouraged me to apply for this fellowship in the first place, and to Jean O'Brien-Kehoe (Ojibwe), who gave me invaluable assistance in improving my fellowship application. Dave and Jeani, colleagues of mine at the University of Minnesota, have made my work as a professor of American Indian Studies both joyful and productive. Moreover, I simply cannot forget to thank Patricia Albers, who until spring semester 2007 was American Indian Studies' intrepid chairwoman and who permitted me an entire year off from teaching the high-enrollment courses I normally tended to for our program.

With respect to the Newberry community, there are several people to acknowledge, beginning with Brian Hosmer, director of the McNickle Center, as well as Daniel M. Cobb, assistant director, and Olivia Littles, office assistant—all of whom not only provided institutional support but more importantly made me feel like I had a home at the Newberry instead of just a work space. Of these three, I must pay special regard to Dan Cobb, a true friend and colleague, who probably spent the most time listening to me expound on my various discoveries and ideas. Dan was not only very patient with me but also an astute listener who often made valuable comments about my work. Speaking of support, I also thank Sara Austin, assistant director of Research and Education, for making my transition from full-time professor to long-term fellow and back again as smooth and painless as possible. The Newberry could not ask for a more conscientious and professional person than Sara to look out for the many and varied needs of its fellows.

One of the many highlights of my fellowship year was partaking in the Newberry's seminar series for long-term fellows. The seminar is a splendid opportunity to have other outstanding scholars conducting their own research at the Newberry read one's work-in-progress and get both written and oral feedback. There is probably no more poignant experience for a scholar than to place your work on the firing line and try to explain and defend what it is you seek to do. Fortunately, in the capable hands of James Grossman, vice president for Research and Education, each meeting turns out to be a very collegial and constructive experience. Perhaps I can say this because in addition to Jim's presence, not to mention that of Sara, Brian, and Dan, I was blessed with the participation of some very special people at my seminar. In attendance were Clara Sue Kidwell (Choctaw), Carol Levin, Eric Slauter, Carolyn Eastman, Anna Lisa Cox, Elizabeth Wingrove, Dror Wahrman, Raymond

Clemens, Paul Solon, Jeff Means (Lakota), Stephanie Leitch, Clay Stein-
man, Jeffrey Sklansky, Ruth McKay, Paula Higgins, John Aubrey (the
wise man tending the Ayer Collection), and Frederick Hoxie. LaVonne
Ruoff, though unable to attend the seminar itself, availed me of her
knowledge, experience, and wisdom on other occasions.

Many thanks as well to the wonderful students I have had the pleasure of working with at both the Newberry, in my graduate seminar,
"Lessons in Assimilation: American Indian Intellectuals, 1890–1934,"
and the University of Minnesota, particularly in my seminar on American Indian intellectuals. Although I was certainly blessed with a room-
ful of interesting and talented students, I have been especially fortunate
to see some of them in the ensuing months and years: Tol Foster
(Mvskoke Creek), who is an assistant professor working for the American Indian Studies program at the University of North Carolina–Chapel
Hill; Kelly Branam, who is a lecturer in the Department of Anthropology at Indiana University–Purdue University Indianapolis; Jamie
Singson (Yaqui), who works for the office of the vice chancellor for student affairs at the University of Illinois at Urbana-Champaign. I was
also honored to be asked by Jennifer McGovern, a graduate student in
the Department of English, University of Iowa, to serve as commenta-
tor for papers presented at the 2004 meeting of the Midwest Modern
Language Association in St. Louis, Missouri. The other presenters were
Tol Foster and Dagmar Frerking, a graduate student in the Department
of American Studies, Purdue University.

Speaking of my students, I feel obliged to thank all of the American
Indian students who enrolled in my courses during my years at the
University of Minnesota. Each in his or her own way got me to think
more deeply about the problems that Eastman faced as an Indian in a
white world and the ideas he tried to express as a Native philosopher.
Specifically, I thank Randi Gibbons (Lakota), Oneida Hayes (Pima/
Ojibwe), Matt Martinez (San Juan), Sasha Bourdeau (Lakota), Kateri
Tuttle (Dakota), Scott Shoemaker (Miami), Kate Beane (Dakota), Amy
Ojibway (Ojibwe), Rainbow Pemberton (Hopi), Brie Ackerman (Mo-
hawk), Carly Beane (Dakota), Marisa Carr (Ojibwe), Kasey Keeler (Maidu),
Lora Pabst (Pawnee/Choctaw), and Sami White (Lakota).

Among the above named students, Kate and Carly Beane deserve
special recognition. As members of the extended Eastman family—they

are direct descendents of the Reverend John Eastman, Charles's older brother—their feedback on the manuscript was both very thoughtful and crucial at turning this book into a work that is worthy of the Dakota readers I hope to attract to its pages. Kate and Carly are well on their way to making their own marks in the world, both as community leaders in their own right and as important proponents of revitalizing the Dakota language. Needless to say, I was deeply honored to be their professor.

A very special acknowledgement needs to be paid to Amy Ojibway, who served as my energetic and talented research assistant and who made the writing of chapter three, "From Enemies to Pan-Indian Allies: Eastman on Dakota-Ojibwe Relations," a possibility and a joy. During 2006, having just finished her junior year at the University of Minnesota, Amy was awarded a Ronald E. McNair Fellowship that enabled her to spend the long days of summer poring over Eastman's various works with an eye to how his portrayal of the Ojibwe Nation metamorphosed over time. Conversing with her about Eastman's work was both very productive and a great pleasure. My heartfelt prayer is that her research experience enlightened her about her gifts and potential and that she takes the lessons learned and applies them to what promises to be a very bright future.

I also thank Lora Pabst for assisting me in locating archival information of the Society of American Indians 1919 meeting in Minneapolis, Minnesota. Lora, working as an intern at the *Minneapolis Star Tribune* newspaper, generously took time out of her busy schedule to help me gather key bits of information on a topic which has never been written about before. Speaking of archives, I thank Robert Preucel, curator, and Alex Pezzati, archivist, at the University of Pennsylvania's museum, who assisted me with my search for the lost Eastman collection. Toward this end, I simply must thank Patricia Nietfeld, collections manager for the National Museum of the American Indian, who came up with the invaluable list of items that are still a part of the Heye Collection, which is stored in the Culture Resource Center in Suitland, Maryland.

Concerning the Minnesota Historical Society Press, I offer a very sincere thank-you to Ann Regan, who has been my wonderful editor and who must have been sent to me from heaven. Little did I know when we spoke at great length at the banquet concluding the 2005 meeting of the American Society for Ethnohistory in Santa Fe, New Mexico, that I was having more than a conversation: I was entering a major turning point of my life. Ann believed in my work from the start and spoke to me of fulfilling my potential as a writer and scholar in ways that had not yet occurred to me. She has clearly worked with Indian authors before and undoubtedly is deeply sensitive to the cultural needs of communicating from a different worldview.

A special thank-you goes to Shannon Pennefeather, who took on the time-consuming job of editing my hefty manuscript. She took to the task with enthusiasm and intelligence and was everything that Ann Regan told me she would be. I especially want to express my gratitude for the patience she showed me, particularly when I was less an enlightened scholar and more a sensitive writer. May there be many blessings on her home.

Speaking of the wonderful people at MHS, I am exceedingly grateful to the Indian Advisory Committee, whose members thought long and hard about the value of this book and found it worthy of their endorsement. May your lands and nations be blessed with happiness and prosperity. Also, a thank-you to Brenda Child, my former colleague at the University of Minnesota, who pleasantly surprised me with her generous remarks about the quality of my work. May you always know friends who will stand by you as you did me.

My list of thank-yous would not be complete without expressing my deepest gratitude to my loving wife, Sharon. She has been by my side since we were both struggling graduate students searching for our place in the world. Despite all the ups and downs that are a part of any academic career, Sharon never let up on her faith in me. Without her love and moral support, writing this book may not have even been possible. In addition to being a wonderfully talented poet, Sharon is also the most perfect partner in life I could ever pray for. I love her very much.

DAKOTA PHILOSOPHER

1

"The Greatest Sioux of the Century"
Eastman and the Pursuit of an Indigenous Philosophy

Do not drop your head because you are an Indian. Be proud!
Charles Eastman, opening address, Annual Meeting of the Society of
American Indians, Minneapolis, Minnesota, October 2, 1919

In 1917, the *American Indian Magazine,* edited by Seneca intellectual
Arthur C. Parker, said of Charles Alexander Eastman: "Dr. Eastman
through all his books gives us a brand of philosophy that while critical is
yet refreshing because it is so evidently true. As a great Sioux, history will
write him down as a great American and a true philosopher." What follows is a long overdue appreciation of Eastman as a "true philosopher"—
or, more specifically, as a true Dakota philosopher. While Eastman's
collected works are not typically spoken of in the same breath as those
of William James, Charles Sanders Peirce, or John Dewey, if only for the
reason that he was an "Indian" who wrote for a wide audience as opposed to an Anglo-American philosopher writing by and large for other
philosophers, they nonetheless hold the distinction of influencing the way
countless readers in several languages perceived and thought about American Indians. Among the people Eastman influenced are other American Indians, including many of us in American Indian Studies today.[1]

This is not to say that, nearly a century after Parker's accolades, Eastman is now beyond criticism, like Shakespeare or the Bible. Certainly,
Eastman's biographer, Raymond Wilson, observed that he was never a
very "systematic thinker" when it came to pressing issues pertaining to
the application of federal Indian policy. By *systematic,* Wilson means
taking a more clearly social scientific approach to his analysis, as did
the sociologist Fayette Avery McKenzie, who used all the tools of his
discipline to analyze the "the Indian problem." In Eastman's hands,
however, in Wilson's opinion, problems always proved to be much more
complex than his narratives on Indian life might lead one to expect.[2]

Perhaps because of the growing sophistication of American Indian Studies since its inception in the late 1960s, there has been much scholarship on Eastman as a man caught in "two worlds," which simultaneously lifts Eastman's work high in the American Indian literary canon yet focuses on the shadows and skeletons that exist behind the dignified image that Eastman effortlessly projected, whether he wore a suit and tie or buckskin and a feathered headdress. As Wilson opines: "[Eastman's] personal experiences in both worlds no doubt contributed to his facile conclusions and the conclusions of others, that since he had achieved fame (if not fortune) in an alien culture, other Indians could also progress and learn to survive and prosper in the modern world." This is to suggest that Eastman, not to mention his peers, were naïve about the role institutional racism played in holding back most American Indians from achieving their objectives in education, business, and politics. However, when one looks at the corpus of Eastman's written work within the broader context of what "educated Indians" were writing at the time, the picture becomes much more interesting and complex, as one can quickly see that Eastman, along with his contemporaries, was quite vigilant in his quest for Indian rights, comprehending the issues and problems as part of a complex process of government machinery and indigenous resistance. Consequently, Eastman was much more than "living proof of the reformers' faith in progress." And while much has been done recently to complicate Eastman's relation to his identity as an Indian and an American—such that he is not merely a victim of assimilationist policies—there is still more to be done at appreciating his work as products of the Dakota/Lakota/Nakota intellectual tradition, which includes Nicholas Black Elk, George Sword, Chauncey Yellow Robe, Zitkala-Sa, and Luther Standing Bear and extends today to include Vine Deloria, Jr., Elizabeth Cook-Lynn, Beatrice Medicine, Susan Power, Delphine Red Shirt, Philip J. Deloria, and Waziyatawin Angela Wilson, to name but a few.[3]

Despite Eastman's prominent position in the Dakota intellectual tradition, his ideas and the example he made with his personal and professional life have not always been revered, even by other Indians. I can remember a time during my own college career when simply knowing that someone was from the "assimilation period" was enough to write him or her off as a "sellout" and "wannabe." In fact, while teaching a graduate seminar at the Newberry Library in Chicago on behalf of the D'Arcy McNickle Center for American Indian History during the 2004 spring semester, I ran into this dismissive mind-set from one of my Indian students. Perhaps because of this predominant attitude that we in the American Indian community do not need Eastman—not to mention other luminaries of the post-1890 generation, such as Zitkala-Sa and Arthur C. Parker—much of the existing scholarship has largely been conducted by non-Indians. The exceptions to this situation are few and fleeting: Eastman appears here and there in the work of Gerald Vizenor, Robert Allen Warrior, Donald L. Fixico, Philip J. Deloria, and Tom Holm.

With respect to Vine Deloria, Jr., his attitude toward Eastman is twofold, revealing an interesting insight into Eastman's status in the contemporary American Indian intellectual community. First, in Deloria's publications, namely his various books, Eastman warrants only a very brief reference in *God Is Red* and then is perfectly absent from everything else. However, influence is not always marked with citations, a reality I encountered firsthand during the fall semester of 2000. Vine partook in American Indian Studies' thirtieth anniversary celebration at the University of Minnesota, at which he gave both a public talk and an informal afternoon seminar. During the seminar, a graduate student asked Vine to name his five favorite books. Without hesitation, Vine named *From the Deep Woods to Civilization* and *The Soul of the Indian* to his list, which also included two books by Luther Standing Bear, *Land of the Spotted Eagle* and *My People the Sioux*. Needless to say, as an American Indian Studies scholar myself I was completely fascinated by this unexpected list of post-1890-generation writers. In fact, I can say that this book is the result of following this fascination to its root, which is a sustained analysis of Eastman's intellectual output as a Dakota writer.[4]

However, with regard to the other Indian scholars named above, Warrior has had the most significant impact on the current analyses and interpretations of Eastman's literary output. Many (non-Indian) scholars, more specifically, seem to have picked up on the ambiguous feelings that Warrior expressed for Eastman and the post-1890 generation in his 1994 book *Tribal Secrets,* in which he opines: "However troubling we might find the [post-1890] generation's support for and advancement of the policies of the U.S. government, we can not fault their sincerity or their commitment to and love for American Indian people." The influence of the latter evaluation may be seen in such articles as "'Good Indian': Charles Eastman and the Warrior as Civil Servant," which appeared in a 2003 issue of *American Indian Quarterly* and began an analysis of Eastman's intellectual agenda with the observation, "Charles Alexander Eastman remains an enigmatic figure in the early days of American Indian activism—a man whose contributions, while unimpeachable in terms of devotion and good will, are often complicated by the lingering shadow of assimilationist values evident in his writings and his career as one of the so-called 'red progressives.' Eastman can be located, by chance or design, on what would seem the 'wrong side' of nearly every major issue he faced at the height of his prominence in the early part of the twentieth century." The article goes on to list the supposedly condemning evidence from Eastman's career, namely support for the 1887 Dawes Act, working as the government physician at Pine Ridge during the Wounded Knee Massacre, as well as obtaining a non-Indian education and becoming a Christian.[5]

Without further consideration, it would be easy under the circumstances to dismiss Eastman as a misguided shill for Anglo-American "civilization." However, when one looks at the details of Eastman's work, a different picture begins to emerge, a complicated hybrid of both Dakota and American values but with priority placed on the Dakota tradition. From the vantage point of his *Indian Boyhood,* if you will, Eastman demonstrates that the decision to embrace mainstream American life was not a simple choice between two evils—assimilation or extinction—but rather an arduous effort at maintaining core Dakota beliefs and principles in a radically different environment than the one in which Eastman's Dakota ancestors dwelled prior to westward expansion. Thus, what makes Eastman a visionary or a "true philosopher" is his capacity to see through to the essence of things, whether it is being a Dakota or a Christian or the nature of modern life. Similar to many premodern philosophers and sages, such as Socrates, one cannot truly appreciate the wisdom without appreciating the life story that generated the insights in the first place. In Eastman's case, not only did he write two volumes of autobiography, but also there are recurring references to his personal experience in his other seven books and assorted articles. It is fair to say that Eastman lived what he spoke and wrote. What is important to remember, though, is that the story begins at and ultimately—at least in spirit—returns to the heart of the Dakota homeland in southern Minnesota. In this sense, Eastman joins the ranks of Samson Occom, William Apess, and Sarah Winnemucca Hopkins as an American Indian intellectual whose personal story has driven how we interpret his political, historical, and religious agenda, all of which are connected to indigenous homelands whose balance has been violently disrupted by Euro-American expansionism.

His lofty reputation for promoting pan-Indian causes notwithstanding, Charles Alexander Eastman (or Ohiyesa, as he was known in his native Dakota) was first and foremost a Minnesota writer and activist. What supposedly undermines this claim is the fact that Eastman spent very little of his life in Minnesota. After his birth around 1858, Eastman, who was then known only as Hakadah, left his home near Redwood Falls in late 1862 as a refugee of the U.S.–Dakota War, an event that virtually emptied the territory of its indigenous Dakota population. Eastman would not return to Minnesota until 1893, when he moved his family from Pine Ridge, South Dakota, where he worked as an Indian Service physician, to St. Paul in the aftermath of the Wounded Knee Massacre. Eastman's return to Minnesota was relatively short lived due to difficulties he encountered while pursuing a private medical practice. Because of financial needs, Eastman took up work as an agent for the YMCA in 1894, which required him to travel extensively throughout the western United States, promoting the founding of YMCA chapters at various reservations. Then, in 1897, the Santee Dakota at Crow Creek Reservation in South Dakota asked him to serve as their lobbyist in Washington, DC, for the purpose of recovering lost treaty annuities that were incurred during their post-1862 exile. The latter was followed by a brief stint in 1899 as an outing agent for the Carlisle Indian School in Pennsylvania. At the turn of the twentieth century, Eastman once again became an Indian Service physician, assigned between 1900 and 1903 at the Crow Creek Reservation. During his time at Crow Creek, Eastman took the job of revising the tribal rolls, a task he did not complete until 1909. However, because his tenure as physician ended before he could complete the rolls, he was compelled to move back to Minnesota, this time to White Bear, from which he soon moved to

Amherst, Massachusetts, where he stayed until 1919. In addition to everything else—including running summer camps for boys and girls in Granite Lake, New Hampshire—Eastman started a career as a popular speaker at colleges and philanthropic societies in both the United States and the United Kingdom. Finally, after separating from his wife, Elaine, in 1921, Eastman continued to lead the itinerant life of an Indian Service employee and public speaker, never really settling down anywhere and always dogged by lingering financial woes. During this time he began visiting his son, Ohiyesa II, in Detroit, Michigan, over the winter months; Eastman passed away in that city on January 8, 1939.[6]

Yet, in spite of the peripatetic lifestyle that Eastman followed throughout his years of writing, speaking, and activism, I make my claim that Eastman is an indigenous Minnesota figure on the basis that he was a Mdewakanton Dakota who not only was born in Dakota Country but also maintained a healthy relationship with his Dakota relatives and a living memory of the indigenous culture as an integral part of his identity as both an intellectual and an American Indian. Even after his father, Jacob Eastman (formerly Many Lightnings), reclaimed him in Manitoba, Canada, and moved them to Flandreau, South Dakota, Eastman was nonetheless conditioned by the customs and values indigenous to southern Minnesota and in which he grounds himself from the beginning of his writing career—namely in the 1902 autobiography *Indian Boyhood,* which he began after his 1893 move to St. Paul. As a struggling physician in his mid-thirties, Eastman began writing, not knowing where it would lead. In fact, Eastman did not even have publication in mind when he began his "sketches." As he recounts in his classic 1916 *From the Deep Woods to Civilization,* the second volume of his autobiography: "While I had plenty of leisure, I began to put upon paper some of my earliest recollections, with the thought that our children might some day like to read of that wilderness life. When my wife discovered what I had written, she insisted upon sending it to *St. Nicholas.* Much to my surprise, the sketches were immediately accepted and appeared during the following year. This was the beginning of my first book, 'Indian Boyhood,' which was not completed until several years later."[7]

Thus began a legacy that is still being felt across the American Indian intellectual community today. However, before we delve into Eastman's contemporary influence, we must take into account the pivotal role he played in defining the literary and political agenda of the post-1890 generation, members of which were attempting to capitalize on the education they were receiving from the American school system at the same time they endured great suffering and insufficient resources. That year is a turning point, not only for the Lakota who suffered through the Wounded Knee Massacre but also for all of Indian Country, which mourned the death of what once was before the reservations. Philip J. Deloria observes the significance of 1890 in *Indians in Unexpected Places*. While other tribes may indeed mark similar watersheds in the course of their own history, Wounded Knee stands as a marker for pan-tribal and even Anglo-American history: "Wounded Knee . . . organizes the big break between the possibility and the impossibility of military struggle, and it does so as a cross-tribal and cross-cultural milepost. For non-Indian Americans, the possibility of nineteenth-century Indian violence existed before Wounded Knee; afterward, it became a thing of representation, perfect for twentieth-century movies and books." In other words, Wounded Knee signaled the abrupt transformation of Indian nations from geopolitical powers (e.g., the Great Sioux Nation) to symbols of conquest (e.g., the University of North Dakota "Fighting Sioux").[8]

Unlike his predecessors, such as Samson Occom (Mohegan), William Apess (Pequot), Joseph Johnson (Mohegan), and George Copway (Ojibwe), Eastman—although he was a Christian—did not write with the narrow mission of converting his brethren in the Indian community to Christianity; rather, he was a university-trained physician who became a professional writer at a time when many thought that social engineering—or progressivism—was key to successfully addressing the so-called "Indian problem." Certainly, this was the clarion call of one commissioner of Indian affairs after another, not to mention the non-Indian leaders of Indian rights groups, such as the Indian Rights Association and the Lake Mohonk Conference. Hence their collective call to pass the 1887 Dawes Act, which they thought would facilitate the transformation of Indians into Christian yeoman farmers and the like. Yet, even though many progressive Indians subscribed to the thinking behind the Dawes Act, we shall see through Eastman's example the American Indian intellectual standing apart from his European and American counterparts by means of the relationship that he ineluctably maintains with his tribe's sense of "Peoplehood," which Cherokee anthropologist Robert K. Thomas defined as the four common elements—homeland, language, kinship system, and sacred history—that bind individuals together into a clear and distinct group. At the same time, Peoplehood is a dynamic relation between historically changing variables as opposed to a timeless identity. For Eastman this meant knowing that he was from southern Minnesota, even as he and other Dakotas were forced into exile after the 1862 U.S.–Dakota War. Eastman also grew fluent in Dakota, which he spoke exclusively until he was compelled into a day school run by a white teacher in Flandreau, forcing him into a bilingual world in which English was considered the dominant language. English would become the lingua franca of the modern pan-Indian community. Eastman, in addition, never failed to honor his Dakota grandmother, uncle, and father. Yet, his mother was half white, the daughter of soldier and frontier artist Seth Eastman. Moreover, Eastman married into Anglo-American society when he took Elaine Goodale as his wife, who bore him six mixed-blood children. How Eastman saw his children's identity, let alone how they perceived themselves, is unknown. What we do know is that by virtue of the stories he learned from Dakota elder Smoky Day, recounted in his first book, *Indian Boyhood,* Eastman saw himself as part of the ongoing story of the Dakota people, which stems back to the time of Creation, specifically to where the Minnesota and Mississippi rivers converge. Fort Snelling stands there now, a rather unimpressive reminder of America's militarized effort at colonizing the Dakota homeland. How is an Indian to deal with such a complicated world?[9]

Frederick E. Hoxie suggested in his article "Exploring a Cultural Borderland: Native American Journeys of Discovery in the Early Twentieth Century" that the Indian writers of "Mourning Dove's generation" became explorers in their own right, the converse of Columbus and Magellan: "Their efforts in the years between 1900 and 1930, which engaged them in fields as various as literature, anthropology, art, religion, and politics, were Native American journeys of discovery, journeys devoted to the search for a new home in a captured land." In spite of the fact that Hoxie is only invoking a metaphor of intellectual exploration, as opposed to conquest, the image still presumes a certain similarity between Indian and European values and motivations regarding such an enterprise. While Hoxie does a commendable job of demonstrating the political and cultural conditions that made these "Native American journeys" a possibility, even a necessity, his analysis would have benefited from taking a closer look at actual journeys. In particular, the writers that comprise Hoxie's focus, namely Mourning Dove, Francis La Flesche, Zitkala-Sa, Luther Standing Bear, and Charles Eastman, pursued literal journeys across the United States and sometimes Europe during an era when different travelers, sojourners, emissaries, and diplomats were making their way between their colonized homelands and the major cities of Europe and the United States. Donald Keene, for example does a wonderful job of recounting the writings of a variety of Japanese travelers during the years 1860–1929 in *Modern Japanese Diaries.* Although Japan was never colonized, as were China and India, the Japanese felt compelled to learn as much as they could about the West, especially its military prowess, so that they could better prepare to defend their interests in a world dominated by western colonialism. Just as important, Hoxie overlooks the travel narratives that were either embedded in American Indian autobiographies, such as *From the Deep Woods to Civilization, My People the Sioux,* and *Black Elk Speaks,* as well as the historically important travel narratives, such as Samson Occom's letters and diary entries regarding his fundraising trip to England with the Reverend Eleazar Wheelock, *Running Sketches of Men and Places in England, France, Germany, Belgium, and Scotland* by George Copway, and *A Papago Traveler* by James McCarthy. Instead, Hoxie makes some major digressions into early modern American Indian art and artists and the burgeoning Native American Church, both of which are interesting in their own way but do very little to advance Hoxie's analysis of the Indian writer as explorer.[10]

So did the Indian writers of the post-1890 generation have a way of describing themselves? With their indigenous heritage in mind, many progressive Indians transformed themselves from "warriors" into "scholars"—or, better yet, into scholars with the hearts of warriors—which is certainly the way Eastman talks about his own transformation in *From the Deep Woods to Civilization.* Before heading south from Flandreau to the Santee Indian School, Eastman's father, Jacob, said to his son, "Remember, my boy, it is the same as if I sent you on your first war-path. I shall expect you to conquer." In this context, *conquering* meant mastering the white man's knowledge, including the ability to speak and write in English. This attitude would be repeated by Luther Standing Bear, who wrote in his 1928 autobiography, *My People the Sioux,* about being a part of the first class to enter Richard Pratt's Carlisle Indian School in Pennsylvania: "My mind was working in an entirely different channel. I was thinking of my father, and how he had many times said to me, 'Son, be brave! Die on the battle-field if necessary away from home. It is better to die young than to get old and sick and then die.' When I thought of my father, and how he had smoked the pipe of peace, and was not fighting any more, it occurred to me that this chance to go East would prove that I was brave if I were to accept it." Similar to Standing Bear, Eastman did not initially trust the whites, even consider- ing them enemies, which was an attitude, in Eastman's case, nurtured by his uncle, who blamed the whites for the Dakotas' expulsion from their Minnesota homeland. Yet they would each overcome their inhibi- tions about joining Anglo-American society and take to it as a new area in which they could distinguish themselves and gain a different kind of honor, that of revered writers and speakers. At the same time, as East- man exemplifies, becoming "educated" did not necessarily entail for- getting one's Native identity. Indeed, Eastman would become a strong proponent of what Standing Bear later called "the Indian School of Thought," which was about applying traditional knowledge to the modern world. "To the end," as Standing Bear put it in *Land of the Spotted Eagle,* "that young Indians will be able to appreciate both their tradi- tional life and modern life they should be doubly educated. Without forsaking reverence for their ancestral teachings, they can be trained to take up modern duties that relate to tribal and reservation life."[11]

Although Standing Bear published his thoughts in 1933, one can eas- ily say that Eastman was a source of inspiration for this kind of think- ing. Yet the compromises Eastman chose to make in his adaptation to modern Anglo-American society were not without controversy. As War- rior says in *Tribal Secrets,* "Eastman's memoirs, for instance, are highly sentimental accounts of his childhood in which he portrays Natives as needy for, worthy of, and ready for inclusion in mainstream civiliza- tion." As such, Warrior regards Eastman and the post-1890 genera- tion—in particular, those who participated in the Society of American

Indians (SAI)—as being blinded by their progressive idealism. Warrior attempts to explain—or perhaps the better word is rationalize—why Eastman and his peers advocated for an assimilationist agenda, saying, "This generation was the integrationist legacy of post–Wounded Knee existence. They were adults at the time of the transition to reservation life, the federal allotment policy, and the land and lease swindles that came along with allotment and western expansion. Faced with the prospect of total dispossession if Natives continued to resist the U.S. government, these figures believed strongly in doing away with special educational and health programs for Natives, abandonment of Native traditional government structures, and full participation in mainstream U.S. life." We must underscore here that many American Indians were not merely faced with the prospect of total dispossession as some horrible possibility; they were already dispossessed, segregated, and disenfranchised as a result of the reservation system and the authoritarian rule with which the Indian Bureau maintained control over its "wards." For the Dakota, in particular, their reservation life began with the 1851 treaty, which was followed after the 1862 conflict with exile throughout the Dakotas and Canada and creation of the Crow Creek Reservation in South Dakota. The Lakota, in turn, suffered through the gross infractions of their 1868 Treaty of Fort Laramie when General George Armstrong Custer led an expedition into the Black Hills and discovered gold, which led to an infamous land grab. This consequently led to the well-known "rubbing out of Long Hair" at the battle of Greasy Grass, which caused the Indian Bureau to tighten the screws on the reservation system that in turn fostered a situation in which the tragedy at Wounded Knee occurred. Reflecting on his nation's travails, Black Elk famously stated, after listening to Red Cloud make a speech cautioning against seeking revenge for the massacre: "When I look back now from this high hill of my old age, I can still see the butchered women and children lying heaped and scattered all along the crooked gulch as plain as when I saw them with eyes still young. And I can see that something else died there in the bloody mud, and was buried in the blizzard. A people's dream died there. It was a beautiful dream."[12]

For Eastman's part, as mentioned above, he served as the government physician at Pine Ridge, entailing that he did not witness the worst moments of the massacre firsthand; however, he did tend to many victims as well as go into the field to search for survivors. Despite his loyalty to the United States, Eastman does not hesitate to call what happened a *massacre,* as opposed to a *battle,* which was the army's official categorization of events, complete with Congressional Medals of Honor. As Eastman tells his story, one can feel his disgust and outrage start to grow: "It took all my nerve to keep my composure in the face of this spectacle, and of the excitement and grief of my Indian companions, nearly every one of whom was crying aloud or singing his death song." Yet, for all that Eastman went through during this time, he managed to practice restraint in how he responded to the situation: "All this was a severe ordeal for one who had so lately put all his faith in the Christian love and lofty ideals of the white man. Yet I passed no hasty judgment, and was thankful that I might be of some service and relieve even a small part of the suffering." At this point it would be easy to explain away Eastman's attitude as simply appeasing the whites working with him on the reservation. However, we must note three things: first, he only withholds his judgment, which is different from offering forgiveness; second, he makes clear that the massacre was in complete contradiction to the Christian ideals that the whites supposedly espoused; and third, he sets an example of what an Indian can do under these trying circumstances by attempting to relieve some of the suffering around him.[13]

How much, then, do Eastman's contemporary critics take his historic predicament into consideration? It varies, of course. While Warrior is still severe in his critique of Eastman's work in his latest book, *The People and the Word,* he does acknowledge that "Eastman was a remarkable person who lived through a remarkable time." However, rather than articulate his own reasons for making this assertion, Warrior turns to Ojibwe intellectual Gerald Vizenor for insight. Specifically, Warrior cites the second chapter of *Manifest Manners,* in which Vizenor states, "Eastman endured the treacherous turns and transvaluations of tribal identities, the simulations of ferocious warrior cultures, the myths of savagism and civilization, federal duplicities, assimilation policies, the rise of manifest manners, and the hardhearted literature of dominance." Significantly, Warrior does not cite what follows the above quote, as Vizenor points out that "[Eastman] wrote to teach his readers that the tribes were noble; however, he would be reproached as romantic and censured as an assimilationist. Others honored his simulations of survivance." This point is significant for the reason that it takes us beyond Warrior's critique of Eastman, which is based on Eastman's supposed romanticism and assimilationist tendencies. Instead, when one examines Vizenor's full analysis of Eastman, one sees a more sympathetic appraisal of what Vizenor calls the "double others," which are individuals who are marginalized twice over due to their ethnicity and their success in mainstream, non-traditionally Indian roles. Eastman epitomizes this state for Vizenor, as the latter summarizes the former's story, stating, "Eastman was raised to be a traditional tribal leader, but that natural course would not be honored" due to the surprising intervention of his father, newly released from a federal prison in Iowa and a recent convert to Christianity. Consequently, as Vizenor continues, "His new name, education, and marriage were revolutions in his time; moreover, he was burdened with the remembrance of violence, the separation and conversion of his father, and the horror of the massacre of Wounded Knee."[14]

Vizenor then criticizes H. David Brumble's analysis of *Indian Boyhood*, in which Brumble focuses on nine lines that Eastman wrote about "the Indian" in the past tense, in which Brumble reads an implication that Eastman promoted social Darwinism. Vizenor argues instead that Eastman's writing style is more symptomatic of someone who has undergone trauma than of a scholar promoting the current theory of social change, i.e., "evolutionism." If Eastman is a romantic—which, in light of books like *The Soul of the Indian*, he may fairly be labeled—then it must be taken within the context of his having endured the emotional turmoil of treating the survivors of a slaughter, in addition to living out the aftermath of the 1862 U.S.-Dakota War. As Vizenor concludes: "[Eastman] celebrated peace and the romance of tribal stories to overcome the morose remembrance of the Wounded Knee Massacre. Could there have been a wiser resistance literature or simulation of survivance at the time? What did it mean to be the first generation to hear the stories of the past, bear the horrors of the moment, and write to the future? What were tribal identities at the turn of the last century?" The answer to the last question was something that Eastman and his peers in the Society of American Indians never tired of trying to figure out. Their existential crisis is also ours. Yet, being persons who by and large preserved their respect for the "old ways," Eastman and his peers were not without some means of alleviating their ethnic uncertainties. More specifically, in the case of Eastman, he always thought back on the examples his elders set for him while he was growing into a man. He thereby distinguishes himself by bringing their indigenous values into the modern American Indian world, setting a precedent for subsequent generations of American Indian leaders.[15]

Among the Dakota, there were persons who bore the distinction of being a *wicasa wakan,* a holy man, who possessed a vision experience, typically gained from a *hanbleceya,* in which a spirit being gave power that the holy man could call upon through ritual actions. He may heal a sick person, aid in hunting or warfare, control the weather, find lost objects, prophesize, or visit the spirit world. Such a relationship with the spirits, in conjunction with helping the community, eventually turned one into a valued elder. Certainly for Eastman, his grandmother, whom he always called "Uncheedah" in his writings, was such a personage. Eastman says of her in *Indian Boyhood,*

> As a motherless child, I always regarded my good grandmother as the wisest of guides and the best of protectors. It was not long before I began to realize her superiority to most of her contemporaries. This idea was not gained entirely from my own observation, but also from a knowledge of the high regard in which she was held by other women. Aside from her native talent and ingenuity, she was endowed with a truly wonderful memory. No other midwife in her day and tribe could compete with her in skill and judgment. Her observations in practice were all preserved in her mind for reference, as systematically as if they had been written upon the pages of a note-book.[16]

Indeed, it was his learned grandmother who taught Eastman that the way of the "medicine-giver," or *pezuta wicasta,* was the ideal to which he ought to aspire, even more so than the warrior, or *akicita.* "She said these things," as Eastman recalls his grandmother's words, "so thoughtfully and impressively that I cannot but feel and remember them even to this day." Such esteem places Eastman within a Sioux literary tradition that includes Zitkala-Sa's regard for her mother in *American*

Indian Stories and Luther Standing Bear's admiration for his father in *My People the Sioux,* not to mention Vine Deloria, Jr.'s laudatory remarks about his father and grandfather in *Singing for a Spirit.*[17]

Of equal importance to Eastman's early education, and another role model for being a learned person—or indigenous intellectual, as I am trying to develop this term—was Smoky Day, who "was widely known among [the Mdewakanton Dakota] as a preserver of history and legend." Smoky Day's influence on Eastman will be examined extensively in chapter two. Suffice it to say at this point that Smoky Day's learnedness in the stories of the Dakota oral tradition would provide Eastman the basis for his understanding of the Dakota Nation's place in the world, not to mention his identity as a Dakota person. From Smoky Day, Eastman learned about where he was from, how the Dakota came to inhabit their homeland in Minnesota, the proper way of living there, and the ancestors, such as Jingling Thunder, who set a standard for subsequent generations of Dakota men, including Eastman.[18]

Complementing the stories Eastman learned from Smoky Day were the practical lessons in being a Dakota man that he got from his uncle. Eastman characterizes him in *Indian Boyhood:* "My uncle, who educated me up to the age of fifteen years, was a strict disciplinarian and a good teacher. When I left the teepee in the morning, he would say: 'Hakadah, look closely to everything you see'; and at evening, on my return, he used often to catechize me for an hour." Eastman's uncle expected him to learn the ways of all the woodland animals, be they birds, fish, or mammals. The immediate concern, of course, was to develop the young Eastman into a good tracker and hunter, as well as a brave and strong person. At the same time, such pedagogy took care of his personal development, especially in terms of building character by instilling an ethical sense appropriate to a tribal community. Eastman summarizes this process:

> With all this, our manners and morals were not neglected. I was made to respect the adults and especially the aged. I was not allowed to join in their discussions, nor even to speak in their presence, unless requested to do so. Indian etiquette was very strict, and among the requirements was that of avoiding the direct address. A term of relationship or some title of courtesy was commonly used instead of

the personal name by those who wished to show respect. We were taught generosity to the poor and reverence for the "Great Mystery." *Religion was the basis of all Indian training* [emphasis added].[19]

Preserving such values in a modern world that was antithetical to such notions (be they Dakota or Christian), then, came neither naturally nor simply. Instead, it took a considerable amount of agonizing reflection on Eastman's part to come to terms with "civilization." Eastman makes this most apparent when recounting the earth-shattering changes he underwent upon his father's unexpected return into his life, after eleven years' imprisonment for participating in the 1862 U.S.–Dakota War. His father, Many Lightnings, who returned to his community as Jacob, ushered civilization and Christianity into Eastman's life.

Eastman writes about his father's reappearance twice: first in the final chapter of *Indian Boyhood* (1902) and then in the opening chapter of *From the Deep Woods to Civilization* (1916). At the end of *Indian Boyhood*, Eastman concludes his account of Jacob Eastman's return with dramatic flourish. The drama of Jacob Eastman's "resurrection" is increased when he announces his intent to take his son to the Indian settlement in Flandreau, South Dakota. Eastman is reluctant, but because of his training he relents to his father's wishes. Their ensuing journey occurs in 1873. Along the way, Eastman's father makes prayers, sings hymns, and reads from the book of his new religion. Referring to his father's curious behavior, Eastman states:

> I listened with much astonishment. The hymn contained the word *Jesus*. I did not comprehend what this meant; and my father then told me that Jesus was the Son of God who came on earth to save sinners, and that it was because of him that he had sought me. This conversation made a deep impression on my mind.
>
> Late in the fall we reached the citizen settlement at Flandreau, South Dakota, where my father and some others dwelt among the whites. Here my wild life came to an end, and my school days began.

For some this concluding passage and much of *Indian Boyhood* signals the death knell for the Dakota way, at least in the life of Charles Eastman. Indeed, it is tempting to compare it with a passage that Luther Standing Bear wrote in *My People the Sioux*, in which he concludes his account of his student days at the Carlisle Indian School and his workdays at Wanamaker's department store with this realization: "So I said farewell to the school life and started back to my people, but with a better understanding of life. There would be no more hunting—we would have to work now for our food and clothing. It was like the Garden of Eden after the fall of man."[20]

However, such a simplistic conclusion is complicated by the fact that in Eastman's case his own father is the one inducing his abrupt transition from "wild life" to "school days," as opposed to an Indian agent or missionary, which is how it occurred for Zitkala-Sa, Luther Standing Bear, and Francis La Flesche. While this situation is hardly completely free from coercion—Jacob Eastman, after all, had spent eleven years in a federal prison—we should not overlook the implicit Dakota context in which this episode takes on its meaning. As Eastman recounts: "My father, who was among the fugitives in Canada, had been betrayed by a half-breed across the United States line, near what is now the city of Winnipeg. Some of the party were hanged at Fort Snelling, near St. Paul. We supposed, and, in fact, we were informed that all were hanged. *This was why my uncle, in whose family I lived, had taught me never to spare a white man from the United States* [emphasis added]."[21]

In the Dakota way, now that Eastman's father had returned to him, along with news that his brothers were alive as well, there was no longer any personal need for vengeance upon any Americans he might encounter on the warpath. This is not to say, however, that all is now forgiven with respect to the Dakotas' loss of land and annuities—a matter the adult Eastman will be asked to address much later in life. For the moment, because "filial duty and affection" outweighed his "prejudices," Eastman gave his father the benefit of the doubt that it was time to "accept their mode of life and follow their teaching." Eastman would do this figuratively in *Indian Boyhood* when he put on the clothes his father brought for him. "At first," Eastman says, "I disliked very much to wear garments made by the people I had hated so bitterly. But the thought that, after all, they had not killed my father and brothers, reconciled me, and I put on the clothes." One can say that at this moment Eastman went from being a future pezuta wicasta to being a future medical doctor.[22]

Furthermore, insofar as we are contextualizing Eastman's work within the historic changes that took place across Indian Country as a result of European and American colonization, then it is accurate to state that Eastman is the spiritual heir to Pequot intellectual William Apess. Although Eastman identifies Samson Occom as his intellectual father, calling him his "countryman," in Apess one can see the paradigm into which Eastman molded himself. Similar to Eastman, Apess wrote a much-read autobiography, *A Son of the Forest*, which appeared in 1831, a year after the infamous Indian Removal Act. As a Christian, Apess was flabbergasted by what whites, led by President Andrew Jackson, were doing to Indians in the name of Christianity. At the same time, as expressed in *The Experiences of Five Christian Indians of the Pequot Tribe* (1833) and *Eulogy on King Philip* (1836), Apess regarded the Jacksonian corruption of Christianity to be the culmination of a political movement that began in 1676, when King Philip's War erupted between the Wampanoag and the English colonialists. One could say, as Eastman did in *The Indian To-day* and elsewhere, that this early epoch of Indian-White relations set a pattern that would be repeated almost endlessly across North America, in which Christian principles would be overshadowed by both an insatiable lust for land and a relentless hate for Indians. Indeed, Apess said as much himself to an audience in Boston's Odeon Theater in 1836: "We often hear of the wars breaking out on the frontiers, and it is because the same spirit reigns there that reigned here in New England; and wherever there are Indians, that spirit still reigns; and at present, there is no law to stop it." In other words, the Indian Removal Act initiated an era characterized by U.S. abuse of power against Indian nations, who were typically coerced into signing land cession treaties as the only alternative to outright annihilation. Or, as Apess emphatically worded the situation, "even the president of the United States tells the Indians they cannot live among civilized people" and that they, the American people, want Indian lands; indeed, "they must have them and will have them." Eastman commented on eastern Indian history by pointing out in *The Indian To-day*,

> There have been but few noteworthy Indian wars in the history of America. In 1629 Powhatan's brother revolted against the colonists in Virginia, and King Philip took up arms in Massachusetts in 1675. The Cherokee war of 1758 in North and South Carolina came next; then the conspiracy of Pontiac in 1763, the Creek War from 1812 to 1830, and the Seminole war from 1820 to 1833. These wars in the South were incited by the insolence and aggressiveness of the

Americans. The struggles of the Algonquins and the Iroquois, however, were not conducted wholly on their own initiative. These tribes were used as allies in the long-drawn-out conflicts between the French and the English, and thus initiated into the motives and the methods of the white man's warfare.[23]

Eastman, in turn, looked back more specifically at what happened to the New England Indians as a lesson and a warning to the Sioux Nation, which had fought much with the Americans during his lifetime but which was also beginning to wane under the relentless pressures of westward expansion. As a young undergraduate at Dartmouth College—and as the only Indian taking classes there—Eastman felt he knew his calling; he reflected on it in *From the Deep Woods to Civilization:*

> I went on to Dartmouth College, away up among the granite hills. The country around it is rugged and wild; and thinking of the time when red men lived here in plenty and freedom, it seemed as if I had been destined to come view their graves and bones. No, I said to myself, I have come to continue that which in their last struggle they proposed to take up, in order to save themselves from extinction; but alas! it was too late. Had our New England tribes but followed the example of that great Indian, Samson Occum, and kept up with the development of Dartmouth College, they would have brought forth leaders and men of culture. This was my ambition—that the Sioux should accept civilization before it was too late!

The irony is that ever since white settlers began colonizing the eastern seaboard, they have made it their policy to "civilize" and "Christianize" the indigenous populations—intentions which frequently devolve in the hands of politicians, soldiers, land speculators, and settlers into very un-Christian crimes against Indians. For those persons like Eastman who made the conversion, the rewards beyond survival have been sparse. Then again, we could not have the revitalization movement we see today among Indian nations if we did not first have survival. Vizenor is adamant about this point when he returns to the topic of Eastman's writings in *Fugitive Poses.* After recounting the major events of Eastman's autobiography, Vizenor reflects on the miracle of his endurance: "[Eastman] encircled the horrors of that massacre in stories of native courage and survivance. That sense of presence, rather than absence or aversion, is natural reason and a source of native identities. The doctor enunciated his visions, memories, and totemic creations as an author. Clearly, his autobiographical stories are native survivance not victimry." Vizenor then goes on to invoke Friedrich Nietzsche's notion of "tragic wisdom" as a way of characterizing Eastman's sense of self. This notion pertains to more than simply learning from tragedy; rather, it is the sense of self that emerges from encountering the force of one's destiny. Like the characters of ancient Greek plays, Eastman is compelled to confront forces beyond his control yet in which he must play a pivotal role. However, rather than curse God or the spirits, Eastman, becoming fatalistic, embraces his destiny as his own and imagines a place for himself—and other Indian people—in the fragmented world where he has been cast. In the end, Eastman shows himself to be the kind of Christian Nietzsche thought was no longer possible when he declared the Death of God.[24]

In turns, Eastman retains the Dakota sense of self that can come only from remembering where one is from, whom one's relatives are, the stories they told, and the language in which they were recalled. Such a sense of self becomes an act of survivance when maintained against a society that does not see a place for such a being outside of museums, history books, and popular media. According to Philip J. Deloria in *Playing Indian,* Eastman represents a complicated attempt at preserving authenticity in a non-Indian world that thrives on inauthenticity. What resulted was a difficult blurring of the boundaries between being a Dakota and being "the Indian." Deloria analyzes this phenomenon: "When Eastman donned an Indian headdress, he was connecting himself to his Dakota roots. But he was also—perhaps more compellingly—imitating non-Indian imitations of Indians." In other words, Eastman had to deal with what Vine Deloria claimed all Indians have had to deal with since the beginning of Indian-White relations—*our transparency.* In *Custer Died for Your Sins,* Deloria points out with all the indignation he can muster: "Our foremost plight is our transparency. People can tell just by looking at us what we want, what should be done to help us, how we feel, and what a 'real' Indian is really like. Indian life, as it relates to the real world, is a continuous attempt not to disappoint people who know us. Unfulfilled expectations cause grief and we have already had our share."[25]

In Eastman's case, though, returning to Philip J. Deloria's analysis, he did something other than merely pander to Anglo-American expectations. At the same time that Eastman attracted readers and listeners with imagery from "real" Indian life, he took the opportunity to change the way his audience thought about Indians, subtly displacing their expectations and stereotypes with cultural and historical knowledge that would, hopefully, inform their understanding of contemporary Indian affairs. In the process, however, Eastman "invariably transformed his construction of his own identity—both as a Dakota and an American." In *From the Deep Woods to Civilization*, Eastman resoundingly concludes his narrative with the assertion that he is both "an Indian" and "an American," insofar as both share spiritual and social values, notwithstanding the American penchant for "commerce, nationalism, or material efficiency." Nonetheless, one cannot adapt an alien language, religion, and education without going through a substantial transformation. As Deloria observes about Eastman: "He lived out a hybrid life, distinct in its Indianness but also cross-cultural and assimilatory. By channeling both a Dakota past and an American-constructed Indian Other through his material body—from mind to pen to paper to book to Boy Scout—Eastman made it ever more difficult to pinpoint the cultural locations of Dakotas and Americans, reality and mimetic reality, authenticity and inauthenticity."[26]

What Eastman generated was a set of narratives that informed his Anglo-American reader about Indian culture and history from a Native perspective, on the one hand, but that also, on the other hand, met the approval of his Dakota relatives, namely his grandmother, uncle, and father, who taught him the ways of the *Dakota wicoh'an*. Such a task is easier said than done, if readers will pardon the cliché. In the case of the Indian population, aside from the precipitous decline in our overall numbers during the nineteenth century, Indian people had to deal with a predicament of poor housing, health, and educational services, which was exacerbated by an ambiguous political status that constantly vacillated between being treated as citizens and as foreigners, on top of which was an Indian Bureau without any interest in easing its hegemonic powers over the reservation system. While some may be tempted to blame Eastman and his generation for putting Indians in the arduous position of having to recover their lost traditions, others can easily regard Eastman as a role model, not only for Dakotas but for people of all Indian nations. On this point, Carly Eastman Beane, a direct descendent of John Eastman, Charles's brother, writes in a 2006 paper,

> Eastman's legacy has influenced, and continues to impact, generations of young native scholars, searching for a place to make their voices heard in an academic world that was not designed with the intent of encouraging and strengthening the most important aspect of their identities—that of their specifically indigenous character...
>
> Years after the first publications of his work, native students today can still relate to many of the conflicts and concerns that Eastman wrote of. Students today struggle with incorporating their traditional teachings and native philosophies into an academic environment that often does not always legitimize their beliefs. The historical suppression of indigenous languages is one important example of how the system has consistently failed native students. Eastman's work lives on in the native students of today who fight for justice by their own standards.

Beane's comments underscore that education is not only one of the battlefields in which Indian people are fighting for their right to preserve and revitalize their cultures; it is also, as Eastman claimed, the most important means available to Indians for achieving success in the modern world into which we have all been thrust. In the end, although Eastman's books were all published in either Boston or New York, with white audiences in mind, it is fair to say that as Eastman wrote he also sought the approval of those he counted as friends and family in the Indian community. And with this in mind we now turn to analyzing and appreciating Eastman's legacy as a paragon of American Indian intellectualism. For us, his Native readers, Eastman's writings still tell our stories and address our concerns. At the same time, they are stories that Eastman wanted all to hear, Indian and non-Indian alike.[27]

2

The Traditions of Their Fathers
Eastman and Dakota Sacred History

*"And who is the grandfather of these silent people? Is it not
the Great Mystery? For they know the laws of their life so well!
They must have for their Maker our Maker. Then they are our brothers!"*
Thus spoke one of the philosophers and orators of the Red men[1]

Thus also spoke Charles A. Eastman in the foreword to *Red Hunters and
the Animal People*. With this publication, Eastman contributed to what
would become a major genre in American Indian literature—traditional
myths and legends retold in English for a wide audience. Zitkala-Sa
(aka Gertrude Bonnin) made a slightly earlier contribution when she
published *Old Indian Legends* in 1901, in which she asserts, "The old legends of America belong quite as much to the blue-eyed little patriot as to
the black-haired aborigine." However, though Eastman and Zitkala-Sa
may have written with both the Indian and non-Indian reader in mind,
the authenticity of the stories is retained through the manner in which
they were acquired, which was firsthand in the native language. Zitkala-
Sa refers to "the Dakota story-tellers," whom she listened to throughout
North and South Dakota, where she "often listened to the same story
told over again by a new story-teller." Eastman, in turn, states, "The
stories contained in this book are based upon the common experiences
and observations of the Red hunter." Moreover, "The scene of the stories
is laid in the great Northwest, the ancient home of the Dakota or Sioux
nation, my people." At the same time, what Arthur C. Parker said later
in the introduction to his 1923 book, *Seneca Myths and Folk Tales,* may also
be said about any collection of stories culled from the oral tradition.
Specifically, Parker admonished his reader not to presume that myths
and legends were sufficient for comprehending a given people's culture.
For example, in the case of the Seneca: "To complete our knowledge we
must have before us works on Seneca history, ethnology, archæology,

religion, government and language. Finally, we must personally know the descendants of the mighty Seneca nation of old. We must enter into the life of the people in a sympathetic way, for only then can we get at the soul of the race." What Parker, Eastman, Zitkala-Sa, and others not mentioned—such as Francis La Flesche, James Murie, and J. N. B. Hewitt—make clear is that the relationship between American Indians and their myths and legends is not based on texts written in an ancient and rarely used language, such as Latin or Sanskrit. Rather, the Dakota and Seneca dialects in which the above-mentioned myths and legends were originally told are still being used to tell these stories today (certainly this was true when these narratives were collected). The implication is that insofar as this kind of work can be done, it indicates that "the soul of the race" still exists in the people.[2]

On the other hand, because nations like the Dakota endured an immense amount of hardship through their relationship with Anglo-Americans, it is easy to become fatalistic about both their traditions and their physical endurance. In *The Dakota or Sioux in Minnesota as They Were in 1834,* which the Minnesota Historical Society first published in 1908, the author, Samuel W. Pond, who, with his brother Gideon, served as a missionary to the Santee Dakota, bemoaned the losses to posterity that the Dakota incurred as a result of the 1862 U.S.-Dakota War, calling it by what the Dakota have always regarded as a misnomer, "the Sioux Outbreak":

> Considerable traditionary information might have been obtained from the Indians in 1834, but probably no one has taken the pains to collect or preserve it, and now it is too late. During the ensuing thirty years, the Dakotas of Minnesota have experienced strange vicissitudes of fortune, such as were calculated to turn their thoughts from the things that formerly engaged their attention. In the midst of the exciting scenes attending and following the Sioux Outbreak, and harassed with anxiety about the future, they have had no time to think of the past or give much heed to the traditions of their fathers. The young men have had their minds occupied with things new and strange, and the old men who had treasured up in their memories things of the past are all gone.

Although Pond goes on to document a still-living oral tradition among the Dakota, he nonetheless maintains a rather romantic lament for the passing—or, as it was more popularly put, the vanishing—of a way of life. Pond's book appeared in 1908, but the publication was posthumous, the missionary having died in Bloomington, Minnesota, on January 20, 1878. Consequently, though Pond knew some of Charles Eastman's elders, such as his grandfather, Cloud Man (Marpiya-wichasta), Eastman and Pond never met. Thus, Pond could not even have gotten a hint of what Cloud Man's grandson was destined to create as a Dakota writer, a body of work that may have allayed some of Pond's distress over the Dakota's loss of "traditionary information." By 1908, Eastman had published the first volume of his autobiography, *Indian Boyhood*, which was followed by *Red Hunters and the Animal People*. While these two books alone are not enough to claim that Dakota culture remained fully intact at the turn of the twentieth century—far from it—they nevertheless signify that some root of the sacred tree, as Black Elk might have said, was still alive.[3]

In *Indian Boyhood*, after completing the opening section regarding his birth, his grandmother's care, and his family's flight from Minnesota in 1862—which we will focus on in chapter four—Eastman does not return to the Dakotas' relationship with Minnesota until section V, "Family Traditions," in which the chapters titled "A Visit to Smoky Day" and "The Stone Boy" appear. With Smoky Day, a much-revered tribal historian, and his stories, the reader is introduced to the narrative paradigm that subtends much of Eastman's writings. The paradigm in question is not so much a theory as it is an extension of the Dakota way of accounting for natural phenomena and historical events, which required equal amounts of imagination and of faithfulness to the facts. As Eastman makes clear in his 1914 book on scouting, "The great secret of [the storyteller's] success was his ability to portray a character or a situation truthfully, yet with just a touch of humorous or dramatic exaggeration. The scene is clearly visualized; the action moves quickly, with successive events leading up to the climax, which must be handled with much dignity and seriousness, or pathos and gravity may be turned upside down in the unexpectedness of the catastrophe." These characteristics describe not only Smoky Day's storytelling style but Eastman's as well. What kind of storyteller Eastman may have been in person we are left to wonder, since there is no known film or sound recording of him. What we do have are his several writings, in which storytelling always plays a central role. Furthermore, Eastman's work with the Dakota oral tradition bears the ulterior motive of promoting and preserving an understanding of the Dakota worldview, which is evident in *Indian Boyhood*, then becomes more apparent in *Red Hunters and the Animal People*, entailing that his work is much more than mere salvage anthropology. On the contrary, what Eastman does with his storytelling may be compared with what Plato does in *The Republic*, in which the narrations, like the Allegory of the Cave, are a way of guiding the mind toward ideas and insights. What makes the Dakota tradition—and Eastman's work with it—different from its ancient Greek counterpart is that the Dakota do not lapse into dogmatism; instead, the Dakota philosopher takes a more indirect approach to edifying his listener or reader. Luther Standing Bear underscores this indigenous pedagogy in *Land of the Spotted Eagle:*

> In Lakota society it was the duty of every parent to give the knowledge they possessed to their children. Each and every parent was a teacher and, as a matter of fact, all elders were instructors of those younger than themselves. And the instruction they gave was mostly through their actions—that is, they interpreted to us through actions what we should try to do. We learned by watching and imitating examples placed before us. Slowly and naturally the faculties of observation and memory became highly trained and the Lakota child became educated in the manners, lore, and customs of his people without a strained and conscious effort. I have known children to become very apt in learning the songs they heard. One singing would sometimes suffice and the child would have the words and tune so well in mind that he could never forget it.[4]

American Indians from all walks of life and tribal affiliations were certainly capable, when necessary, of being didactic, even scolding, in their remarks to soldiers, politicians, and bureaucrats who were either unable or unwilling to appreciate indigenous attitudes regarding land and community. Frederick E. Hoxie does a magnificent job of demonstrating this tradition in *Speaking Back to Civilization*, in which he anthologizes an array of Indian leaders who were exposed to and educated about mainstream institutions, such as "schools, courts, art museums, publishing houses, and newspapers," as well as capable of expressing themselves through the media they were acquiring in their modern lives, such as "books, paintings, lawsuits, and perceptive commentaries on contemporary issues." With new tools in hand, Indian leaders were far from coy about speaking up about the issues and problems that concerned them. "Indians began to talk back to American society," Hoxie writes. "By talking back to those who considered themselves superior, Indians could show that they rejected the self-serving nationalism they heard from missionaries and bureaucrats. The Natives made it clear that they refused to accept the definitions others had of them—savage, backward, doomed. And they attacked people who thought white culture epitomized the virtues of 'civilization.'"[5]

One result of the Dakota practice of storytelling is that Eastman deepens his portrayal of the Dakotas' relationship with their Minnesota homeland—as well as the Great Sioux Nation—by demonstrating the extent to which this relationship is integral to the people's collective memory and knowledge. Essential to the Dakota myths are place names referring to locations that are farther north than the historic southern Minnesota home in which European explorers found them, thereby signifying a lengthy and involved relationship with the land that antecedes the written, non-Indian historical record. Turning primarily to the oral tradition—as well as his personal experience—enables Eastman to set a Dakota-centered agenda to his autobiographical, historical, and literary discourses, which, above all, do not rely upon meeting any of the prevailing non-Indian, Euro-American notions of nonfiction writing. In this sense, Eastman is well ahead of his time: even as late as 1967, non-Indian historians, such as Roy W. Meyer, were still determined to write about Indian history from a strictly Euro-American point of view. As Meyer states in his preface to *History of the Santee Sioux*, "Despite the obvious advantages of a book about Indians written from the 'inside,' this one is quite frankly written from the 'outside.' History is based largely on written records, and most of the records from which the history of the Santee Sioux must be reconstructed were kept by white men."[6]

To the contrary, what Eastman aspires to throughout his nine books is extending the Dakota oral tradition—complete with its attendant values and precepts—into his written English works. In other words, he is working toward what Zitkala-Sa set out to do in *Old Indian Legends*: "And now I have tried to transplant the native spirit of these tales—root

and all—into the English language, since America in the last few centuries has acquired a second tongue." This necessitates, of course, an
act of "translation" that westernizes Eastman's narratives as much as it
indigenizes them. In light of this, familiarity with some of the concepts
of the Dakota oral tradition is in order.[7]

Ella Deloria observed, in *Dakota Texts,* that there are two major categories in the Dakota storytelling tradition: *ohunkakan* and *woyakapi.*
Ohunkakan are stories that are the most well known among the Dakota
and thus the most often repeated by storytellers; they are the "farthest
removed from the events of every day life of the Dakota people."
Ohunkakan, moreover, are the residuum of a very remote time when a
different order of beings dwelled on the earth: "These tales, in which
generally some mythological character like Iktomi, Iya, the Crazy Bull,
the Witch, or Waziya (the Cold), takes part together with human beings,
are part of the common literary stock of the people." Another type of
ohunkakan contains fictional or "novelistic" elements. These stories are
not nearly as well known as the first group of ohunkakan. What distinguishes this group is that the sacred beings have stepped out of the picture. Nonetheless, wondrous things still happen to people who are
much like the people of today, and these things are regarded as within
the realm of possibility.[8]

The woyakapi, like the ohunkakan, are divided into two types. The
first type includes those stories that are thought to have "happened to
our people in comparatively recent times, perhaps in the lifetime of the
aged narrator's grandfather or great-grandfather." The first type of woyakapi may also pertain to specific localities, and "while the miraculous
still runs through many of them, they are regarded as occurrences that
may happen to someone aided by supernatural powers." The second
type of woyakapi consists of the mundane but often entertaining stories
about a local band, of which every Dakota band has its own stories.
"These stories," meaning the entire breadth of the oral tradition, "were
the libraries of our people," Luther Standing Bear states on behalf of
the Lakota. "In each story there was recorded some event of interest or
importance, some happening that affected the lives of the people. There
were calamities, discoveries, achievements, and victories to be kept. The
seasons and the years were named for principal events that took place."[9]

Woyakapi, in particular, is the appropriate way to either entertain guests or introduce visitors to the ways of the community. Such is the agenda, not only in *Indian Boyhood* but also in *Red Hunters and the Animal People.* Written while Eastman and his family resided in Amherst, Massachusetts, *Red Hunters* consists of a dozen stories about animals indigenous to the Old Northwest: "The Great Pipestone Quarry, Eagle's Nest Butte, the Little Rosebud River, and all the other places described under their real names are real and familiar features of that country." Further indigenizing, if you will, Eastman's narratives is the proposition that the stories invoke a time, "before 1870, when the buffalo and other large game still roamed the wilderness and the Red men lived the life I knew as a boy." Eastman will return to this theme in *The Soul of the Indian:* "I have attempted to paint the religious life of the typical American Indian as it was before he knew the white man." In particular, Eastman wants to invoke an image of Indian culture and religion that is purified—in the same sense as an *inipi* or sweat lodge purifies—of the demoralizing effects of "civilization," be it from alcoholism, poverty, or materialism. In this context, remembering stories is good medicine. Some stories, as Standing Bear recounts, "taught the virtues—kindness, obedience, thrift, and the rewards of right living" that many Indian nations need to recover.[10]

Integral to this native pedagogy is the notion that virtues and other concepts can be taught through the wisdom of animals, which is the impetus for *Red Hunters.* Indeed, the stories therein are far from autobiographical—in fact, they are typically written from the animal's perspective. Yet the truth of these stories is the truth that comes from experiencing something for oneself, entailing that Eastman understood the animals he writes about because he observed these creatures for himself and, further, his observations have been corroborated by generations of other Dakotas. Or, as Eastman has one of his characters say, "Of course, we have all heard the traditions of the old hunters as they have been handed down from our fathers, but the things that we ourselves have seen and known are straight and strong in our minds as a newly made arrow." Moreover, with regard to the continuum that exists between woyakapi and ohunkakan, Eastman also states, "The main incidents in all of them, even those which are unusual and might appear incredible to the white man, are actually current among the Sioux and deemed by them worthy of belief."[11]

The stories that follow are an engrossing array of tales of "wild" animals engaging in life and death struggles with hunters and other animals. Similar to their human counterparts within the Indian community, buffalo, beavers, prairie dogs, and mice live in their own tribes, complete with kinship ties and customs. Other animals, like mountain lions and wolves, exhibit warrior-like qualities yet show a grave concern for their children. When they face peril, the reader immediately sympathizes with their fate. This is the case in "A Founder of Ten Towns," in which Pezpeza, a prairie dog, lives to see his villages overrun by Indians who are disturbed by their presence near the scaffolds bearing their deceased relatives. The Indians, naturally thinking only of their dead, drive Pezpeza's tribe from the area by stopping the entrances to their homes and scorching the grass. In the end, only Pezpeza and his wife are left. Unavoidably, one is tempted to read this story as an allegory for what happened to the Indian nations across the continent. Specifically, that the Indians were treated like animals whom the invaders did not think to consider when they decided, for their own interests, to drive them out.[12]

With the Pezpeza story in mind, it is pertinent to point out here that the only creatures in *Red Hunters* that seem out of place in Eastman's landscape are the white settlers who intervene into the ancient rhythm of season and hunt, hunger and feast, birth and death that existed long before homesteading, railroads, and Manifest Destiny overran the region. In "On Wolf Mountain," Eastman describes the disdain sheep ranchers have for the gray wolves that occasionally prey upon their stock—and the comparable feeling they have for Indians. After recounting a vicious and seemingly very organized attack upon a sheep ranch, in which all the sheep were slaughtered, one of the survivors, ranch owner Hank Simmons, makes his way to the local army post, where he tells his incredible tale to a man referred to only as a sutler. Upon hearing about the wolves' attack, the sutler declares: "Oh, the devil! You don't mean it . . . Well, I told you before to take out all the strychnine you could get hold of. We have got to rid the country of the Injuns and gray wolves before civilization will stick in this region!"[13]

What may be all the more astounding to consider is the possibility that a reader could come across such statements and be completely unaffected. Although the term *genocide* was not coined until after World War II, the average reader still knew that slaughter, murder, and massacre were both illegal and immoral. Yet, the proposed and actual annihilation of Indian communities is often treated like a natural catastrophe—unfortunate but inevitable. For many readers of *Red Hunters*, it may have been too easy to slip into the attitude that the stories were little more than children's entertainment, complete with talking animals. Alas, even for the rare reader who realizes there is something much more profound occurring in the narrative, books like *Red Hunters* were not enough to counteract the overwhelming production of savage stereotypes generated by western novels, wild west shows, and a burgeoning film industry. Nonetheless, *Red Hunters* is a paragon of the indigenous practice of adapting traditional storytelling skills to the modern paradigm of the book. Although it would have been wonderful if *Red Hunters*, and other books like it, had been issued in a bilingual edition—which during Eastman's time was the domain of anthropologists—the book nevertheless accomplishes the remarkable feat of transporting the reader into a Dakota-centered world, in which animals are not only "persons" but also, in some cases, "sacred beings," complete with concern for family and community and often possessing great wisdom and medicine.

Nowhere is this reverence more apparent than in "The Mustering of the Herds." The plot is about the death of a white buffalo, Ptesanwee, the matriarch of a large herd, and the birth of a new white calf, which just took place at a distance, "in a hidden nook upon the Shaeyela River, that flows through the Land of Mystery." Meanwhile, the Two Kettle band prepared for their "great spring hunt." Preparations include the lighting and ritual smoking of the long-stemmed pipe, a "spirit talk," and singing, which "is done to call the spirits of the bison, and charm them into a happy departure for the spirit land." When the hunt begins, the hunters are surprised by the tenacity with which the buffalo bulls defend the herd. A hunter is even killed in the fray. It is not long, however, before the people discover the dead white buffalo left behind by the wandering herd. Befitting the status of this sacred being, the people "tied or hobbled their ponies at some distance, and all came with tobacco or arrows in their hands. They reverently addressed the dead cow and placed the tobacco gently around her for an offering."[14]

As the seasons cycled through the year, the herd became quite excited one summery day upon learning of the new white calf now in their midst, the daughter of one of their own, Hinpoha. The news became a time of feasting and celebrating. Once again, though, the hunters prepared—this time with the intention of capturing Hinpoha's daughter. A person is fortunate to see such a creature even once in a lifetime, but to capture one safely is to be truly blessed. As an elder in the story explains, "They who see her shall be fortunate in hunting and in war. If she be captured, the people who take her need never go hungry." Given that the competition for food, including buffalo, became more intense the farther west white settlements expanded, such medicine was eminently vital to a people's future well-being. In *Indian Boyhood*, Eastman bemoans the buffalo's demise in the Old Northwest, which he witnessed as the Dakota endured their years of exile after the 1862 conflict: "It must now be thirty years since our long journey in search of new hunting-grounds, from the Assiniboine river to the Upper Missouri. The buffalo, formerly so abundant between the two rivers, had begun to shun their usual haunts, on account of the great numbers of Canadian half-breeds in that part of the country. There was also the first influx of English sportsmen, whose wholesale methods of destruction wrought such havoc with the herds. These seemingly intelligent animals correctly prophesied to the natives the approach of the pale-face."[15]

On the day of the hunt in "The Mustering of the Herds," the hunters gather, ready as if for war: "Their dusky faces and naked bodies were extravagantly painted; their locks fantastically dressed; even the ponies were decorated." In the middle of the large herd, the infant white calf stood with her mother. The hunters, awestruck, speak in hushed whispers: "To them she looked like an earth-visiting spirit in her mysterious whiteness." When the hunters succeed in capturing Hinpoha's young daughter, they return home to great rejoicing, for they have captured, more than a mere trophy, a symbol of hope and well-being. The white buffalo is now their talisman against hunger. By the same token, the white robe made from the calf's flesh "shall be handed down from generation to generation, and wherever it is found there shall be abundance of meat for the Indian." Ultimately, *Red Hunters and the Animal People* is about changing the image of animals that dominates the popular American imagination, already substantially industrialized and urbanized, in which nature is something "out there" as opposed to the Dakota of Eastman's memory, who regarded it as "right here." At the same time, Eastman averts from merely turning the "right here" into a romanticized landscape by reminding the reader that, just as his tales and insights are the product of personal experience, so too must the reader take care to make his or her own connections with the natural world, lest he or she be overcome with the innervating effects of civilization. "In civilization," Eastman writes in *Indian Scout Craft and Lore*, "there are many deaf ears and blind eyes. Because the average boy in town has been deprived of close contact and intimacy with nature, what he has learned from books he soon forgets, or is unable to apply. All learning is a dead language to him who gets it at second hand."[16]

At the same time, Eastman's sense of nature consistently displays elements of nostalgia. One can say that this longing to "return to the woods" takes on some very poignant cultural and political qualities in light of the fact that the one doing the recollecting, namely Eastman as storyteller, comes from an exiled Indian nation. To understand Eastman's acts of cultural revitalization, we need to look to *Indian Boyhood*. While this book has been criticized recently as an example of Eastman's attempt to distance himself from his Dakota past, these arguments are based on the superficial adjustments Eastman made in adapting to life outside the reservation and inside the non-Indian community. In which case, Eastman neither distances himself from nor dispenses with his Dakota heritage; rather, he wraps his Dakota identity around his shoulders like a war shirt covered with medicine symbols that will protect him from the destructive forces of so-called civilization. Similar to the way Eastman dressed when he first headed off to school in Flandreau, he willingly acquired some of the accoutrements of those who now dwell among his people. What this means for his storytelling is that Eastman not only writes rather than speaks but also does so in English (with some assistance from his white wife, Elaine). Moreover, although the storytelling event that Eastman recounts in *Indian Boyhood*, specifically in the section titled "Family Traditions," occurs outside of

Minnesota, in the Dakotas' exilic home in Manitoba, the stories themselves take the listener—and reader—back to the Dakota's original homeland and the mythic time intrinsic to the ohunkakan.[17]

Before Smoky Day begins his narrations, his young listener presents him with a gift of tobacco and an eagle feather, as both compensation and a token of respect for the aged storyteller. Upon accepting Eastman's gift, Smoky Day proceeds to regale the young Eastman, still known as Hakadah, with a brave story about his paternal grandfather's family, beginning with Cloud Man. Smoky Day wants to teach Hakadah about the line of ancestors from which he is descended, many of whom are great warriors and leaders. It is important that Hakadah hear these things, not only for his growing self-esteem but also so that he will strive to model himself after his revered ancestors.

The first story begins with Cloud Man's two brothers being murdered by a band member, one of the worst crimes that can befall such a small, tightly knit community. Naturally, there were those who were completely outraged and argued that the murderer ought to be killed for his offense. When Cloud Man is given the opportunity to slay his brothers' murderer, however, he declines, but not out of fear of killing. As prominent warriors, Hakadah's grandfather and his brothers never had their courage in question, yet Cloud Man did not let loose his rage. "This, my boy," as Eastman recalls Smoky Day's words, "is a test of true bravery. Self-possession and self-control at such a moment is proof of a strong heart." A lesser man would have simply given in to his baser emotions, thereby creating more hardship and the possibility of a blood feud in the community.[18]

Smoky Day then moves on to the story of Jingling Thunder, to whom Ohiyesa is related through his grandfather, Cloud Man. The story takes place, according to Smoky Day, "forty winters before the falling of many stars, which event occurred twenty winters after the coming of the black-robed white priest; and that was fourteen winters before the annihilation by our people of thirty lodges of the Sac and Fox Indians." Yet the story is invoked as if it happened only yesterday. In Smoky Day's skillful narration—which Eastman artfully re-creates for us—the words take us back over time and space to when the Dakota still owned the land from which they would be driven in 1862. "Our people lived then on the east bank of the Mississippi, a little south of where Imnejah-skah, or White Cliff (St. Paul, Minnesota), now stands. After they left Mille Lacs they founded several villages, but finally settled in this spot, whence the tribes have gradually dispersed. Here a battle occurred which surpassed all others in history. It lasted one whole day—the Sacs and Foxes and the Dakotas against the Ojibways." The Dakota met their Sac and Fox allies along the St. Croix River. Among the combatants was a grandmother and her only grandchild, the very last of their band. The grandson now sought "a just revenge for the annihilation of his family." Furthermore, he would do so bearing the familiar name of "The Little Last," or Hakadah. Jingling Thunder, of course, distinguished himself in battle, slaying the Ojibwe's great chief, which caused the Ojibwe warriors to lose heart and give up the fight. The Dakota, on the other hand, were emboldened by Jingling Thunder's deed and routed their enemy, driving the Ojibwe "out of their territory." Jingling Thunder not only went on to attain further distinction but also, as Smoky Day told Ohiyesa, "became the ancestor of a famous band of the Sioux, of whom your own father...was a member."[19]

Smoky Day speaks of Eastman's father, Many Lightnings, in the past tense because at the time it was presumed that the Americans had executed him for his participation in the 1862 conflict. But, as Ohiyesa learns, being killed is the risk any true warrior willingly takes when going to war. Knowing this does not make the mourning for men lost in battle any less severe, however, as illustrated by Smoky Day's story of Morning Star and Winona. Morning Star was one of three brothers, also Ohiyesa's ancestors, who partook of a war party into Ojibwe Country at the behest of "Wakinyan-tonka, the great medicine man." The Dakota war party fought seven battles and was successful all seven times. However, during their return trip, in which they used the enemies' birch-bark canoes, the war chief sensed that there was misfortune at hand. None among the war party consequently seemed willing to lead the Dakota fleet—until Morning Star volunteered to ride in the first canoe. True to the war chief's premonition, the Dakota warriors were ambushed, a rain of arrows washing over them. The Dakota warriors nevertheless managed to fend off their Ojibwe adversaries, but not without casualties.[20]

"At home, meanwhile," Smoky Day relates, "the people had been alarmed by ill omens." Among those worried about the war party's fate was Winona, the eldest daughter of a great chief, whose heart belonged to Morning Star. Winona took it upon herself to seek out the missing warriors, setting out in a canoe up the Mississippi River. Eventually, she thought she heard the sounds of "young men giving courtship calls in the distance." Suddenly, above her, she spotted six sandhill cranes. Winona thought to herself that they must be the spirits of the six warriors lost to the tribe, and she sensed that Morning Star was with them. At that moment, floating by her canoe, she saw the body of her beloved. Winona cried out to the Great Mystery. She begged to join Morning Star. "It was evening," Smoky Day concludes his story for Ohiyesa, "The pale moon arose in the east and the stars were bright. At this very hour the news of the disaster was brought home by a returning scout, and the village was plunged in grief, but Winona's spirit had flown away. No one ever saw her again." Smoky Day then tells Ohiyesa that this is enough storytelling for the evening.[21]

As Smoky Day begins the next and longest story, "Little Stone Boy," Eastman recalls the unexpected way in which the learned storyteller prefaces his narrative, announcing to Hakadah, "I will tell you one of the kind we call myths or fairy stories." Moreover, the so-called "myth or fairy story" is about "men and women who do wonderful things—things that ordinary people cannot do at all. Sometimes they are not exactly human beings, for they partake of the nature of men and beasts, or of men and gods." What follows in actuality is a subtle transition from the woyakapi to the ohunkakan, as Ella Deloria defined these terms. It should also be noted that Eastman tells a slightly different version of the Little Stone Boy story in *The Soul of the Indian,* a project in which such tales served as the foundation to Dakota identity and culture:

> Every religion has its Holy Book, and ours was a mingling of history, poetry, and prophecy, of precept and folk-lore, even such as the modern reader finds within the covers of his Bible. This Bible of ours was our whole literature, a living Book, sowed as precious seed by our wisest sages, and springing anew in the wondering eyes and upon the innocent lips of little children. Upon its hoary wisdom or proverb and fable, its mystic and legendary lore thus sacredly preserved and transmitted from father to son, was based in large part our customs and philosophy.

As such, "Little Stone Boy" places the Dakota in their original Minnesota homeland—long before the whites came. Such an effort, in some hands, would be little more than romantic musings, especially in the maudlin sense of the word. In Eastman's, however, one might argue that it is an act of decolonization before decolonization was invented. In other words, Eastman sought in his retelling of Dakota stories what contemporary Dakota historian Waziyatawin Angela Wilson refers to in her introduction to *Remember This!* as *hipi itokab,* "which literally means *before they came.*" The "they" Wilson refers to is of course the Europeans, Americans, and Canadians who infiltrated and colonized Dakota lands. "So," as Wilson asserts, "in reference to seeking decolonization of our [indigenous peoples'] minds, we might seek *tawacin suta wan hipi itokab,* or *a strong mind before they came.*" As Eastman might say, all of this begins at the beginning, with the stories of first things.[22]

The story of Little Stone Boy begins with ten brothers and their sixteen-year-old sister. The sister is especially skilled at embroidery, while all of the brothers are outstanding hunters. Together they live quite happily apart from anyone else. One evening, the eldest brother fails to return from hunting, and the sister has a premonition that something bad has befallen him. The second eldest volunteers to look for him and heads out to make his search first thing the next morning. However, when evening rolls around again, the second eldest brother does not return. So the third eldest brother decides to look for the other two, but he does not return either. And so it continues with the remaining brothers until all are missing, leaving their sister alone and terribly worried. With no one left to help her, the sister sets out on her own to find her brothers. But search as she may, she cannot find them anywhere. Assuming that they are lost to her for good, she begins to grieve for them.

One day, while in a state of mourning, the sister is walking along the edge of a stream when she spots a most beautiful pebble. She cannot resist picking it up, and when she does she becomes inexplicably happy. Holding it to her bosom, she soon forgets about her sorrow. Although she cannot account for what happened to her, she nevertheless goes home in a much lighter mood than she has felt for some time.

The next morning she decides to return to the same place along the stream where she found the pebble. Soon after reaching this spot she is overcome by sleep. Upon awaking she is amazed to find a baby boy with her. She immediately picks up the baby and kisses him, naming him Little Stone Boy because he is so heavy. The sister takes the newborn child home to raise him as her own son.

Little Stone Boy grows more quickly than an ordinary child, and soon he is talking and asking questions. He notices the bows and arrows around the lodge and inquires about their owners. Little Stone Boy's mother explains what happened to her brothers. Little Stone Boy says that he will go and seek out his uncles. His mother fears that he will only be lost like the others, however, and so implores him not to go. Little Stone Boy feels confident about his search and assures his mother that all will be fine. Before heading out, Little Stone Boy sets a pillow upright in the lodge and tells his mother that as long as that pillow stands up she may assume that he is all right. With that, Little Stone Boy begins the search for his uncles.

Little Stone Boy first asks every animal he finds if any of them know of his uncles' whereabouts. None of them can help him. Eventually, he confronts a Bear who is more interested in attacking Little Stone Boy than in speaking with him. Seeing the great animal charge at him, Little Stone Boy turns himself into stone, foiling the Bear's attack. Unable to dig its teeth into the boy's flesh, the Bear is killed by an arrow Little Stone Boy shoots into its heart.

Little Stone Boy continues his search. At some point he comes upon a pine tree that looks as if it has been struck by lightning. There are also signs of a recent struggle. Suddenly, Little Stone Boy is confronted by a Whirlwind covered in dark clouds and shooting out lightning. The Whirlwind challenges Little Stone Boy to combat. Little Stone Boy accepts, and they begin to fight. Despite all the chaos that the Whirlwind is able to kick up, Little Stone Boy prevails as the winner. As a token of victory, Little Stone Boy takes the scarlet down that the Whirlwind had on his scalp.

Little Stone Boy blows on the scarlet down, which is carried on the wind and which he follows into the sky. The scarlet down leads Little Stone Boy to where the Whirlwind lives in the land of the Thunderbirds. In order to reach this place, Little Stone Boy has to follow the scarlet down to the top of a very tall mountain. After achieving the pinnacle, Little Stone Boy looks out over "a beautiful land, with lakes, rivers, plains and mountains." Little Stone Boy also sees many lodges throughout the valley, "as far as the eye could reach." In the distance, Little Stone Boy notices a majestic tree that towers above all the others. He heads down the mountain until he reaches the foot of the tree.[23]

Little Stone Boy blows again on the scarlet down, and it leads him to the highest branches, where there is a great nest. In the nest Little Stone Boy discovers countless red eggs of various sizes. As he examines the eggs, he begins playing with them recklessly. Suddenly, an excited group of people rushes toward him from the many lodges below. Assuming that he is under attack, Little Stone Boy throws an egg, killing one of the men. The people become very distraught, shouting to Little Stone Boy, "Give me my heart!" He immediately realizes that each red egg is a heart that belongs to one of the people clambering below. But since these are the people who took his uncles, he decides to break them all.

Little Stone Boy spares four of the eggs, bringing them down the tree with him and walking into the village. Four little boys are there, and he asks them to show him to his uncles' bones, which they do. Little Stone Boy tells the four boys to bring him wood, water, stones, and willow wands. As soon as the requested items are brought, Little Stone Boy builds a sweat lodge. He brings his uncles' bones into the sweat lodge, where he slowly and methodically resurrects each of them.

All this time, Little Stone Boy's mother waits nervously for her son, hoping and praying that he will return safely, and with his uncles in tow. For an untold amount of time, the mother watches the pillow that Little Stone Boy left standing as a sign of his well-being. Each day it stays standing, until at last Little Stone Boy returns from the land of the Thunderbirds, followed by his uncles. "Mother," Little Stone Boy exclaims, "your ten brothers are coming—prepare a feast!" Together they all live quite happily for a long while. But the story does not end here.[24]

Sometime after successfully bringing his uncles home, Little Stone Boy took to killing animals wantonly. Little Stone Boy was advised not to treat animals so carelessly, but he was certain that his supernatural powers would protect him from any repercussions. One day, however, Little Stone Boy caught wind of a conspiracy that the animals were hatching to overthrow him and his family. He told his uncles what he had heard, to which they responded by scolding their nephew, saying, "we told you that you would get into trouble by killing so many of our sacred animals for your own amusement." Nevertheless, the uncles agreed to assist their nephew in defending their home.[25]

Little Stone Boy prepares for the upcoming battle by tossing pebbles into the air; they turn into stone walls that surround their lodge. Little Stone Boy builds two stone lodges, one sitting atop the other. For their part, the uncles make many bows and arrows while their sister fabricates several pairs of moccasins and cooks plenty of food, particularly for her son, who declares that he will defend their home by himself.

The day of battle arrives at last. The great animals launch a terrible and massive attack. Armies of buffalo, muskrat, beavers, badgers, bears, or sparrows, each led by their own chief, charge at the stone lodges. Little Stone Boy shoots volleys of arrows at blinding speed, slaying animals by the thousands. Still, the animals come, aided now by a torrential rain. Little Stone Boy's uncles and mother stay deep inside the stone lodges as the battle wages. Alas, Little Stone Boy cannot stop the water from flooding the stone structures, and his uncles and mother drown in the deluge. Little Stone Boy nonetheless is not entirely defeated: he stands to this day, half-buried where the animals left him, forever unable to walk.[26]

At the end of the "Family Traditions" section of *Indian Boyhood*, Smoky Day finishes tracing out a genealogy that goes from Hakadah to his father (Many Lightnings) and grandfather (Cloud Man) and then on to Jingling Thunder, Morning Star, and Little Stone Boy. Reinforced through these connections is the idea that Hakadah is the latest link in a long chain of well-respected individuals going back to mythological times. By virtue of connecting Hakadah with Morning Star and Little Stone Boy, Smoky Day asserts that the virtues Hakadah must acquire are grounded in the ohunkakan. This path only Hakadah can choose for himself, and he will as he makes the transition from being Hakadah to Ohiyesa and on to Charles Eastman. Moreover, this path can only be seen within a culture unified by a common mythology. Remembering this and maintaining the connection is the difference between remaining grounded and entering an existential crisis. The connection is important, not only at the individual level but also at the tribal.

With this in mind, Smoky Day invokes through his stories an axis mundi that connects the Dakota Nation to their homeland, the only place from which Dakota identity and values may be derived. This impulse is particularly poignant in light of the fact that Hakadah is learning about his ancestors not long after his family's forced removal from Minnesota. By means of placing the stories in concrete locations, like Imnejah-skah or the site where Little Stone Boy rests, Smoky Day is making a clear claim to a particular area as being *where the Dakota belong,* in which "belong" is defined by the phenomenon of being indigenous to a *given place,* in which "given" means set aside by the Creator. This claim, of course, only comes to light when one situates these stories within a Dakota context. Otherwise, in, say, the context of a Christian evangelical mission, Dakota stories may too easily be taken for mere entertainment at best or blasphemy at worst. Pond, fortunately for the Dakota, tended toward the former category, as he did in *Dakota Life in the Upper Midwest,* in which he listened to these stories and called them "fables" that exhibit an "inventive genius and active imagination." Pond went on to observe,

> These fables are full of the supernatural and are made up of many strange events and wild adventures, but they will hardly bear a literal translation into English, and to civilize is to spoil them.
>
> Years ago the Dakotas were in the habit of repeating these tales for the entertainment of company, and I have known a crowd to fill a tepee and listen with fixed attention to the recital for hours during the long winter evenings.

Pond is flattering the Dakota intellect by describing, as best he can, their stories as being tantamount to poetry or literature, albeit unwritten. Nonetheless, he does not take these tales seriously as "history," although he acknowledges that many of the Dakota stories were of "high antiquity." In this vein, Pond notes that some of the Dakota "fables" bear no trace of any items acquired from the white man, such as firearms, and also mention trees and plants that exist farther north than the southern Minnesota area where he conducted his field research. To Pond's credit, he at least did not have the kind of virulent and self-righteous reaction to Dakota stories and their inherent beliefs as have some who thought they bore "the truth."[27]

In *The Soul of the Indian,* Eastman recounts an unnamed missionary's visit to an unnamed tribe, though one may presume that the visitor is a Jesuit among the Dakota. During his visit, the missionary told
the Indians how the earth was created in six days, as well as the story of
Adam and Eve. The Indians listened to everything the missionary
wanted to tell them, quietly and respectfully. The Indians in turn told
the missionary their story about the origin of corn, which the missionary responded to with disdain, consequently chastising the Indians for
spouting "mere fable and falsehood." Taken aback, the offended Indian,
according to Eastman, rebutted the missionary, stating, "My brother . . .
it seems that you have not been well grounded in the rules of civility.
You saw that we, who practice these rules, believed your stories; why,
then, do you refuse to credit ours?"[28]

The missionary's attitude is symptomatic of not only religious but
also intellectual intolerance toward the validity of the oral tradition.
Vine Deloria, Jr., quotes Eastman's missionary story in *God Is Red.* Deloria
first points out that a major problem with the Christian doctrine regarding the story of Creation is that it has typically been taught as "historical fact." This ongoing and pervasive problem has caused endless
conflict in American society and politics, as evidenced in the infamous
1925 Scopes trial and the recurring attempts to require the teaching of
the biblical story in the public school system, in some instances even
asking that the Genesis story replace any references to Charles Darwin
and evolution. Since American Indians generally do not divide up their
knowledge into conflicting bodies of doctrine, the result for them has
been a much more harmonious relation between belief and empirical
fact. As Deloria states with regard to the science versus religion debate
that recurrently assails modern American society: "Indian tribal religions have not had this problem. The tribes confront and interact with
a particular land along with its life forms. The task or role of the tribal
religions is to relate the community of people to each and every facet of
creation as they have experienced it. Dr. Charles Eastman, the famous
Sioux physician, relates a story in which the Indian viewpoint of the
historicity of creation legends is illustrated." Deloria then goes on with a
mix of direct quotes and paraphrases to cite Eastman's missionary story.
The missionary's outrage toward his hosts' story and beliefs, Deloria explains, stems from Christianity being an intrinsically time-based religion.

From Creation to Adam to Christ and so forth, the basis of Christian belief in redemption is grounded in the belief that events of sacred history,
most notably the life of Jesus Christ, were preordained in the historic
creation of the world. Acknowledging any other account of how the
world was formed, be it a Dakota story or a scientific theory, entails
accepting the possibility that the Christian mythology is merely one
worldview among others at best or completely invalid as an explanation at worst.[29]

At this point it is worth noting that Eastman never expressed any
concerns about the incompatibility of Dakota and Christian beliefs.
Unlike what Deloria does in God Is Red, Eastman always made the argument—articulated in The Soul of the Indian—that Christianity and the
"Indian religion" were fundamentally the same in "spirit." This symbiosis, however, was mostly based on comparable ethical principles
and ritual practices rather than on notions about creation or the fate of
the universe. Eastman instead focused on how each tradition, as he saw
them, relates to the here and now. However, this did not mean that
Eastman accepted the institutionalization of Christianity uncritically.
While he was still a medical student in Boston, Eastman recalls, "I continued to study the Christ philosophy and loved it for its essential
truths, though doctrines and dogmas often puzzled and repelled me."
What Eastman could not condone was the pedantry, not to mention intolerance, that comes from a dogmatic approach to religion and that
was often at the basis of much persecution of Indian religions and their
adherents, such as outlawing the Sun Dance or attempting to stamp out
Hopi clowning. In the Dakota way, on the other hand, "Our faith might
not be formulated in creeds, nor forced upon any who are unwilling to
receive it; hence there was no preaching, proselyting, nor persecution,
neither were there any scoffers or atheists." On the contrary, religious
truth was something that one could seek only for oneself, and what that
person experienced firsthand was the only suitable basis for formulat-
ing his or her beliefs about the nature of things.[30]

The doctrines and dogma attitude, unfortunately, is not limited to
the religious community. In the area of historiography there has always
been reluctance among historians, of whom Roy Meyer stands—alongside Samuel Pond—as an example, to include the oral tradition as a
valid form of history. In this regard, Waziyatawin Angela Wilson points

to David Henige as another example of this hesitancy. More specifically, Henige makes the distinction in his book *Oral Historiography* that the oral tradition is sacred and static, while oral history is much more recent and basically secular in nature. This distinction is difficult to maintain in light of the above analysis of ohunkakan and woyakapi, both of which allowed for innovations prompted by either changing events or the storyteller's imagination. Furthermore, the Dakota stories display an ongoing belief that "supernatural" forces can affect even an ordinary person's life, as opposed to those of mythic heroes exclusively. With this in mind, Wilson states in her article "Grandmother to Granddaughter: Generations of Oral History in a Dakota Family," in contradistinction to Henige (not to mention Pond and Meyer): "From a Native perspective, I would suggest instead that oral history is contained within oral tradition. For the Dakota, 'oral tradition' refers to the way in which information is passed on rather than the length of time something has been told. Personal experiences, pieces of information, events, incidents, etc., can become a part of the oral tradition at the moment it happens or the moment it is told, as long as the person adopting the memory is part of an oral tradition." For Wilson, this clearly implies "necessitating an understanding of history as being encompassed in oral tradition." With respect to how a Dakota storyteller compares to a modern historian in terms of quality and accuracy, Wilson turns to her predecessor—maybe the better word is ancestor—for an example of the depth and sophistication that goes into learning the oral tradition. "Almost every evening a myth, or a true story of some deed done in the past, was narrated by one of the parents or grandparents," Wilson quotes Eastman from *Indian Boyhood,* and the boy was expected to listen very intently. On a subsequent evening, the boy was called on to repeat the story he was told. "If he was not an apt scholar," Wilson further quotes, "he struggled long with his task; but as a rule, the Indian boy is a good listener and has a good memory," enabling him to perform more than adequately in his storytelling duties. The result is a person knowledgeable in the stories and traditions that are *grounded* in the needs and concerns of the people whom these narrative actions ultimately benefit in terms of collective memory and social cohesion. As such, the storyteller is an intricate part of the tribe in the sense that he or she shares an identity with the audience.[31]

Characteristic of the mythic storytelling style is a tendency to regard time as nonlinear. Consequently, *Indian Boyhood* is arranged topically, beginning with "Earliest Recollections" and "An Indian Boy's Training." As Eastman's topics expand to cover things like games and playmates, along with making his first offering, learning about prestigious ancestors, and partaking in a Bear Dance and a Maiden's Feast, it slowly becomes apparent that Eastman's real subject is not merely himself but the Dakota Nation. Yet the arc of Eastman's narrative was defined less by the *longue durée* of Dakota social and political history and more by an admiration for how the Dakotas developed character in their young people and made them adults. At the same time, Eastman's discourse was far from an emic example of ethnography. In fact, it was not an ethnography at all: Dakota culture was not something Eastman *studied*—it was something he *lived*. As Crow intellectual and educator Janine Pease Pretty On Top observes about the connection between Eastman's life and writings: "Ohiyesa is a fully inculcated Santee Sioux of his era ... As an individual Santee Sioux, he has full membership in the culture, its knowledge, beliefs, art, morals, laws, customs, capabilities and habits. Ohiyesa learned the life attributes of the Santee Sioux from his contemporaries, elders, his relatives and the past." With respect to what Eastman contributed to the preservation of Indian cultures, Pretty On Top acknowledges that growing up in a given culture is not enough in itself to enable one to write insightfully about one's people or nation. She states, "Only unusually knowing individuals can perceive their own actions and behaviors and reflect upon their attachment to the entire endowment of their culture." In other words, it takes an especially gifted person to evoke the "soul" of a culture, and this effort is made all the more difficult when that culture is undergoing drastic changes. Eastman's secret, at least in *Indian Boyhood*, may be found in his original desire to write with his children in mind. Thinking of them, Eastman does not "dumb-down" his recollections; rather, he concentrates on portraying his family and community as ordinary, even familiar, people. At the same time, given that Eastman knew the audience for his book would mainly be white readers, his anecdotes are also about Indian people who have a lot in common with Americans, save the superficial differences that divide all peoples from one another. However, as these "differences" inevitably accumulate, we begin to see that Eastman is making a subtle argument about the advantages that Indians had before the imposition of white civilization. One such advantage is the earlier rate at which Dakota children gain maturity compared to their Anglo-American counterparts.[32]

Chapter four of *Indian Boyhood*, "Hakadah's First Offering," is an especially fascinating example of Eastman's indigenous style of storytelling and philosophizing. In one respect, the story demonstrates a culturally unique manner through which a Dakota boy achieves a major stage in his personal development, one which does not have a parallel example in modern American society—at least, not for the early-twentieth-century New Englanders that Eastman likely had in mind as typical Americans. In another respect, it is a compelling demonstration of the intimate knowledge Eastman possessed about Dakota custom and belief. The latter is important to remember because the same story that substantiates Eastman's claim to a Dakota identity is referred to by others as an example of his attempt to distance himself, even dissociate himself altogether, from traditional Dakota culture as a thing of the past.

Indeed, the offering in question is an integral part of the maturation process upon which Dakota youths ought to attend if they are to become assets to the community. What is most interesting about this ritual is, given that Eastman—or Hakadah—is only "eight summers" old, the Dakota clearly believe that a child is never too young to begin growing into an adult. Naturally, Uncheedah took charge of leading her grandson through this turning point in his young life. As Eastman recounts this episode, the time for his "first personal offering . . . to the 'Great Mystery'" came up without warning. It was simply time for it to happen, according to Uncheedah's judgment, which was always considered sound. After all, Uncheedah took responsibility for regulating and developing her sons' characters, including that of Hakadah's father, Many Lightnings. All of Uncheedah's sons were renowned as hunters and warriors, as Smoky Day would emphasize during a later phase of Eastman's education.[33]

After calling Hakadah in from small game hunting with his dog, Ohitika, Uncheedah explains to Hakadah his pending duties, now that he is "almost a man." The idea of making a sacrifice causes Hakadah to feel a little stunned. Still, at Uncheedah's behest, he grapples for the thing that is "most dearest" to him, which will serve as an appropriate offering to the Great Mystery. As he comes up with only trivial ideas, Uncheedah asks Hakadah to think deeper. Hakadah seems puzzled at this; then, he mentions his spotted pony as a possibility. Surely nothing can be worth more than that? Uncheedah meanwhile realizes that her grandson is avoiding the thought of sacrificing Ohitika. But she does not impose her will over his choice; instead, she reminds him of what the Great Mystery means to all the people, regardless of their stature in the tribe. Uncheedah emphasizes her point by saying, "I know you wish to be a great warrior and hunter. I am not prepared to see my Hakadah show any cowardice, for the love of possessions is a woman's trait and not a brave's."[34]

Hakadah's boyish sense of manhood is inflamed, but still he cannot think of the most fitting sacrifice. At last, Uncheedah tells him that it must be his dog. Hearing this, Hakadah wants to cry, but he holds back. Instead, hoping to look like a man, Hakadah asks for permission to dress his dog for sacrifice, which he is allowed to do. On the day of the sacrifice, Hakadah adorns his faithful hunting partner in black and red paint. He also sings a death song, followed with a promise: "Be brave, my Ohitika! I shall remember you the first time I am upon the war-path in the Ojibway country." Considering the event a somber one, Hakadah has dressed himself for mourning by loosening his hair and painting his face black. At the sight of him, Uncheedah almost relents, but then she remembers the gravity of the ritual. She tells Hakadah to wash his face, for he must not mourn his first sacrifice.[35]

A small party then goes to the appropriate place along the Assini-boine River, where they seek out a cave underneath a particular cliff: "A feeling of awe and reverence came to the boy. 'It is the home of the Great Mystery,' he thought to himself; and the impressiveness of his surroundings made him forget his sorrow." Ohitika, already dead, is brought to the scene. Paints and tobacco are scattered about according to tradition. Grandmother concludes the ceremony by offering up a prayer, which finishes with the supplication, "Behold this little boy and bless him! Make him a warrior and a hunter as great as thou didst make his father and grandfather." Later, the value of going through this rite of passage is substantiated by the "family traditions" he learns about from Smoky Day. More specifically, at this point Hakadah learned the value of serving the Great Mystery. Everyone who became widely respected among the Dakotas knew the value of this lesson.[36]

George Sword, a Lakota who was a major resource for James R. Walker, states that there are basically three types of offerings: "A Lakota can secure the favor of *Wakan Tanka* [whom Eastman refers to as the 'Great Mystery'], or of any spirit, if he will make a suitable offering. The offering may be made in either one of three ways. It may be abandoned in the name of the one to whom it is offered, or it may be given to one whose hands are painted red to show that they are sacred. Or it may be burned in the name of one to whom the offering is made." Although Eastman does not account for what happened with Ohitika's body, we may assume, based on Sword's analysis, it was left as is inside the cave. This conjecture seems more plausible than speculation that the dog was eaten, as proposed by one of Eastman's critics, Anna Lee Stensland. She criticizes Eastman for omitting this explanation, portraying it as an unfortunate example of his Christian influence. Stensland overlooks that in Dakota/Lakota culture, partaking in such a meal occurs during the *Heyokakaga*, the making of sacred clowns ceremony, but it does not appear likely to have occurred with Hakadah's sacrifice. In other words, just because something is "edible" in one context does not mean that it is eaten in every context. In which case, Eastman does not mention that Ohitika's body was eaten because it was not eaten but simply left for "the spirits" to consume.[37]

With regard to the way Eastman tells the story of his first offering, another critic, David J. Carlson, has argued that it provides evidence of Eastman's attempt to detach himself from his former life as a pre-assimilated Dakota. Carlson writes: "The role that third person point of view plays in suggesting a sense of distance from the Indian past appears even more strikingly in a chapter called 'Hakadah's First Offering.' Here, more than anywhere else in the book, Eastman works in a particularly literary (one might even say 'fictional') narrative mode. Hakadah appears to the reader very much as a character; were one to take this section out of its larger context in the book, it would be impossible to tell that he and Eastman are the same person." The obvious question to ask at this point is: what do we see when we do *not* take the chapter on Hakadah's first offering out of context? It is imperative to pursue this question because Carlson's construal of Eastman's text fails to take into account not only the inner logic of *Indian Boyhood* but also the Dakota values that are expressed in the stories told. Aside from coming before "Family Traditions," "Hakadah's First Offering" is told after chapter three, "My Plays and Playmates," in which Eastman gives an account of the kind of activities that were common for Dakota boys to engage in, alone and together. In one respect, chapter three portrays a very rugged and appealing boy's life, the relevance of which is determined by the presumption that such games as squirrel hunting, foot races, swimming, fighting bees, and playing lacrosse are preparing the boy to become a man, that is, that Dakota boys want to become like the men they admire around them, such as Many Lightnings or Jingling Thunder. Throughout the first part of chapter three, "Games and Sports," Eastman uses the collective "we" and "our" to tell his stories. Only toward the very end of the section does he switch to the first-person singular. In the entire second section, titled "My Playmates," Eastman talks about his older brother Chatanna and his younger female cousin, Oesadah, among others, from a first-person perspective. This practice continues through to the end of the third section, titled "The Boy Hunter." The sum result of this chapter, as far as how Eastman represents himself, is with a first-person account of his boyhood life. So, then, why does Eastman begin referring to himself in the third person in chapter four, "Hakadah's First Offering"?[38]

A more plausible answer than dissociating himself from his pre-assimilated boyhood is that his first offering marked a transition in how he saw himself as a growing and maturing Dakota person. Eastman's grandmother had explained that the first offering signified that "Hakadah" was approaching the threshold of manhood. Passing through this doorway entailed leaving behind his boyhood ways for the much loftier status of being a man, complete with a different name and new responsibilities. Obviously, at eight years of age Hakadah still has more to accomplish before he can seriously think about having truly achieved adulthood; nonetheless, "being a man" about sacrificing Ohitika signified a turning point in Eastman's life that would not be matched until his father returned to reclaim him seven years later. Speaking of himself in the third person, then, connotes two important things about Eastman's life at this juncture. First, it recognizes that

Hakadah names the little boy he once was before the first offering, when he "was a prince of the wilderness" and "His principal occupation was the practice of a few simple arts in warfare and the chase." Secondly, speaking about his experience in the third person places this event in a domain apart from everyday life. Eastman, after all, is not recounting a birthday; he is recalling an important first sacrifice to the Great Mystery. Speaking about this ritual in the third person places the emphasis on the ritual itself; in other words, the story is not driven by Hakadah's ego but by the expectations placed on everyone for honoring the Great Mystery. Lastly, we may add that using the third person makes the story of his first offering consistent with the stories that Smoky Day tells him about his ancestors:

> [Uncheedah] scattered paints and tobacco all about. Again they stood a few moments silently; then she drew a deep breath and began her prayer to the Great Mystery:
>
> "O, Great Mystery, we hear thy voice in the rushing waters below us! We hear thy whisper in the great oaks above! Our spirits are refreshed with thy breath from within this cave. O, hear our prayer! Behold this little boy and bless him! Make him a warrior and a hunter as thou didst make his father and grandfather."
>
> And with this prayer the little warrior had completed his first offering.[39]

And for us, Hakadah qua Eastman has passed on the blessings of this story as testimony to the power of blending myth, ritual, and prayer into our lives. On a more theoretical basis, if you will, Eastman's manner of storytelling is done with regard to the epistemological necessity of giving the indigenous perspective a distinct form of expression. Rather than privileging the prevalent social science theories pertaining to American Indian cultures, languages, and origins, Eastman instead grounds his discourse in a form of explanation that enables him to incorporate the cultural, historical, and environmental variables that are related to a given topic of discussion, be it Dakota religious rituals, the relationship between animals and humans, a philosophy of history, or the origin of the Dakota Nation. With respect to the Peoplehood paradigm mentioned in chapter one, a people's sacred history is fundamental to understanding their kinship and communal relations, their sense of purpose within a given homeland, the disruptive impact of westward

THE TRADITIONS OF THEIR FATHERS

expansion, and the potential for healing the more deleterious effects of colonialism through language revitalization. In the final analysis, what Eastman inaugurated with his books is a storytelling tradition that extends through the work of Ella Deloria's *Dakota Texts,* Elizabeth Cook-Lynn's *Aurelia: A Crow Creek Trilogy,* Vine Deloria's *Red Earth, White Lies,* and Waziyatawin Angela Wilson's *Remember This! Dakota Decolonization and the Eli Taylor Narratives.*

An important aspect of the Dakota oral tradition, which we will examine more closely in the next chapter, pertains to Dakota-Ojibwe relations. The Ojibwe, the Dakotas' traditional enemy for generations, are a critical component of Dakota identity, which Eastman must mull over at the same time he is reflecting on what it means to be an American Indian at the start of the twentieth century.

3

From Enemies to Pan-Indian Allies
Eastman on Dakota-Ojibwe Relations

The waters of Menesotah have been crimsoned with the blood of both nations; and the upper Mississippi has witnessed their unrewarded contest; and their shouts and groans have alike resounded among the mountain passes, and echoed from cliff to cliff on the rock-walled shore

George Copway, The Traditional History and Characteristic Sketches of the Ojibway Nation

One of the least understood aspects of Eastman's writings is the consideration he gave to the Dakotas' historic relations with the Ojibwe. In all but one of his books, Eastman makes references to the Dakotas' traditional enemies in ways that reflect his growing awareness of pan-Indian affairs in turn-of-the-century American society. Eastman thus goes from recounting stories, both mythical and historical, about Dakota-Ojibwe warfare to emphasizing the camaraderie he feels with the Ojibwe in their common struggle to adapt to white society. Setting aside personal bias and ameliorating a historic feud that defined generations of Dakota warriors was not something that happened immediately for Eastman, even though by his own admission he never got the opportunity to go on the warpath against his tribe's ancient adversary. Missing the opportunity did not preclude Eastman from being inculcated with prejudices that were generations old and which he only outgrew the more he reflected on the nature of Indian religions, in addition to the causes behind key events in American Indian history, from King Philip's War to the massacre at Wounded Knee. Eastman's reflections unfold within the stories and anecdotes that turn up throughout his books, which were written in tandem with the development and prominence of the Society of American Indians (SAI), an organization he eventually served as president in 1919, presiding over its annual meeting in Minneapolis.

A pivotal change in Eastman's views most likely came about because of the time he spent with the Ojibwe in northern Minnesota and Canada during the summer of 1910, while on a collecting mission for George Gustav Heye and the University of Pennsylvania Museum of Archaeology and Anthropology. Up until then, the Ojibwe, in Eastman's eyes, were no more than respected rivals whose role in Creation was on a different path from their Dakota enemies. Indeed, it is a commonplace among Indian nations that each received a different homeland and way of doing things from their Creator, entailing that their respective interests and concerns did not extend beyond their boundaries. Although they might share resources—due to the typically hazy boundaries separating nations and their respective hunting grounds—as well as complementary histories—due to traditional rivalries or alliances—Indian nations generally did not regard themselves as one race. Only in situations of great urgency did otherwise disparate nations band together in common cause, be it in terms of confederacies like the Iroquois, which Hiawatha and Deganawidah established to end the relentless blood feuds afflicting the region, or, even more dramatically, the fleeting but brilliant alliances initiated by Pontiac and Tecumseh, who each sought a bulwark against the deleterious effects of westward expansion and colonization.

By the time Eastman emerged as a major American Indian intellectual in the early twentieth century, the grand era of Indian prophets that stretched from Neolin to Wovoka was a thing of the past. What Eastman sought, then, along with his post-1890 peers was a stable and long-term way of adapting to the non-Native forces of modern life, which valued competition, money, accumulating material goods, and political power. Entering into such a situation necessitated going through a transvaluation of traditional customs and beliefs, which for Eastman in particular meant reconsidering how he thought about the Ojibwe. Consequently, what emerges is a race consciousness that previously did not exist in Indian culture, this in addition to a political identity, i.e., the American Indian, which also did not exist before but around which Indian people, however tangentially, could identify their individual and tribal needs, thereby augmenting the SAI's effort at gaining justice and restitution for the price Indians paid so that the United States could grow and prosper.

In *The Indian To-day*, Eastman makes a very casual but by no means insignificant observation about the Ojibwe's relationship to the Dakotas: "The great Siouan race occupied nearly all the upper valley of the Mississippi and Missouri rivers and their tributaries. North of them dwelt the Ojibways, an Algonquin tribe with an entirely different language." Such a seemingly minor difference, however, was sufficient for maintaining a mutual tradition of warfare, in which honors could be gained and the welfare of the nation preserved. This is not to say that the Dakota and Ojibwe somehow practiced an idyllic form of combat in which no one was killed. While it is surely the case that American Indians traditionally maintained notions about warfare that differed substantially from those of their Euro-American counterparts, nonetheless Indian warfare was a dangerous venture, in which lives were lost and territorial boundaries shifted. The Ojibwe historian William W. Warren recounts the Ojibwe migration west as causing an inevitable and increasingly violent infiltration into the Dakota Country of Minnesota and Wisconsin. The process took generations and was initiated by a prophecy that foretold of finding food that grows on the water—wild rice, *manoomin*—if they would only follow the megis shell that would show them the way.[1]

Of particular interest was the region surrounding the source of the Mississippi River in what is today northern Minnesota. "In former times," Warren writes, "this region of country abounded in buffalo, moose, deer, and bear, and till within thirty years past, in every one of its many water courses, the lodges of the valuable and industrious beaver were to be found." However, it was not imperial or colonial ambitions on the part of the Ojibwe that drove them into Dakota territory; rather, it was the wars for empire between European powers that compelled the Ojibwe to search out sustainable resources. This resettlement was a consequence of the drastically changing political map, which was redrawn by the French and Indian Wars, the American Revolution, and the War of 1812. Needless to say, a significant portion of Indian Country was in a state of chaos during this era. Moreover, Indian nations were certainly not blind to the impact Europeans were having on the balance of things. However, while many fought valiantly against the unlawful seizure of their lands, Turtle Island still seemed vast enough to allow others to migrate away from sources of conflict and decay and start anew.[2]

For the Ojibwe this meant entering a territory, as Warren observes, making reference to its advantageous natural bounty, that "has always been a favorite home and resort for the wild Indian, and over its whole extent, battle fields are pointed out where different tribes have battled for its possession." Within this context, there is nothing extraordinary about the Ojibwe fighting with the Dakota over this terrain. Thus, when an Ojibwe leader, Bi-aus-wah, sought revenge for his father's death, many Ojibwe answered the call. The object of Bi-aus-wah's vengeance was the Dakota settlement at Sandy Lake. Though the Ojibwe warriors were outnumbered, they were "armed with the murderous weapons of the pale face," and thereby forced the Dakota to remove themselves, leaving the Ojibwe to eventually settle the location. Then, as Warren summarizes events,

> From this central location, they gradually increased their conquests in western, northern, and southern directions, and drawn by the richness of the hunting grounds in this region of country, many families from Lake Superior, of both the northern and southern divisions of the tribe, who had separated two centuries before at Sault Ste. Marie, moved over, and joined this band of hardy pioneers, increasing their strength and causing them to be better able to withstand the powerful Dakotas, and gradually to increase their new possessions. Sandy Lake or Kah-me-tah-wung-a-guma, signifying "lake of the sandy waters," is the site of the first Ojibway village about the head-waters of the Mississippi.
>
> It is from this point that the war parties proceeded, who eventually caused the Dakotas to evacuate their favorite seats at Leech, Winnepeg, Cass, and Red Lakes, and also from Gull Lake, Crow Wing, and the vicinity of Milles Lacs.

For generations afterward, the Dakota and Ojibwe would remain enemies, but the push for new territory would cease and a kind of symbiosis would ensue.[3]

Tensions began to rise again, however, as the United States took more of an interest in the region, beginning with Zebulon Pike's 1805–6 expedition. Before settlement, trade, and commerce could take place, though, the Americans stipulated that peace must be made between the various Indian nations of the region, which, in addition to the "Sioux and Chippewa," included the "Sacs and Fox, Menomonie, Ioway, Sioux,

Winnebago, and a portion of the Ottawa, Chippewa, and Potawattomie Tribes." Like many an American Indian critic of U.S. federal Indian policy, Eastman clearly implies that the American-imposed 1824 treaty, which ostensibly proclaimed peace between Indian nations, instead fomented war by arbitrarily inserting a boundary line between cultures that did not possess such a notion in their thinking or language. Thus, as Eastman critiques events, "In 1824, the United States required of the tribes in this region to define their territory, a demand which intensified and gave a new turn to their intertribal warfare. The use of gun, horse, and whiskey completed the demoralization, and thus the truly 'savage' warfare had its origin, ever increasing in bitterness until it culminated in resistance to the Government, in 1862, one hundred years after the struggle and defeat of the great Pontiac." Eastman's remarks suggest that what the Americans did in Minnesota and Wisconsin had been tried before in other regions with other Indian nations, only to result in the same tragic state of affairs. This reading further suggests that there is something deliberate in the way that American authorities created unnecessary friction between tribes who otherwise knew how to handle their differences. In other words, the Americans wanted to incite savagery for the sake of justifying the enforcement of their own sense of civilization.[4]

From the beginning in the Upper Midwest, the Americans were warned that positing an artificial boundary between tribes would not work between people who did not find such things to be either valid or comprehensible. On this point, Roy W. Meyer quotes Caramonee, a Ho-Chunk leader of the time, who stated,

> The lands I claim are mine and the nations here know it is not only claimed by us but by our Brothers the Sacs and Foxes, Menominees, Iowas, Mahas, and Sioux. They have held it in common. It would be difficult to divide it. It belongs as much to one as the other... I did not know that any of my relations had any particular lands. It is true everyone owns his own lodge and the ground he may cultivate. I had thought the Rivers were the common property of all [Indians] and not used exclusively by any particular nation.

Nonetheless, the purpose of articles two through nine of the 1824 treaty is to establish territorial boundaries between the various tribes named

above. All of which culminates in article ten, in which all of the participating tribes supposedly "acknowledge the general controlling power
of the United States," thereby disclaiming any alliance or affiliation
with any other powers, namely, the British (the French having largely
become a nonentity in North America). Yet, for all this pretense of
power and supremacy, the United States could not keep the peace.[5]

In his 1850 book, *The Traditional History and Characteristic Sketches of
the Ojibway Nation*, Ojibwe missionary and writer George Copway adds
his own interpretation of the Dakota and Ojibwe's historic conflict.
Instead of blaming U.S. federal Indian policy for the ongoing hostilities
between the Ojibwe and Dakota, Copway instead appropriates the attitude—common among many white settlers—that the Dakota are a warlike
people who would not hesitate at slaughtering innocent and honorable
Ojibwe. Referring to a recent battle at Lake St. Croix, Copway illustrates
the endemic pugnacity of the Dakota, stating, "The Siouxs may have
killed a large number of Chippeways, but the warfare was not an hon-
ourable one. The day previous, a pipe of peace was received from the
Sioux nation by the Chippeways, who had a desire for peace." Copway
goes on to suggest that it will be through the strength and authority of
the Americans that any chance at peace will take hold in the region. "I
was glad," Copway writes, "during my short stay at Minisota, to see the
beneficial results of Governor Ramsey's efforts among the Indians. They
must be induced to give up war and petty strifes before they can be
benefited, morally or physically." Of course, territorial governor Alexander Ramsey was trying to negotiate a treaty with the Dakota that, as of
1851, would be more beneficial to the whites than to the Indians. One
wonders, of course, what Copway would have said about the 1862
conflict that arose between starving and desperate Dakota and the white
settlers who were profiting from Indian land. Although he passed away
in 1863, Copway did not leave us his thoughts about this dire episode in
Dakota history.[6]

With respect to Eastman's personal experience and what he wrote
about it, the Dakota-Ojibwe rivalry was far from settled when Eastman,
then still known as Hakadah, was a little boy growing up in Lower
Sioux. Despite a subsequent treaty between the Santee Dakota and the
United States in 1851—which mostly served to divest the Dakota of more
of their land in exchange for annuities—conflict continued between the

Dakota and Ojibwe. Indeed, when one looks through the pages of *Indian Boyhood,* there is a clear and unquestioned presumption that the Ojibwe are an "enemy" tribe, in the sense of being an ongoing and real threat to the physical well-being of the Dakota people. This is evidenced straightaway in a song that Uncheedah sings to her newborn grandson, Hakadah:

> Sleep, sleep, my boy, the Chippewas
> Are far away—far away.
> Sleep, sleep, my boy; prepare to meet
> The foe by day—the foe by day!
> The cowards will not dare to fight
> Till morning break—till morning break.
> Sleep, sleep, my child, while still 'tis night;
> Then bravely wake—then bravely wake!

Eastman quotes this song without any explanation of its content. Instead, he simply goes on to describe the various activities that occupied his grandmother's life as a traditional Dakota woman. This unconscious preconception that the Ojibwe are an adversary recurs throughout every section of *Indian Boyhood,* making it the work in which the Ojibwe are mentioned the most.[7]

Even though their books were published more than half a century apart, the nature of Dakota-Ojibwe relations that Eastman evokes is similar to the attitude and actions that Copway recounts with respect to Ojibwe children. Copway writes,

> The quarrels have been kept alive and the war-fires fanned by the songs of each nation. As soon as children were old enough to handle a bow and arrow, representations of the enemy were made, and the youngsters taught to shoot at them, for exercise and practice. The old men narrated to them deeds of bravery, and thus were they inspired with a desire to grow up, and when men, act like their fathers, and scout the wide forests for each other. Even the mothers have taught their offspring, before they leave their breast, to hate their enemies.

Eastman, perhaps as a reflection of the post-1890 times in which he wrote, never shows any signs of palpably "hating" the Ojibwe. He neither reviles nor disdains them. This attitude may be attributable to the changes that Dakota-Ojibwe relations underwent during the intervening years separating Eastman from Copway. Whatever the reason, the Ojibwe are simply a part of the Dakota world, though a very meaningful one. This is not to say that Eastman's portrayals were free from bias. For example, when Eastman describes an Ojibwe person being killed in battle, it was usually credited as an act of bravery on the part of a Dakota warrior, but when a Dakota person was killed, it was a tragedy and not typically regarded as an act of bravery on the part of the Ojibwe. Still, as connoted in *Indian Boyhood,* the Ojibwe are the Dakota's equal in bravery and warfare, making them worthy foes for the Dakota warrior seeking honor and distinction. This status is readily apparent in two of the stories that Ohiyesa hears from Smoky Day: specifically, the legend of Jingling Thunder and the tale of Morning Star and Winona. Both have been recounted before; however, what is essential in this context is the way in which the Ojibwe are described as an enemy.[8]

In the story of Jingling Thunder, the Dakota and their Sac and Fox allies are engaged in a battle with the Ojibwe near the St. Croix River; the Sac and Fox warriors are the first to encounter the enemy. "It seemed to be an equal fight," as Smoky Day tells his story, "and for a time no one could tell how the contest would end." The battle tide turned when the Sac and Fox were compelled to retreat, at which time the Dakota entered the fray. The Dakota advantage was not held long, however, as Ojibwe reinforcements turned up to fight just as the Dakota warriors were becoming weary from the daylong battle. Everything nevertheless came down to a confrontation between two men: a "great Ojibway chief" and Jingling Thunder, a very young and inexperienced Dakota warrior. As Smoky Day tells it, "The powerful man flashed his tomahawk in the air over the youthful warrior's head, but the brave sprang aside as quick as lightning, and in the same instant speared his enemy to the heart. As the Ojibway chief gave a gasping yell and fell in death, his people lost courage; while the success of the brave Jingling Thunder strengthened the hearts of the Sioux, for they immediately followed up their advantage and drove the enemy out of their territory." This was an abundantly important moment in the life of Jingling Thunder, for not only did he determine the outcome of the battle but he did so by slaying a very prominent Ojibwe warrior who more than likely earned his great distinction by fighting the Dakota. In the final analysis, Jingling Thunder became a distinguished warrior because of the distinction of the one he fought and conquered.[9]

In the story of Morning Star and Winona, the meaningfulness of going to war against the Ojibwe is signified by the role that the medicine man plays. It is because of Wakinyan-tonka's vision, "whereupon a war-party set out for the Ojibway country," that the events leading to Morning Star's tragic demise take place. In the Dakota way, as in many Indian traditions, a vision is more than a mere dream; it is a sacred experience in which any messages must be respected and any directives must be fulfilled, lest the recipient incur misfortune upon himself, his family, or his community. As such, Dakota warriors surely did not hesitate to take up Wakinyan-tonka's call to make a war party. Nonetheless, despite the success that the warriors enjoyed against their enemy, misfortune was at hand when Wakinyan-tonka had a sense of foreboding during the canoe trip back home. At this juncture of the story, the Ojibwe reappear as a force of nature: "Just as the sun peeped through the eastern tree-tops a great war-cry came forth from the near shores, and there was a rain of arrows." Because of this brave venture, undertaken at the behest of a medicine man's vision, Morning Star's death is genuinely tragic, in the epic sense of encountering one's destiny as determined by the spirit world.[10]

Because the Dakota-Ojibwe relation goes back to mythic times, the idea that the Ojibwe are an adversarial force in the Dakota world is taken for granted as a fact of life. Even when Eastman played as a boy, he saw himself setting out on the warpath against the Ojibwe. "One of our most curious sports," Eastman recalls, "was a war upon the nests of wild bees. We imagined ourselves about to make an attack upon the Ojibways or some tribal foe." Later on, while still a boy, Eastman prepares to sacrifice his dog to the Great Mystery as his first offering, saying to his faithful companion, "Be brave, my Ohitika! I shall remember you the first time I am upon the war-path in the Ojibway country."[11]

Even everyday activities were prone to sudden attack by an Ojibwe war party. In the case of Eastman's account of a sugar camp in *Indian Boyhood*, we not only see the Ojibwe regarded as an enemy but we also can sense the American influences that would ultimately reshape the historic Dakota-Ojibwe dynamic. More specifically, the sugar camp, in which "old men and women and the children" participated after the "first March thaw," required an essential but nonindigenous utensil, namely "the huge iron and brass kettles for boiling. Everything else could be made, but these must be bought, begged or borrowed." In turn, the narrative on making sugar is a strictly Dakota affair, in which no white man appears. The scene takes place "in the midst of a fine grove of maples on the bank of the Minnesota river," the bulk of the narration demonstrating how the sugar making was done, including emphasis on Uncheedah's industriousness. The Dakota sugar-making tradition is not frozen in time, however, for the sugar camp in question is, Eastman acknowledges, "our last sugar-making in Minnesota, before the 'outbreak.'" Further signifying how much life was about to change for the Dakota, not to mention the Ojibwe, Eastman concludes "An Indian Sugar Camp" by introducing Cloud Man, his great-grandfather. Cloud Man arrives carrying kinnikinnick along with the disturbing news that a nearby Dakota sugar camp was recently attacked by "roving Ojibways."[12]

As of 1862, traditional warfare between the Dakota and the Ojibwe had already intensified with the introduction of firearms throughout the Great Lakes region, and the situation was about to become more volatile as Americans continued their growing colonization of what was now the state of Minnesota. With respect to this, Eastman discloses an important part of his heritage: "[Cloud Man] was the first Sioux chief to welcome the Protestant missionaries among his people." One may wonder, though, if Cloud Man had any sense of just how much havoc the whites, namely the Americans, would wreak upon the Dakota when he received the missionaries and even accepted their religion at his "original village . . . on the shores of Lakes Calhoun and Harriet." But now, Eastman laments, they are "in the suburbs of the city of Minneapolis," and the memory of what was would exist only in the minds of his descendants and in the pages of *Indian Boyhood*. The mystery of why the whites and Christianity came to Dakota Country is something still pondered today. Katherine Elizabeth Beane, another of Charles Eastman's brother John's descendents—and Carly's twin sister—writes about this topic with respect to her own family history:

The details behind my family's relationship with the Christian faith, and the subsequent loss of our traditional teachings are complex. Our history, not unlike many other American Indian families, is made up of situations of turmoil, plundering, and forced removal, all of which were brought upon us by white Europeans. We fought hard to endure. The introduction of Christianity to my family began in the mid 1860s, before the settlement at Flandreau and the construction of our church. In a short essay my grandmother Grace Moore wrote about how the settlement of Flandreau, which is known in Dakota as *Wakpaipaksan* (Bend in the River) came to be, she writes, "To trace the history of the Indian community and the First Presbyterian Church, you have to go back many years to the time when the Christian missionaries came among the Indian people in Minnesota." She goes on to explain that Dr. Thomas S. Williamson and Rev. Stephen R. Riggs chose the area of Fort Snelling and Lac qui Parle to do their missionary work, and that it took them forty years to translate the bible into the Dakota language. But she never really gives any reason why these men were so extremely committed to converting my people. These missionaries, and their children after them, would make it their life's work to make sure that Dakota people learned the bible so that they could be saved. But what exactly was it that they were being saved from?

One can easily imagine that there were Ojibwe families asking themselves the same question with respect to their own missionaries.[13]

The Dakota and Ojibwe, it must be acknowledged, were not without common ground. Symbolic of the values shared by both the Dakota and the Ojibwe, as opposed to the whites and Indians, is the story Eastman tells about two female Ojibwe captives. His own uncle at one time brought home two women after a battle. Since none of the Dakota were slain in the skirmish in which the Ojibwe women were captured, they were treated kindly. The women remained for the next two years in Eastman's grandmother's family, only to be returned when "a great peace council" was held between the traditional adversaries. The eldest of the two women, before leaving, turned and spoke lovingly of Eastman's grandmother. She called Uncheedah brave and "a true mother," complimenting her son, Eastman's uncle, for sparing their lives and doing what her father, brother, and husband would have done. Finally, the woman departed, promising that she would raise her sons to be like the Dakota warriors she came to know. The younger of the two women, on the other hand, chose to remain with the Dakota and in time married one of them. Then, perhaps as a sign of his growing awareness of inter-tribal unity, Eastman recalls that the younger woman justified her deci-sion by stating, "I shall make the Sioux and the Ojibways ... to be as brothers." Such a union between Dakota and Ojibwe was not unusual, according to Eastman: even the "mother of the well-known Sioux chieftain, Wabashaw, was an Ojibway woman."[14]

After *Indian Boyhood*, Eastman's references to the Ojibwe in *Red Hunters and the Animal People* and *Old Indian Days* consist of brief allu-sions to their traditional role as enemy tribe. For example, Eastman tells about a young Dakota man who was having difficulties finding a woman, commenting, "If it had been anything like trailing the doe, or scouting the Ojibway, he would have ridiculed the very notion of miss-ing the object sought." This passing reference to the Ojibwe shows how casually the rivalry still arose in Eastman's thoughts. After the two aforementioned books were written, though, Eastman made his fateful 1910 journey through Ojibwe Country, which we will examine below. Suffice it to say that Eastman gained a more intimate understanding of and appreciation for Ojibwe people and their culture and history than he had ever possessed before.[15]

In *The Soul of the Indian*, there are three substantial examples of Eastman's growing realization that the Dakota and the Ojibwe are a part of something that transcends their cultural differences, something defined by the era in which they now lived. In the first instance, in which Eastman accounts for the power of prophecy among some Dakota medicine men, Ta-chánk-pee Hó-tank-a, His War Club Speaks Loud, foretells of a war party against the Ojibwe a year before it hap-pens. Echoing the story of Morning Star and Winona, seven battles were fought to seven victories, only to end in utter defeat at the hands of an Ojibwe ambush. In a subsequent episode, still concerning the topic of medicine men, Eastman makes mention of a medicine man born near Rum River "during a desperate battle with the Ojibways," at a point when the tide was turning against the Dakota. The child's grandmother, sensing her family's annihilation, placed her grandson's cradle "near the spot where his uncle and grandfathers were fighting" so that the child might die a warrior's death. However, an old man spotted the child and saved it, stating that one never knows what will be the value of even a single warrior to his people. "The child lived to become great among us," Eastman recalls, then states much more cryptically that the child's greatness "was intimated to the superstitious by the circumstances of his birth." Lastly on the topic of prophetic medicine men, Eastman recounts the story of a Dakota who had a "twin spirit" among the Ojibwe. The unnamed medicine man one day informed others during a hunting trip that they would encounter an Ojibwe party led by the twin medicine man. The Dakota medicine man asked his brethren to resist the temptation of engaging their ancient enemies in combat. They agreed, and, as soon as word came back with some scouts that the Ojibwe hunting party had been spotted, they prepared to greet them with the sacred pipe. Once the Ojibwe party knew of the Dakotas' intention, they signaled that they were ready to gather in peace. As the twin spirits met, both the Dakota and the Ojibwe members of each party were amazed by the close resemblance the two medicine men bore to each other. Eastman concludes this story, and the pages of *The Soul of the Indian,* with this parting image of intertribal amity: "It was quickly agreed by both parties that they should camp together for several days, and one evening the Sioux made a 'warriors' feast' to which they invited many of the Ojibways. The prophet asked his twin brother to sing one of his sacred songs, and behold! it was the very song that he himself was wont to sing. This proved to the warriors beyond doubt or cavil the claims of their seer."[16]

With respect to his portrayal of Dakota-Ojibwe relations, this scene from *The Soul of the Indian,* which appeared the same year the Society of American Indians held its first meeting on October 12, 1911, would prove to be a turning point in Eastman's writing career. Afterward, Eastman would no longer uncritically portray the Ojibwe as the Dakotas' enemy. Instead, he would be more conscientious about showing respect for the Ojibwe, their history and culture, as well as be more critical of the alien forces that infiltrated the Dakota-Ojibwe world, causing political corruption and spiritual imbalance to occur, in particular, as a result of American colonization.

Beginning anew, if you will, with *Indian Scout Talks*, Eastman speaks about his friend, Simon Bonga, "a three-quarters blood Ojibway at Leech Lake in Minnesota." What is immediately distinctive here is that Eastman not only regards Bonga as a "friend," complete with a name (all previous Ojibwe went nameless), but also as an equal in the knowledge of woodland arts. More specifically, Eastman tells an anecdote about Bonga taming a fawn, which, though it remains in the wild, regarded Bonga's home as a safe haven. As a further sign of how Eastman's regard for the Ojibwe has changed, he refers to a letter he wrote to Bonga, in which he mentions the incident with the fawn, to which Eastman's friend answers with a cheerful update. The significance of the latter is that, as of 1914, when *Indian Scout Talks* appeared, at least one pair of Dakota and Ojibwe men were both friends and corresponding in English, implicitly setting an example for Indian life today.[17]

In *The Indian To-Day*, there is no mention of bloody warfare with the Ojibwe or even any reference to their traditional rivalry. Although Eastman does not go out of his way to write about the Ojibwe in an unusually high regard, he continues to show signs of personal growth in his respect for this tribe. This approach parallels Eastman's development as an American Indian intellectual: *The Indian To-day* marks the first time Eastman writes about the urgent future of American Indians as students, intellectuals, and American citizens, as opposed to recounting traditional Dakota stories. One could even say that the scope of this book more than likely influenced the way in which Eastman characterized the Ojibwe—more as victims of the colonialism and federal Indian policies that impacted all tribes rather than as simply an enemy tribe. Eastman realizes more explicitly that the best way of improving life for the Dakota is to make life better for all Indian nations through political reform. While he would still write as if "the Dakota" and "the Indian" were synonymous terms, he would set aside previous biases and work toward improving conditions for all American Indians, thus creating a pan-Indian agenda.

In chapter one of *The Indian To-day*, "The Indian as He Was," there is a subsection titled "The Transition Period," in which Eastman accounts for the social and political metamorphosis that many tribes underwent in changing "from their natural life to the artificial life of civilization." For the most part, according to Eastman, the transition was gradual and tribes such as the Cherokee handled their situation with integrity. Which is not to say that Eastman endorsed the policy of forced removal but rather that he admired how the Cherokee approached their predicament with fortitude. Eastman even extols the virtues of those Indian individuals who, as scouts, swore allegiance to their white neighbors, then kept their word "at any cost." Such emphasis on loyalty was important at a time when many prominent Indian intellectuals, such as Eastman, were still fighting for universal American citizenship for all Indians, as opposed to fostering more stereotypes of untrustworthy savages.[18]

With respect, on the other hand, to the history of Indian-White relations, we see a different story. Because of the competition between Britain, France, and America, the alliances between Indian nations and their Euro-American counterparts became a part of the conquest and imperialism that the three foreign powers sought throughout North America. Along with the spread of colonialism came "a kind of warfare that was cruel, relentless, and demoralizing" for the Indian nations who suffered through these conflicts. Giving historical depth to his proclamation in *The Soul of the Indian* that there is no such thing as a Christian nation—at least not when that nation places more value on materialism than on its spiritual beliefs—Eastman makes the observation that the "two great 'civilizers'... were whiskey and gunpowder, and from the hour the red man accepted these he had in reality sold his birthright, and all unconsciously consented to his own ruin." With respect to the Dakota, to appreciate the veracity of Eastman's claim one need only refer to the stories told about the 1862 conflict, which we will examine in the next chapter.[19]

What resulted from colonialism was social decay, in which tribes began to split their loyalties between themselves and the white nations that sought to exploit their differences. For a few medals, some men were even willing to betray the greater interests of their nation in return for money and prestige among the whites. In other words, the Americans in their lust for land often appointed someone "chief" without the consent of the tribe, which typically led to jealousy and fractioning. "Chief Hole-in-the-Day of the Ojibways and Spotted Tail of the

Brule Sioux," Eastman points out as examples, "were both killed by tribesmen for breaking the rule of their respective tribes and accepting favors from the Government." Like smallpox and alcoholism, the disease of political corruption was a scourge on any tribe that came into contact with it.[20]

Unfortunately, corruption is far from a thing of the past, in spite of claims from the Indian Bureau that its officers are fully taking care of Indian interests. It was not that Indian commissioners were deaf to Indian complaints—they often echoed these concerns in their annual reports; rather, it was a lack of commitment on the part of the Indian Bureau to actually solve the problems it ostensibly declared as its priorities. In a section of *The Indian To-day* titled "Inheritance and Other Frauds," part of chapter seven, "The Indian as Citizen," Eastman speaks of an incident at White Earth, Minnesota. The context for this event involved determining heirs to allotted tribal land. Even when the twenty-five-year time limit, which normally protects the title, was not expired as of the allottee's death, the land could nonetheless be sold "for the benefit of their legal heirs." The potential for fraud sprang from the fact that the Indian Bureau handled thousands of cases during the 1910s in which the vast number of heirs were either minors or "incompetent Indians." In the case of twenty-one thousand Oklahoma Indians, Warren K. Moorehead of the Board of Indian Commissioners reported that the average cost of handling their estates was 30 to 90 percent, "whereas the average rate in thirty states is 3 per cent." In answer to the question of why the law could not protect Indian people from being swindled, Eastman states, still citing Moorehead, that the law went baldly unenforced. Eastman then illustrates his point further by recounting an investigation Moorehead conducted in Minnesota: "[He] uncovered a scandal of large proportions, relating to the theft of over two hundred thousand acres of valuable land, as a result of suddenly removing all restrictions on the mixed bloods at that agency, many of whom were incompetent to manage their own affairs." The bitter irony here is that mixed-bloods were designated as "competent," according to the 1906 Burke Act, precisely because they were mixed-blood, meaning they possessed a sufficient amount of white blood as opposed to full-bloods, who were typically labeled as "incompetent" regardless of their actual ability to conduct their own affairs. In light of this, the root of the problem of inheritance fraud, Eastman acknowledges, has less to do with the state of Indian "competency" and more to do with an inherently corrupt Indian Bureau.[21]

Blood quantum, as has been written about numerous times, was a federal imposition meant to encourage intermarriage between whites and Indians, with the objective of eliminating Indian blood altogether through biological assimilation. In the meantime, "mixed-blood" was a kind of political status, which labeled one as being physiologically and mentally more "civilized," depending upon the admixture of white and Indian. Of course, given the epidemic hypocrisy of American race politics, *mixed blood* in contexts other than "the Indian problem" was also a derogatory term, signifying the taboo of miscegenation and mongrelism. Mixed-blood people, if living within an Indian community, could tip the balance in their favor by ingratiating themselves to the whites, siding with them on policy issues and treaties, or serving as army scouts, interpreters, informants, and policemen. For Eastman, being technically a mixed-blood himself, what mattered more than blood quantum was where one placed his or her heart. Was it with one's people and their well-being? Or was it only for oneself, pursuing one's selfish interests? With respect to Eastman and where he falls along the spectrum of Indian-White blood quantum, we must first observe that the topic of race and ethnic identity is largely absent from any of Eastman's works. The topic of race seems to be more of a preoccupation among white Indian agents, commissioners, politicians, and social scientists. Since Eastman regarded himself as nothing more or less than a Dakota, the greater issue was the lack of citizenship and citizens' rights for all Indians. Citizenship and the right to participate in the political process belonged to all persons regardless of race or any admixture thereof. In Eastman's opinion, a full-blooded Navajo has as much right to the vote as a blond-haired, blue-eyed Cherokee.

In chapter three of *The Indian To-day*, titled "The Agency System: Its Uses and Abuses," Eastman mentions in a subsection labeled "Indian Claims" the fate of the Oneida and Stockbridge tribes of New York. In essence, the Oneida and Stockbridge peoples were two of the many indigenous nations to see their treaty relations with the United States blatantly violated on behalf of those coveting their lands. In their case, not only did they make a treaty with the Americans, they also converted to Christianity and took up the ways of "civilization." The Oneida, in particular, even took the side of the Americans during the Revolutionary War. Unfortunately, these two peaceful peoples were swept away in the wave of ethnic cleansing that permeated the eastern United States during the 1830s. Because of their Christian ethos, they did not choose to fight either militarily or in the courts. Instead, they conceded their New York homelands for a new reservation in Kansas. Fortunately, when the Oneida and Stockbridge reached Green Bay, Wisconsin, they were warmly received by the Ho-Chunk Nation, who offered to "share their reservation, as they had plenty of good land." In turn, as westward expansion continued and the Americans took more land farther west, the Ojibwe opened their doors to the now displaced Ho-Chunk and even further displaced Oneida and Stockbridge, offering them land and hospitality.[22]

As for the federal government representing the white interests that took over the Oneida and Stockbridge lands in New York, it subsequently and without conscience allowed the Kansas lands to be overrun by white settlers. In spite of the fact that this land technically belonged to the Oneida and Stockbridge peoples, the federal government for the next seventy-five years refused to offer the Indians any compensation. Only in 1905, after years of congressional investigations, did the Indians receive any payment. "The fact," Eastman notes, "that the two tribes remained in Wisconsin and settled there does not invalidate their claim, as those wild Ojibways had no treaty with the Government at that time and had a perfect right to give away some of their land." Nevertheless, the Oneida and Stockbridge were compelled to retain an attorney at considerable cost to each tribe in order to acquire what anyone with common decency would consider to be just. "If anything is proved in history," Eastman reflects, "it is that those who follow in the footsteps of the meek and gentle Jesus will be treated unmercifully, as he was, by a hard and material world."[23]

With respect to the Ojibwe, their magnanimity toward the Oneida and Stockbridge is not the only example Eastman mentions. Later, in chapter eleven, "The Indian's Gifts to the Nation," Eastman recounts a heroic episode in which Catherine, "the Ojibway maid," serves as an example of "Historic Indian Women." In the same section in which Eastman mentions Pocahontas and the Oneida and Stockbridge women "who advised their men not to join King Philip," he tells about an episode in which, perhaps, "no greater service has been rendered by any Indian girl to the white race" than what Catherine did at the height of Pontiac's rebellion. As Eastman portrays events, "Had it not been for her timely warning of her lover, Captain Gladwyn, Fort Detroit would have met the same fate as the other forts, and the large number of Indians who held the siege for three months would have scattered to wipe out the border settlements of Ohio and Pennsylvania." Eastman writes with the assumption that American settlement of the Ohio Valley was an inevitability, in which victories for Pontiac's forces would have only led to a more prolonged and bloodier conflict, the result of which still would have been the same for the Indians. As things turned out, Eastman proclaims, Catherine "was civilization's angel, and should have a niche in history beside Pocahontas."[24]

Eastman delves even further into the lives of the Ojibwe in *From the Deep Woods to Civilization*. In this book, he writes about time spent traveling among the Dakotas' now former enemy, tribal warfare having long since ended. Throughout most of the descriptions, he speaks fondly of the people he encounters. As an aside, we should note that as of the writing of *From the Deep Woods*, Eastman's interest in pan-Indian politics was already fully developed. By the time *From the Deep Woods* appeared in 1916, the Society of American Indians had hosted nearly half a dozen national meetings. On a more personal level, Eastman's awareness of the needs of all Indian nations had grown during his work with the YMCA, in which he was "constantly meeting with groups of young men of the Sioux, Cheyennes, Crees, Ojibways, and others, in log cabins or little frame chapels, and trying to set before them in simple language the life and character of the Man Jesus." However, as Eastman tells his life story, one could say that the first sign that he was sympathetic to the common Indian good occurred at the Santee Indian School in Nebraska. During Eastman's orientation, he was at one point left in the chapel with another Indian boy, a Mandan from Fort Berthold. The Mandan were another of the Dakotas' traditional enemies. In fact, as Eastman recalls, not "more than two years before that time my uncle had been on the war-path against this tribe and had brought home two Mandan scalps." For Eastman, however, the Mandan boy was just another student like him, bewildered and a bit apprehensive about the unfamiliar surroundings. "My heart at once went out to him," Eastman confesses, "although the other pupils were all of my own tribe, the Sioux." Eastman especially admired this boy for his traditional appearance, complete with two long braids, as opposed to the other students, including himself, who had all had their hair cut. He notes, "This boy, Alfred Mandan, became a very good friend of mine." One could say that only under the social and historical conditions that led Eastman to the Santee Indian School in the first place was such a friendship possible.[25]

It was in the same spirit of adapting to modern Indian life that in 1910 Eastman accepted a commission "to search out and purchase rare curios and ethnological specimens for one of the most important collections in the country." Although Eastman never names his benefactor, the collection in question belonged to the University of Pennsylvania Museum of Archaeology and Anthropology. And the benefactor? In spite of Eastman's reticence, the benefactor was the well-known collector George Gustav Heye. Such information was far from hidden, as the *Museum Journal,* the Pennsylvania Museum's own publication, announced in a 1910 issue,

> The George G. Heye collection illustrating the culture of the American Indians has been materially enlarged since its first opening in February last. Among other things a fine carved wooden bowl from the Sauk and Fox Indians, a sun robe, and a collection of pipes from the Northwest Coast have attracted special attention. At the present time Mr. Heye is maintaining three expeditions in the field, one among the Plains Indians, another among the Ojibways and still another in Ecuador. No reports have yet been received from the last. The first has had very remarkable success, obtaining rare specimens, such as sacred medicine bundles and objects used in ceremonies. From Dr. Eastman, who is in charge of the work among the Ojibways, there have been received two very fine birch bark canoes and a collection of very remarkable specimens, which will be enumerated and described in a later issue.

Thus, the "rare curios and ethnological specimens" that Eastman speaks of in *From the Deep Woods* were mostly utilitarian, with a handful of sacred items belonging to various Ojibwe communities throughout northern Minnesota and Ontario, Canada. As unnerving as this sort of collecting may seem to a contemporary reader, Eastman underscores the deference he showed for his Ojibwe hosts, summarizing his approach thus: "My method was one of indirection. I would visit for several days in a camp where I knew, or had reason to believe, that some of the coveted articles were to be found. After I had talked much with the leading men, feasted them, and made them presents, a slight hint would often result in the chief or medicine man 'presenting' me with some object of historic or ceremonial interest, which etiquette would not permit to be 'sold,' and which a white man would probably not have been allowed to see at all."[26]

The irony of Eastman's ostensive mission is seen in the metamorphosis he underwent as he traveled deeper into Ojibwe Country. More to the point, the further Eastman pursued his museum work, the more the Ojibwe reawakened in him the deep connection he once felt for the woods and the life he lived there. Consequently, rather than being a tale about the expropriation of sacred items, Eastman's real story is about how the Ojibwe are the only true Indians left. "I know of no Indians," Eastman claims, "within the borders of the United States, except those of Leech, Cass and Red Lakes in Minnesota, who still sustain themselves after the old fashion by hunting, fishing and the gathering of wild rice and berries." In a world where Eastman and many of his intellectual peers regarded the old ways as gone, maintaining a traditional life is nothing short of extraordinary.[27]

With respect to Eastman's portrayal of Dakota-Ojibwe relations, the clearest indication of how much things have changed is the extent to which the Ojibwe not only welcomed their Dakota visitor but also obviously accepted that the rivalry between the two Indian nations was now a thing of the past. Indicative of the new world order is the story that Eastman tells about his visit to Boggimogishig, a prominent leader of the Sugar Point band. Eastman's meeting with the old Ojibwe war chief takes place twenty years after Eastman's Pine Ridge experience and thirty-eight years after the 1862 U.S.-Dakota War. Much has changed in both Minnesota and the United States as a whole with respect to Indian affairs. Not only is the reservation system firmly in place; the ramifications of the Dawes Act (1887), the Burke Act (1906), and Indian boarding schools, which began with Carlisle in 1879, have taken their toll on the maintenance of traditional cultures. While Eastman never buys into the notion that Indians are a "vanishing race," he did regard their pre-reservation cultures, even for the Ojibwe, as necessarily giving way to modern life, as defined by the exigencies of mainstream American society. In this view, traditional Indian warfare can seem like something from a completely different time and place. Boggimogishig, for example, was once well known for his many successful war parties against the Dakota, attributed "to the influence of the sacred war club, which had been handed down through several generations of dauntless leaders." By utilizing his wit and humor, Eastman won the affections of the chief and was able to obtain the club, as well as stories and traditions. Another band of Ojibwe with whom Eastman came into contact was at Red Lake. Eastman claims that he was able to obtain objects he was looking for (although the specific objects were not mentioned), including stories. One of the more important stories was about how Red Lake got its name. He was told of a battle between the Dakota and the Ojibwe so violent that the lake became red with blood.[28]

Eastman's travels into Ojibwe Country eventually took him as far north as International Falls. Along the way, at North Bay, Eastman met with someone whom we may rightly call the counterpart to his own grandmother. Without mentioning her name, Eastman recounts "a remarkable old woman, said to be well over ninety years of age." The daughter of a once prominent chief, this woman still lived in a birch-bark lodge, and when she came upon Eastman waiting for her at her home, she was carrying a heavy load of bark. The woman was not fazed by Eastman's presence, however, and agreed to have her picture taken, followed by "some old stories of her people," which she told "with much vivacity." Included in the old woman's tales was an account of her disdain for the white traders who wanted to take her as a wife but whose hairy faces repulsed her. The traders in turn paid her back by giving her a "shockingly irreverent" nickname.[29]

Continuing farther north, Eastman passed Massacre Island, named for an incident involving French traders, a Jesuit priest, and some whiskey. After plying the Ojibwe with alcohol in hopes of gaining all of their furs for a trifle, the traders were surprised by the hostile response they received instead of the bargain they expected. The Ojibwe killed everyone in the trading party, including the priest, and the island is now considered haunted by the Jesuit's wandering spirit, "and no Indian ever sets foot there." Probably without fully realizing it, Eastman's rather critical references to whites in northern Minnesota history is symptomatic of the growing discomfort he feels between the civilized society he has grown to accept and the life in the woods that he truly loves. "Every day," Eastman admits, as he draws nearer to International Falls, "it became harder for me to leave the woods." Toward the end of this trek, he came upon a stark reminder of how vulnerable Indians were to the onslaught of colonization. Near the Seine River stood a small village of perfectly preserved birch-bark lodges, none of which were inhabited. Even more surprising was the fact that whoever once lived there left all their belongings behind, as Eastman found clothing and utensils throughout the camp. Eastman soon learned from his guide that "a band of Indians had lived here every winter for several years, hunting for the Hudson Bay Company. One winter many of their children were attacked by a disease unknown to them, and after several had died, the people fled in terror, leaving everything behind them." As Eastman heard this story, it was a mere eleven years after these events occurred. The chapter on Eastman's journey finally ends with an anecdote about a very large turtle intruding upon Eastman's camp, unafraid of either the Dakota traveler or his guide, "as if to tell us that he was at home there and we were the intruders." For anyone familiar with the notion that this land is regarded as Turtle Island, the symbolism of this incident speaks for itself.[30]

It is probably fair to say that the Ojibwe taught Eastman something quite valuable about being Indian in the early twentieth century. After his experiences at Pine Ridge, then working for the YMCA, followed by serving as a lobbyist in Washington, DC, it could easily seem to Eastman that the Indian in America was being swept away by so-called progress, that it was only a matter of time before all Indians disappeared into the melting pot. In the woods of northern Minnesota and Canada, however, Eastman saw that it was still possible to maintain a vigilant stance against the push of civilization, a posture which, even if futile in some respects, is worth holding on other levels. Eastman surely appreciated this when he met Majigabo during the early stages of his trip into Ojibwe Country. Eastman said that although members of the tribe were traditionally his band's "fiercest enemies," he was made to feel welcome by the principal chief, Majigabo. Eastman was even allowed to witness certain rites that were being performed during his visit. Majigabo held the distinction of being the last Indian leader to defy American forces, including slaying commanding officer Captain Wilkinson, among those sent to Bear Island to pressure the Ojibwe into submission. While his act of defiance is less well known than Geronimo's, which occurred just a few short years earlier, unlike his Apache counterpart, Majigabo could claim victory in the end. Majigabo continued his vigilance even when Eastman met him, having recently refused to allow his nation to partake in the 1910 U.S. census. "[The whites] can take everything else," Majigabo said to Eastman, "but they must let me and these island people alone," to which Eastman said, "I could not but sympathize with his attitude."[31]

One can say that Eastman's sympathy for Majigabo and the Ojibwe carried over into his last book, *Indian Heroes and Great Chieftains*. Significantly, the piece on the Ojibwe leader Hole-in-the-Day (Bug-o-nay-ki-shig) is the concluding story, following four essays on the lives of Dull Knife, Roman Nose, Chief Joseph, and Little Wolf. The fact that the first ten stories are about Lakota and Dakota leaders means, given Eastman's tendency for Dakota-centric discourses, that the five exceptions had to have been particularly impressive in order to catch his attention. With this in mind, one can argue that Hole-in-the-Day is especially meaningful to Eastman as a symbol of all that he has learned about Indian leadership. For Hole-in-the-Day was born during the early nineteenth century, just as the Americans were beginning to implement their plans for controlling all of the land, "regardless of the rights of its earlier inhabitants."[32]

Although Hole-in-the-Day's father, who bore the same name, was a noted war leader who fought the Dakota many times, he and his peers did not choose to fight the newcomers. They cautioned that there was enough land for both peoples to coexist, not knowing just how many whites were ultimately on the way, let alone how much the Americans would covet Ojibwe land. After all, as Eastman has noted before, many Indians were unfamiliar with the notion of conquest and colonization. Even the Dakota and Ojibwe had once customarily held "peace meetings" each summer, "at which representatives of the two tribes would recount to one another all the events that had come to pass during the preceding year."[33]

Eastman's personal description of Hole-in-the-Day, the younger, is nothing if not flattering. Although Eastman obtained his information secondhand from Reverend Claude H. Beaulieu, he nonetheless developed a glowing admiration for the legendary Ojibwe. Describing him as tall, handsome, and graceful, Eastman also points out that he was a natural diplomat of very refined manners and speech. However, like most of the exemplary people about whom Eastman writes in *Indian Heroes,* there are some revealing anecdotes about Hole-in-the-Day's boyhood that are part of the story. Of particular interest here is the one about father and son during a day of fishing. The story takes place at Gull Lake when the younger Hole-in-the-Day was not quite ten years old. Because the father was fishing in a different canoe apart from his son, when screeching war whoops suddenly burst forth the father "could not think of anything but an attack by the dreaded Sioux." As it turned out, the younger Hole-in-the-Day was merely having trouble with a fish he caught that was too big for him to handle. To which the father said with exasperation, "if a mere fish scares you so badly, I fear you will never make a warrior!" What is particularly noteworthy here is the reference to the "dreaded Sioux," a figure of speech hitherto unseen in any of Eastman's writings.[34]

In the same vein, Eastman tells a daring tale of the elder Hole-in-the-Day, who successfully attacked and scalped a Dakota carrying pelts to a trading post. Pursued by the rest of the Dakota party, the elder Hole-in-the-Day made a desperate canoe crossing of the Mississippi River, reaching a small island near Fort Snelling. Still under hot pursuit and nearly cornered, the Ojibwe warrior managed to lose his pursuers by hiding behind the waters of Minnehaha Falls. Such deft and daring on Hole-in-the-Day's part was subsequently honored by the Dakota as they made this episode a part of their oral tradition. More important, as Eastman tells Hole-in-the-Day's story, the example that the father set for the son, in the common Indian tradition of emulating elders, sets the stage for the son to become the man that the people would both revere and revile: "Like Philip of Massachusetts, Chief Joseph the younger, and the brilliant Osceola, the mantle fell gracefully upon his shoulders, and he wore it during a short but eventful term of chieftainship."[35]

Unfortunately for the younger Hole-in-the-Day, he ascended to his leadership position at a time in Ojibwe history when it became increasingly difficult for any Indian leader to maintain the integrity of his tribe. Hole-in-the-Day had to deal with the threatening effects of American imperialism. Or, as Eastman describes this era, giving poetic influx to the political analysis he made in *The Indian To-day*, "It was [Hole-in-the-Day's] to see the end of the original democracy on this continent. The clouds were fast thickening on the eastern horizon. The day of individualism and equity between man and man must yield to the terrific forces of civilization, the mass play of materialism, and the cupidity of commerce with its twin brother politics." Obviously, this system was very different from the various alliances and rivalries that Indian nations once knew amongst themselves. In time, Hole-in-the-Day found himself in the same predicament as Little Crow and Spotted Tail, having to play at the white man's politics, much to the chagrin of the people each represented. More specifically, Hole-in-the-Day enacted a policy of gradual adaptation of the "white man's way," which included establishing territorial boundaries between the various Ojibwe bands and recognizing chiefs in the treaties with the United States, agreements that included compensating Indian leaders such as himself. "This was a serious departure from the old rule but was tacitly accepted," although tensions arose between the Mississippi River branch of the Lake Superior Ojibwe and the Leech Lake and Red Lake bands. Furthermore, in the 1855 treaty and in a subsequent treaty, Hole-in-the-Day did not fail to benefit himself and those close to him by securing more land and monetary compensation in exchange for giving the Americans land and power over what was once the collective Ojibwe dominion. Indeed, as Eastman now describes him, Hole-in-the-Day did not hesitate to flaunt his wealth, wearing an elaborate mix of Indian and white clothing. Hole-in-the-Day even employed "many white servants and henchmen" in addition to demonstrating a fondness for entertaining, thereby becoming quite the favorite "among army officers and civilians," not to mention being "especially popular with the ladies."[36]

While Eastman does not absolve Hole-in-the-Day for giving in to the temptation of wealth, power, and sex, he does point out that there is more to the story than the mere weakness of an individual before mammon. In an effort to more fully exploit the Old Northwest, the United States sought to forge a peace between the Dakota and Ojibwe; therefore, the Americans arranged for a peace council at Fort Snelling. Hole-in-the-Day was not bashful about ingratiating himself with the attending whites, including the white women who wanted to witness the spectacle of the peace council and whom he invited to sit on the Ojibwe side of the meeting when seating on the Dakota side grew crowded. During his many trips to Washington, DC, Hole-in-the-Day consistently attracted attention from a host of bureaucrats and politicians, who immediately became quite curious about the exotic Ojibwe chief. Eastman even recounts an affair that Hole-in-the-Day had with a white reporter, who followed him as far as Minneapolis and even bore him a son. Not only did Hole-in-the-Day violate the racial divide that existed between Indians and whites, he also already had other wives back home.[37]

Unsurprisingly, much resentment developed toward Hole-in-the-Day, whose prominence as an Ojibwe chief was largely due to the chicanery of Indian agents and Washington politicians. In spite of two attempts on his life, Hole-in-the-Day held onto his lucrative position until the 1860s, when successive Republican administrations changed federal Indian policy. Regardless of the proclamation to be more Christian with their Indian wards, the new generation of Indian Bureau agents turned out to be bigger grafters than their predecessors. Consequently, Hole-in-the-Day's wealth and power diminished substantially. Only in his state of decline did he finally realize the extent to which the Americans were mistreating the Ojibwe. Similar to Little Crow, Hole-in-the-Day was accused of betraying the interests of the people for the fleeting rewards of power and wealth. Also similar was Hole-in-the-Day's belated attempt at regaining his people's respect by turning on the ones who were at the root of every Ojibwe's problems.[38]

When the 1862 U.S.–Dakota War erupted, federal authorities plotted to humiliate Hole-in-the-Day by accusing him of conspiring with the Dakota, after which they would arrest him and install a more "friendly" chief. According to Eastman, Hole-in-the-Day never had any intention of aligning himself with the Dakota. When he was out on the road, he learned from a messenger of the plot against him, which was soon followed by the appearance of some soldiers sent to apprehend him. Hole-in-the-Day managed to give the detachment the slip, get word out to his warriors, and move his family safely to the other side of the Mississippi River. When the soldiers caught up to Hole-in-the-Day and he refused to surrender, they quickly fired upon him, and Hole-in-the-Day responded with his own rifle. However, the Ojibwe chief did not wait to be overwhelmed by the numbers opposing him. Instead, "with a whoop" he "disappeared among the pine groves." Because of this confrontation, the Ojibwe rallied behind their controversial chief, many of them holding camp with him while demanding an explanation from the government. Eastman recounts what happened as a result: "Presently Judge Cooper of St. Paul, a personal friend of the chief, appeared, and later on the Assistant Secretary of the Interior, accompanied by Mr. Nicolay, private secretary of President Lincoln. Apparently that great humanitarian President saw the whole injustice of the proceeding against a loyal nation, and the difficulty was at an end."[39]

Despite this reprieve from American connivance against Ojibwe interests, the lust for Ojibwe land ensued unabated. Treaties were concocted in 1864, 1867, and 1868, compelling the Ojibwe to remove themselves to the White Earth Reservation. Hole-in-the-Day "declared that he would never go on the new reservation, and he kept his word," remaining on a land grant near Crow Wing. Such relentless defiance, however, did not spare Hole-in-the-Day from the resentment that some still harbored against him, "especially among the Pillager and Red Lake bands." As a consequence of the epidemic fractioning of tribes during colonization, Hole-in-the-Day was assassinated "by a party of these disaffected Indians." Eastman concludes his article with a fitting eulogy for the slain Ojibwe leader: "Thus died one of the most brilliant chiefs of the Northwest, who never defended his birthright by force of arms, although almost compelled to do so. He succeeded in diplomacy so long as he was the recognized head of his people. Since we have not passed over his weaknesses, he should be given credit for much insight in causing the article prohibiting the introduction of liquor into the Indian country to be inserted into the treaty of 1858." Finally, Eastman notes that although Hole-in-the-Day had many children, none, at least when *Indian Heroes* was first published in 1918, had risen to the same level of prominence as their illustrious father. Nonetheless, Eastman hoped that someday the world will see in "one of his descendants that undaunted spirit . . . rise again."[40]

Eastman's notion of being American Indian did not end with the realization that the Dakota and Ojibwe ultimately share a common history. On the contrary, the pan-Indian agenda took on a decidedly political dimension, replete with reformist fervor, when he and other "educated Indians" formed the Society of American Indians in 1911, thereby setting the stage for a growing movement toward self-determination.

4

"For the Honor of the Race and the Good of the Country"
Eastman and the Progressive Indian Agenda

I looked back on the past and recalled my people's old ways,
but they were not living that way any more
Nicholas Black Elk, *Black Elk Speaks*

In the penultimate chapter of *The Search for an American Indian Identity,* after recounting what amounted to the epic story of the rise and decline of the Society of American Indians—the first Indian-run rights organization, its core membership consisting exclusively of Indians from communities across the continental United States—Hazel W. Hertzberg laments that the story of early twentieth-century Indian progressivism was not well known when she undertook what remains the single most important book on the subject. "It is highly doubtful," Hertzberg wrote in 1971, "whether any contemporary reform Pan-Indians have even heard of the Society of American Indians or of Indian reformist efforts antedating the National Congress of American Indians." So, has much changed in the intervening years between Hertzberg's book and my own? Somewhat. When I was a professor of American Indian Studies at the University of Minnesota during the years 2000-2007, I learned that my students, both graduate and undergraduate, knew about the NCAI but were more familiar with the American Indian Movement; however, they knew nothing about the SAI. Among my fellow scholars in the field of American Indian Studies, there is evidence of a growing awareness of the SAI and the concomitant generation of individuals, groups, and movements that also defined this pivotal epoch in American Indian history, including an attempt at updating the SAI's story, as seen in Lucy Maddox's 2005 book *Citizen Indians.*[1]

Hertzberg's book, on the other hand, appeared at the peak of the Red Power movement, which was ushering in a sea change in Indian political history. Moreover, Hertzberg's analysis of Progressive Era Indian

83

intellectuals underscored, by implication, just how far the fight for Indian rights had come since the time when "assimilation" was the prevailing ideology driving federal Indian policy. The Society of American Indians' dignified meetings between 1911 and 1920, which are at the core of Hertzberg's analysis, contrast starkly with the early 1960s "fish-ins" in the Pacific Northwest, not to mention the late sixties occupation of Alcatraz Island, followed by what would soon become known as the Second Wounded Knee in 1973. Paradoxically, Red Power activists, despite their militantism, were fighting about the same issues and problems as their turn-of-the-century predecessors, namely, treaty rights and Indian services reform. Indians may have grown in their political sophistication over the years, particularly after World War II; unfortunately, white Americans were lagging behind, consequently creating the same obstacles as their "Friends of the Indian" predecessors, namely paternalism and romanticism. Indeed, one thing Indian intellectuals have always had to tend to is educating predominantly white audiences about Indian cultures, histories, and politics. The language used may have changed from the gentlemanly moralistic works of Charles Eastman to the caustic legal analysis of Vine Deloria, Jr.; nevertheless, the objective has remained the same: specifically, to attain political freedom from American hegemony, as epitomized by the Bureau of Indian Affairs. On the latter point, it is worth pointing out that both Carlos Montezuma, in his self-published newsletter *Wassaja,* and the American Indian Movement, in its Twenty Points, called for abolishing the BIA.

Maddox's book, *Citizen Indians,* appearing a generation after Hertzberg's, turns out to be less of a radical departure from Hertzberg's discourse and more of a complement to it. I say this not because Maddox provides an indigenous perspective—she does not—but because she provides—from the same point of view as Hertzberg—a cultural critique of American society that explains more fully the possibility and necessity of the progressive Indian intellectual. With respect to Eastman, Maddox picks up on a laudatory remark that Hertzberg made, in which Eastman's name is virtually synonymous with Indian progressivism. After summarizing the vastly different assessments of Eastman's intellectual career, specifically as articulated by H. David Brumble III and Gerald Vizenor, Maddox goes on to make her own appraisal:

For Eastman as a writer and public figure, representing identity usually meant deliberately turning away from the disturbing details of specific recent histories [e.g., the Wounded Knee Massacre], tribal or personal, and toward a more optimistic and idealized representation of "the Indian" as a figure grounded in history but not bound by it, a particular type of a universal ideal. The old Indian that Eastman had known as a child was no more to be found, he acknowledged, except in memory and imagination; but "as a type, an ideal, he lives and will live!" The new Indian carried the internalized ideal with him into the civic and cultural life of America. For Eastman, the Indian ideal provided a model of democratic citizenship that set into relief the debasements of a society driven by materialism, greed, a love of ease and the corruptions of political ambition. Eastman's writings, taken together, constitute a sustained argument for the conclusion he stated in a 1918 article for the SAI journal—that the American Indian is in fact the most appropriate representation of all that America has professed but failed to be: "I am proud to say," he wrote, "that the Indian has exemplified the American spirit; it is his contribution to mankind." Eastman's presentation of his case fits comfortably with the general ethos of the SAI, at least as it was articulated by Arthur Parker, and perhaps even more comfortably with the ethos of those reform organizations that seemed to have more direct appeal to Eastman than did the SAI—the YMCA and the Boy Scouts of America. In his public presentation of himself, Eastman is both the SAI's representative man and the voice of one important strand of American progressivism.

What Maddox fails to observe, but what Hertzberg does a superior job of documenting, is that Eastman's 1918 proclamation about "the Indian," quoted above, only came after years of keeping his distance from the SAI.[2]

In *The Indian To-day*, Eastman provides his own account of how the Society of American Indians was founded. In a subsection of chapter eight titled "Problems of Race Leadership," Eastman claims that around 1900 he and his brother, John, along with Sherman Coolidge, began discussing the creation of a "national organization of progressive Indians." Their greatest concern, however, was with the reaction from the Indian Bureau, which was at the height of its authoritarian powers on the reservations. More specifically, the three were worried about retribution against the significant number of Indians who worked for the Indian Bureau across the reservation system, as it was typically the only place where "educated" Indians could obtain employment. Eastman's own case was an example of this peculiar situation: when he acquired his medical degree he did not go straight into private practice but to the Pine Ridge Agency as a government physician. What was true for Eastman was true for a great many Indians. "Very few Indians," Eastman observes, "are sufficiently independent of the Bureau to speak and act with absolute freedom." Even at the turn of the twentieth century, the lack of independence in the reservation system went beyond political impediments to include physical ones as well. Luther Standing Bear recounts in *My People the Sioux* a rather peculiar project: "When the agent called for more men, I went to him, and was assigned to help build a fence around the entire Indian reservation. This seemed like a funny proposition to us—fencing us in like a lot of wild animals—and the Interior Department had approved such an order! However, we all got busy fencing ourselves in, at $2.50 per day for a man and his team. It seemed like a positive disgrace to construct this fence around a race of people who had always been free to roam where they chose." Despite Eastman's growing reputation as an independent American Indian thinker, as of 1900 he had returned to working for the government at Crow Creek, which, similar to his Pine Ridge experience, was characterized by long hours treating patients and an ongoing confrontation with the local Indian agent. The inspiration, however, for forming a national organization for progressive Indians had as much to do with the increasing number of "educated" Indians coming out of the boarding school system as it was motivated by multiplying cases of Indian Bureau corruption. This is not to say that creating such an organization would be simple, as the American Indian community, Eastman notes, has many unique obstacles built into it: "I have been asked why my race has not produced a Booker Washington [a founder of the NAACP]. There are many difficulties in the way of efficient race leadership; one of them is the large number of different Indian tribes with their distinct languages, habits, and traditions, and with old tribal jealousies and antagonisms yet to be overcome. Another, and a more serious obstacle, is the dependent position of the Indian, and the almost arbitrary power in the hands of the Indian Bureau."[3]

With respect to the first obstacle, we saw in the previous chapter that Eastman had to undergo his own transformation: from a Dakota who thought of intertribal relations along traditional alliances and rivalries to an American Indian who comprehended the common values and interests that bound all Indian people together. In fact, it is probably worth repeating that the year before the Society of American Indians held its first meeting on October 12, 1911, in Columbus, Ohio, Eastman made his life-altering trip through Ojibwe Country in northern Minnesota. While it is true that, as Eastman states, he had been thinking about the future of pan-Indian politics several years prior to his 1910 collecting mission for George Gustav Heye, we should not underestimate the effect that this experience had on his understanding of the "Indian problem" and how to address it. Recall that Eastman's account of his Ojibwe journey ended with the discovery of an abandoned village, inhabited by a lone but very large turtle, simultaneously signifying both the aboriginality of indigenous people and the fate of their old traditions. The following summer, on July 28, 1911, Eastman gave a presentation at the University of London for the First Universal Races Congress. Eastman reflects, in *From the Deep Woods to Civilization*, on the value of what he experienced during this international meeting: "What impressed me most was the perfect equality of the races, which formed the background of all the discussions. It was declared at the outset that there is no superior race, and no inferior, since individuals of all races have proved their innate capacity by their standing in the universities of the world, and it has not seldom happened that men of the undeveloped races have surpassed students of the most advanced races in scholarship and ability." Eastman, of course, did not have to wait until he went to England to learn these things. A part of the Dakota tradition is to think of people around one in terms of kinship: "The family was not only the social unit, but also the unit of government... The very name of our tribe, Dakota, means Allied People." Complementing the Dakota notion of family was the Christian idea of brotherhood. After encountering moments of racism while searching for summer employment among Wisconsin farmers, Eastman eventually found work from a man who accepted his letter of introduction from President Chapin, which he obtained while a student at nearby Beloit College. One can only assume that the unnamed employer moved Eastman enough to inspire him to reflect on the possibilities when Christian ideals are upheld in people's daily lives and not just at the pulpit. Eastman writes,

> It was here and now that my eyes were opened intelligently to the greatness of Christian civilization, the ideal civilization, as it unfolded itself before my eyes. I saw it as the development of every natural resource; the broad brotherhood of mankind; the blending of all languages and the gathering of all races under one religious faith. There must be no more warfare within our borders; we must quit the forest trail for the breaking-plow, since pastoral life was the next thing for the Indian. I renounced finally my bows and arrows for the spade and the pen; I took off my soft moccasins and put on the heavy and clumsy but durable shoes. Every day of my life I put into use every English word that I knew, and for the first time permitted myself to think and act as a white man.[4]

As for excelling beyond the abilities of his white counterparts, Eastman experienced this on more than one occasion during his prestigious academic career. Consequently, with the reinforcement of the Ojibwe and United Kingdom trips, Eastman came to the realization that the pursuit of Indian rights in early twentieth-century America must acknowledge the impracticality of reverting to a pre-reservation world, on the one hand, while, on the other, arguing that more than ever society needs to find an antidote to the deteriorating effects of modernity, especially as evidenced on the reservations. In his writings, Eastman proposed a two-pronged approach, consisting of advocating for citizenship and education in addition to maintaining Indian values and principles. "I am an Indian," Eastman famously proclaims at the end of *From the Deep Woods to Civilization,* "Nevertheless, so long as I live, I am an American."[5]

Once inaugurated, the SAI held the distinction of being the first major national organization run by American Indians for the purpose of promoting American Indian legal and political issues. As expected, there were several individuals, including Eastman, who played great and small roles in the origin story of this social phenomenon. Fayette McKenzie, in particular, a non-Indian sociology professor at Ohio State University, is typically given a great deal of credit for successfully coordinating the SAI's first meeting in October 1911. Eastman corroborates this recognition to an extent when he recounts in *The Indian To-day* that it was McKenzie who, in 1910, invited him, along with Sherman Coolidge and Carlos Montezuma, to Columbus, Ohio, under the pretense that "the time was now ripe to organize our society." The following year McKenzie convinced six key figures in the progressive American Indian community, Thomas L. Sloan (Omaha), Charles E. Daganett (Peoria), Laura Cornelius (Oneida), Henry Standing Bear (Lakota), and Eastman, to form a tentative group called the American Indian Association, which would set about promoting to other progressive Indians and their supporters the benefits of creating a national pan-Indian organization. Toward this end the AIA issued a statement that declared "the time has come when the American Indian race should contribute, in a more united way, its influence and exertion with the rest of the citizens of the United States in all lines of progress and reform, for the welfare of the Indian race in particular, and humanity in general."[6]

In Hertzberg's estimation, Eastman was an ideal leader for the post-1890 generation. Anointing him "the dean of progressive American Indians," Hertzberg goes on to describe Eastman in her seminal study of the SAI as "a lithe and handsome man with the classic features of the Sioux, one who looked as much at home in a Boston business suit as in a feathered Plains war bonnet." Fortunately, we can honestly claim that Eastman's credentials as a national Indian leader extended far beyond his good looks. Indeed, by the time the SAI became a national sensation, Eastman had already garnered a lofty reputation in the American Indian community as well as among Anglo-Americans interested in Indian affairs. As of 1911, he had published five of his nine books, completed his YMCA service, lobbied for the Santee Dakota, worked as a Carlisle Indian School outing agent, and served Crow Creek as a physician in addition to revising its tribal rolls. Just as important, lest we forget, Eastman also had substantial experience battling against the forces of federal bureaucracy, which he first encountered in the wake of the Wounded Knee Massacre. While Eastman was initially taken aback by the Ghost Dance, regarding it as "a craze," he later learned that the

Lakota had good reason for being attracted to its urgent message of hope. Eastman then observed the inhumane conditions prevalent on the reservation, many of which caused the ailments he treated as their physician. The arising of the Ghost Dance, then, "meant that the last hope of race entity had departed, and my people were groping blindly after spiritual relief in their bewilderment and misery." Consequently, Eastman recalls this time as a loss of innocence: "I had faith in every one, and accepted civilization and Christianity at their face value—a great mistake, as I was to learn later on. I had come back to my people, not to minister to their physical needs alone, but to be a missionary in every sense of the word, and as I was much struck with the loss of man-liness and independence in these, the first 'reservation Indians' I had ever known, I longed above all things to help them to regain their self-respect."[7]

Before facing further disenchantment with the federal government as the Santee Dakota lobbyist, Eastman first got a lesson in Native re-sistance to assimilation during his tour of western reservations for the YMCA. Undertaken when the organization was still overtly Christian, Eastman's job was to convince members of these Indian communities to take an interest in the Christian lifestyle the YMCA promoted. But Eastman encountered a very astute spiritual resistance to the demands of modern American Christian life. By turns, Eastman was compelled to recognize from one reservation to the next that what survived of the old ways was still more fulfilling than what the YMCA or the federal government had to offer. Among the "Sioux, Cheyennes, Crees, Ojib-ways, and others," Eastman kept meeting the same response—that what he preached with respect to Jesus and Christianity was already practiced by the Indians. "Why, we have followed this law you speak of for untold ages," exclaimed one. Another proclaimed, "I have come to the conclusion that this Jesus was an Indian." In turn, a leader of the "Sac and Fox tribe in Iowa" stated, "As for us . . . we shall still follow the old trail." Eastman concluded at the end of his arduous but fascinating mission,

> My effort was to make the Indian feel that Christianity is not at fault for the white man's sins, but rather the lack of it, and I freely admitted

that this nation is not Christian, but declared that the Christians in it are trying to make it so. I found the facts and the logic of them often hard to dispute, but was partly consoled by the wonderful opportunity to come into close contact with the racial mind, and to refresh my understanding of the philosophy in which I had been trained, but which had been overlaid and superseded by a college education. I do not know how much good I accomplished, but I did my best.[8]

Eastman, as mentioned, now faced further disillusion with the nature of politics and politicians during his tenure as the Santee Dakota lobbyist, as recounted in a chapter titled "At the Nation's Capital." "I learned," Eastman recalls, "that scarcely one of our treaties with the United States had been carried in good faith in all of its provisions," including the treaties made in 1824 and 1851. Among the violations on the part of the United States against the Dakota was the arbitrary withholding of annuities as a punishment for participation in the 1862 conflict. As Eastman points out, not every Dakota supported going to war against the American settlers and traders, even though there was good reason for holding the United States in contempt. Still, there were many, Dakota Christians in particular, who chose to abide by their decision not to wage war against the United States. Nonetheless, the whole tribe was punished for the instigation of a few desperate individuals. Eastman would not be asked for his assistance until nearly forty years after the conflict had ended. What he discovered firsthand about the "machinery of government" was just as eye opening as what he learned about the corruption of the Indian Bureau on the reservation. Patronized and often given the runaround, Eastman had to work hard at attaining the attention and respect of those in power. By equal measure, Eastman had his patience tested by many "minor politicians and grafters": "Armed with a letter of introduction from one of my staunch eastern senatorial friends, I would approach a legislator who was a stranger to me, in the hope of being allowed to explain to him the purpose of our measure. He would listen a while and perhaps refer me to some one else. I would call on the man he named, and to my disgust be met with a demand for a liberal percentage on the whole amount to be recovered." In the end, Eastman was more successful at learning about the problems of politics and bureaucracy than he was at recovering the Dakotas' lost annuities.[9]

With respect to this endeavor, Eastman concludes the chapter "At the Nation's Capital" with some very interesting observations. First, he expresses his disappointment with the administration of Teddy Roosevelt, who was once regarded as the best hope for American Indian interest in reform: "Spotted Horse said of him, 'While he talked, I forgot that he was a white man.'" Unfortunately, once in office, especially during Roosevelt's second term, things took a turn for the worse: "There were more frauds committed; and in the way of legislation, the Burke bill was distinctly a backward step." Whereas the 1887 Dawes Act, in Section 6, sought to expedite the American Indian transition into citizenship, the 1906 Burke Act decidedly impeded this process. Instead of a fixed twenty-five-year trust period for allotments, the length of time was now at the secretary of Interior's discretion. Furthermore, citizenship was now granted at the end rather than the start of the trust period. Worst of all was the proviso granting the secretary of Interior the power to judge an individual Indian's "competency" at handling his affairs. Second, Eastman comments on the status of the Indian boarding school system and its long-term effect on the Indian community. At the same time that Indian students have been thoroughly inculcated with a mainstream education—at the expense of their language and traditional ways—"they have really become an entirely different race." Third, Eastman observes an effect of the land allotment policy in South Dakota: many of the Dakota and Lakota have become American citizens in enough numbers that they carry the swing vote in some counties. With respect to these things, Eastman makes the statement, "Some persons imagine that we are still wild savages, living on the hunt or on rations; but as a matter of fact, we Sioux are now fully entrenched, for all practical purposes, in the warfare of civilized life." As such, Eastman advocated the formation of the Society of American Indians with this "unexpected"—to borrow Philip J. Deloria's term—reality in mind.[10]

During the SAI's first two successive meetings in Columbus, Ohio, a constitution was drawn containing a Statement of Purposes, which espoused seven key principles, all of which were promoted for "the honor of the race and the good of the country," and would define the progressive Indian agenda:

First.—To promote and co-operate with all efforts looking to the advancement of the Indian in enlightenment which leave him free, as a man, to develop according to the natural laws of social evolution.
Second.—To provide through our open conference, the means for a free discussion on all subjects bearing on the welfare of the race.
Third.—To present in a just light a true history of the race, to preserve its records, and to emulate its distinguishing virtues.
Fourth.—To promote citizenship among Indians and to obtain the rights thereof.
Fifth.—To establish a legal department to investigate Indian problems, and to suggest and to obtain remedies.
Sixth.—To exercise the right to oppose any movement which may be detrimental to the race.
Seventh.—To direct its energies exclusively to general principles and universal interests, and not allow itself to be used for any personal or private interests.[11]

Eastman quoted these same principles, which are really a kind of manifesto, in *The Indian To-day*. However, as Eastman acknowledges, after listing the SAI's accomplishments following a mere four years of operation, the inherent problems of the Indian community have not been entirely overcome. Moreover, there are issues relating to the SAI itself; in particular, the question of how the organization can be most effective. Eastman poses the dilemma thus: "Should we [the SAI] devote ourselves largely to exposing the numerous frauds committed upon Indians? Or should we keep clear of these matters, avoid discussion of official methods and action, and simply aim at arousing racial pride and ambition along new lines, holding up a modern ideal for the support and encouragement of our youth? Should we petition Congress and in general continue along the lines of the older Indian associations? Or should we rather do intensive work among our people, looking especially toward their moral and social welfare?" Eastman aligned himself with "the latter plan" of moral and social welfare. After all, Arthur C. Parker proclaimed in his first editorial for the SAI's journal that its members were pursuing their work "Without the hope of personal gain, of financial reward or advanced position." This selfless approach was consistent with Eastman's notion, as expressed in both *Indian Boyhood* and *From the Deep Woods to Civilization*, that he "was consciously trained to be a man; that was, after all, the basic thing; but after this I was trained to be a warrior and a hunter, and not to care for money and possessions, but to be in the broad sense a public servant." The idea of service carried over into Eastman's academic and professional pursuits, specifically in terms of figuring out which career to choose in order that he might "share with my people whatever I might attain." Magnifying this ideal of service in a way that was suitable to a national pan-Indian organization proved more difficult. As Parker further states, "The open plan is to develop race leaders, to give hope, to inspire, to lead outward and upward, the Indian American as a genuine factor in his own country and lead him to see that upon his individual effort depends his share in the salvation of his race and his value to his country." As Eastman had summarized, there was no clear consensus on which direction to devote the SAI's limited resources. At the same time, the one thing the SAI was good at was generating debate among its members. Perhaps because of the broiling factionalism, Eastman kept the SAI at arm's length. The situation that grew more divisive as "peyotism" became a major religious movement, creating a problem the SAI never resolved and leading to its eventual dissolution after 1920.[12]

Unsurprisingly, Eastman's contributions to the *Quarterly Journal of the Society of American Indians* and the *American Indian Magazine* were sporadic. Eastman was spoken about rather than published in the first volume of the *Quarterly Journal.* Specifically, he is quoted briefly as saying, "The white race is impatient." Then, a little further on, Eastman is named, along with other "well known Indians," such as Carlos Montezuma and congressman Charles D. Carter, as endorsing the SAI. Eastman stands again as an example in an article by Dennison Wheelock (Oneida) titled "Not an Indian Problem but a Problem of Race Separation," in which Wheelock avers, "If Dr. Montezuma, Dr. Eastman, Rev. Coolidge, Rev. Roe Cloud, and scores of other noted Indian men and women who are successfully living and practicing their professions among the most refined and cultured of the white race, are not strong affirmative living answers to the question propounded, then attempting to reason with the powers that be, and urging the establishment of a policy which shall contemplate the mixing of the races, becomes a senseless agitation and a mockery." Eastman's own voice came through loud and clear in 1915, when he published an article in the *Quarterly*

Journal titled "The Indian's Gift to the Nation," which appeared sub-sequently as chapter eleven of *The Indian To-day*. More specifically, Eastman makes his contribution to a tradition of celebrating the Native genius that continues through today, in which a range of culturally sig-nificant innovations and some historically important individuals are highlighted as evidence that the indigenous peoples of North America were anything but "primitive." For the post-1890 generation, contribu-tions to this subgenre of American Indian scholarship include "Indian Gifts to Civilized Man" (1918) by Zitkala-Sa, *The Indian How Book* (1931) by Arthur Parker, and "What the Indian Means to America," the con-cluding chapter of *Land of the Spotted Eagle* (1933) by Luther Standing Bear. The purpose of such pieces, beyond generating pride in their Indian readers, typically consists of making the argument that Ameri-cans in general owe a huge debt to American Indians for influencing and shaping the United States into the distinct society and world power it is today. Integral to this argument is pointing out that Indian nations were not simply looking after the land until Europeans arrived and "discovered America"; nor were they intractable "savages" looking to kill white settlers at every opportunity. Moreover, despite Indian partici-pation in the Wild West shows and early cinema, such popularizations of Indian stereotypes only served to cloud a much more interesting and complex relationship between Indians and whites.[13]

In fact, an ongoing criticism among SAI members concerned the harm that the Wild West show in particular was doing to the progres-sive Indian's efforts at informing the public about contemporary Indian affairs. Parker, in a 1914 editorial, states unequivocally, "The Wild West show has done a lot of harm in the way of deceiving the public." It made the work of improving the lives of Indians all the more arduous, since the public and those in government were left with the impression that Indians were still running "wild" across the plains and deserts of the American West, suggesting that the Indian's wildness still needed to be subdued before the civilization process could begin in earnest. Obvi-ously, this impression obscured the fact that many Indian communities, in some cases for several generations, had successfully endured the transition to modern American life—the SAI itself being a prominent example of Indian progress. Yet the Wild West show caused droves of Anglo-Americans to "think that every Indian of whatever tribe wears, or once wore, the Sioux war bonnet; it has made them believe that Indian women all wore a feather in their hair standing up straight behind."[14]

Interestingly, Parker does not limit his criticism to the white producers of Wild West shows but also reprimands the Indians who make the conscious choice of working for them. "There would be no such degenerate antics," Parker argues, "if the public opinion of the Indians themselves was against it. When white showmen are assailed for recruiting actors 'at a dollar a day and feed' the class of Indians who misrepresent their people should likewise be criticized." In the same issue as Parker's editorial, Chauncey Yellow Robe, a Lakota and former Wild West performer, also came out against this form of so-called entertainment in a short article titled "The Menace of the Wild West Show." After recounting an anecdote in which two former adversaries, an old army general and a Lakota chief, shared tales of their life and conflict on the plains, Yellow Robe distinguishes this example of authenticity and amity between those who actually lived the history that others can now only read about in books from the shams perpetrated by Wild West showmen. What the likes of William Cody staged before thousands across the United States and Europe, Yellow Robe observes, has been going on since the time Columbus exhibited live Indians before the Spanish throne. Even worse than whiskey, the Wild West show led many Indians down the road to ruin, at the end of which they were often broke and drunk. The situation was exacerbated by the Wild West "craze" that swept the nation, in which audiences were taught that "the Indian is only a savage being." All the more egregious is the manner in which the Wild West show mentality distorted historic events, including the most traumatic episodes in Indian history. Yellow Robe writes about an appalling example:

> Before the closing history of the nineteenth century an awful crime was committed in this great Christian nation. It was only a few days after the civilized nations of the world had celebrated the message of the heavenly host saying, "Fear not, for behold I bring you good tidings of great joy which shall be to all people;" and "Glory to God in the highest and on earth peace, good will towards men." A band of Sioux Indians, including women and children, unarmed, were massacred. The wounded were left on the field to die without care at

Wounded Knee by the United States troops just because they had founded a new religion called "The Indian Messiah." This was a cowardly and criminal act without diplomacy. Twenty-three years afterwards, on the same field of Wounded Knee, the tragedy was reproduced for "historical preservation" in moving-picture films and called "The Last Great Battle of the Sioux." The whole production of the field was misrepresented and yet approved by the Government. This is a disgrace and injustice to the Indian race.

Yellow Robe concludes his piece with an appeal for equal rights and opportunities for Indians, as well as for fighting the inequities and misconceptions that seem to be always driving Anglo-American attitudes toward the so-called "Indian problem."[15]

In the same spirit of dispelling ignorance and stereotypes about Indians, Eastman provides his readers in "The Indian's Gift to the Nation" an encomium of Indians and their achievements that have clearly benefited their white brethren across the United States. By the same token, one can read Eastman's narrative for the examples it provides Indian readers of what Indian people have accomplished in the past and may yet achieve in the future. In other words, the example of the progressive Indian has always been a part of Indian culture and history, at least insofar as progressiveness may include any Indian who works for the good of the people. In this vein, Eastman honors the Indian's natural leadership capacity in both diplomacy and military strategy, naming Red Jacket and Chief Joseph as examples. American forces have benefited greatly from the tactical support they received from their Indian allies as soldiers and scouts, beginning with General George Washington's reliance on Delaware warriors during the revolution. Indeed, the Indian reputation for producing excellent soldiers and scouts had even led to some astounding appeals from earnest whites. For example, Eastman recalls a request made to him personally: "It is interesting evidence of the world-wide respect for our strategy and methods, that when the Boer commission came to Washington a few years ago Mr. Wessel called upon me to advise him how he might secure one thousand Sioux and Cheyenne scouts in their war against Great Britain. Of course I told him that it could not be done: that I would not involve my country in an international difficulty. I was similarly approached during the Russo-Japanese war." While there is abundant evidence of Native acumen in the field of conflict, one may count the warrior and scout alongside other stereotypes that modern Indians face. By implication, Eastman shows that he is aware of the warrior image that many non-Indians have of Indian people when he makes it a point to emphasize that, by equal turns, there were many instances when the Indian voice was the voice of reason, cautioning against war and retaliation. Here, he names the Cherokee chief Ottakullakulla, who admonished against unmitigated revenge for the murder of Cherokee warriors who had recently assisted Washington in his campaign against Fort Duquesne. Ottakullakulla advised instead that the Cherokee take into consideration the whites who pledged friendship to them and who were not guilty of any crime. The latter should be escorted back to their homeland, where they would be safe, and only then might the offended Cherokee "take up the hatchet!" Another example came from the Dakota, a "man named Arrow," who protected white prisoners during the 1862 U.S.-Dakota War. Eastman then proclaims that the ideals articulated through Christianity are not the exclusive property of any one nation or people but may be practiced by a "very simple and unpractical people" like the Dakota or any other Indian tribe.[16]

After naming and honoring the contributions of Indian women in history, such as Pocahontas, Catherine ("the Ojibway maid"), and Saca-jawea, Eastman concludes his chapter with a section titled "The Children's Hero," in which the "new race" is recognized as an important component in the future of modern America. What makes the current generation of Indians "new" are the results from gaining an education, the influence of Christianity, and the necessity of engaging in the vocations of modern life. "Yet," Eastman assures his reader, "the inherent racial traits are there: latent, no doubt"—due to the inertia of reservation life—"but still there. The red man still retains his love of service," and, despite what one might see in a Wild West show, "his love for his country. Once he has pledged his word to defend the American flag, he stands by it manfully." Colonel Ely S. Parker and George Guess, known as Sequoyah, endure as towering examples of Indian probity in America: Parker for being an aid to General Ulysses S. Grant during the Civil War and Sequoyah for inventing the "Cherokee alphabet" and being the only Indian "admitted to the nation's Hall of Fame" in Washington, DC.[17]

In turn, such luminaries may also serve as role models for young Anglo-Americans; at least, such is the suggestion Eastman makes in an appeal to support the Boy Scouts and Camp Fire Girls, which depend upon "the wisdom of the first American" and which may provide America the possibility of raising a generation of young people imbibed with the "spiritual and philosophical" principles that Indian people still embody. One could say that Eastman was making a very interesting attempt at encouraging the average American to "Indianize" himself; indeed, one could say, based on Eastman's evidence of the "painter, sculptor, author, scientist, [and] preacher," that this is exactly what Americans seem to naturally want to become—a more Indian and, hopefully, less puritanical version of their forefathers. The difficult task for intellectuals like Eastman is to get Americans to see the connection between addressing the "Indian problem" and preserving the "Indian wisdom" that otherwise means so much to them. The tendency, evidenced by attendance at Wild West shows, is for Anglo-Americans to simply appropriate Indian images and turn them into "entertaining" stereotypes—always at the expense of valuable lessons in history and culture, not to mention the Indian's integrity.[18]

The following year, 1916, in the *American Indian Magazine,* another chapter from *The Indian To-day* appeared. On this occasion, "The Indian's Health Problem" was featured. Here, Eastman accounts for the current health crisis that exists throughout the reservation system, which is made all the more distressing when compared with the vibrant existence, as Eastman portrays it, that Indians knew before colonization. Miraculously, the evidence of the last three U.S. censes demonstrates a turnaround in the rate of decline of the overall Indian population: "This indicates that the race has reached and passed the lowest point of its decline, and is beginning slowly but surely to recuperate." Nonetheless, the reservation is anything but conducive to healthful living, which is exacerbated by all the obstacles a government physician faces while trying to do his job. Eastman recounts a story told with dramatic effect in *From the Deep Woods to Civilization* of his days at the Pine Ridge Agency. As the only doctor serving a population considered potentially "hostile," Eastman was forced to deal with the ongoing problems of being understaffed and underfunded, worsened by the racial prejudice of the Indian agent.[19]

Fortunately, because of reforms in the Indian Bureau, the situation had improved, as it had for the reservation system entire. "At Pine Ridge," Eastman points out, "where I labored single-handed, there are now three physicians, with a hospital to aid them in their work." Despite the evidence of progress, all was not rosy: Eastman refers his reader to the "poor sanitary" conditions of the Indian boarding schools. While improvements had been made in this area of Indian life, Indians were still in a state of recovery from the effects of policies mismanaged by government agents. Nonetheless, Eastman counsels against being pessimistic, noting there is clear indication that when provided the right conditions, Indian people thrive in the modern world just as much as their white counterparts. Eastman's message of hope is fascinating for the fact that much of his expectation hinges on the "mixed-blood" or the "new Indian," the product of increased participation in the "melting-pot." Eastman observes: "[American Indians] now intermarry extensively with Americans and are rearing a healthy and promising class of children. The tendency of the mixed-bloods is toward increased fertility and beauty as well as good mentality. This cultivation and infusion of new blood has relieved and revived the depressed spirit of the first American to a noticeable degree, and his health problem will be successfully met if those who are entrusted with it will do their duty." Eastman's remarks respond to a number of issues, not the least of which was the opinion of many in mainstream Anglo-American society that the mixing of races resulted in "mongrelism." He also countered the assumption that, because intermarriage was taking place, there were therefore fewer "real Indians." As a "mixed-blood"—at least in the sense of being related genealogically to whites through his mother's branch of the family, most notably his grandfather, Seth Eastman— Eastman, himself married to a white woman, surely wanted to dismiss such a misguided notion. Lastly, Eastman makes a statement against the irrepressible belief that the Indians were a "vanishing race." They may have been transforming, but they were hardly disappearing.[20]

In 1917 the *American Indian Magazine* released an issue devoted exclusively to the Sioux, featuring an article by Eastman titled "The Sioux of Yesterday and Today." It additionally included an homage to "The Fighting Sioux" by Chauncey Yellow Robe, a commemoration of "The Sioux Outbreak of 1862" by Arthur Parker, a poem about "A Sioux

Woman's Love for Her Grandchild" by Zitkala-Sa (aka Gertrude Bonnin), and an informational piece regarding "The Situation at Santee" by S. M. Brosius, which originally appeared in the thirty-fifth annual report of the Indian Rights Association. All these pieces were respectful and even laudatory of "Sioux Indian" culture and values as well as complemented with insightful criticisms of federal Indian policy and replete with special retorts for the Indian Bureau.

According to a footnote, Eastman's article first appeared in an issue of the *Sioux City Journal*. Its focus is Ogallala Fire, whom Eastman eulogizes after the elder Lakota's recent passing. Given the time of this article's publication, the story of Ogallala Fire could very well be taken as an inspiration for Eastman's last book, *Indian Heroes and Great Chieftains*. At the very least, one can say that, as Eastman portrays him, Ogallala Fire was worthy of having his story told alongside those of Red Cloud, Sitting Bull, and Crazy Horse. Indeed, this venerable old warrior was the contemporary of these illustrious figures in Lakota history. "Ogallala Fire," Eastman writes, "was already middle aged when Custer, Crook, Terry and Gibbons invaded the Sioux territory." Eastman excoriates the United States for violating the 1868 Fort Laramie Treaty, a blatant act of greed for land clearly acknowledged as Lakota and for the gold in the Black Hills that made the whites go crazy: "Ogallala Fire was one of the gallant warriors who made their last stand then and there, while General Crook moved upon them from Wyoming, and General Terry came up the Missouri River and over to the Yellowstone to attack the so-called 'hostile Sioux.' As well call the Belgians and the Servians 'hostiles' because they resisted the invading armies of their aggressors!" Making the bold implication that the United States was to the Lakota in 1870 what the Germans were to the Belgians and Serbs in 1914, Eastman compels his reader to think about whether the United States had really progressed beyond the culpabilities of the past. Whereas the Battle of the Little Bighorn may have been a dramatic episode from a bygone era for most Americans, for the Lakota, "For more than a quarter of a century after this time [1876], at every 'Big Issue Day' on any of the western Sioux agencies, certain old men would seat themselves in a circle on the dry prairie grass and pass the long pipe while they told over again the stories of their celebrated battles. They usually ended with this one," the annihilation of Custer and the Seventh Cavalry.

Eastman then gives the heroic account of how the Lakota and their Cheyenne allies took advantage of Custer's gross strategic errors and routed the American detachment.[21]

In turn, Eastman does not hide or sugarcoat the fact that the Lakota were eventually subdued and placed on reservations, having lost both Crazy Horse and Sitting Bull to political assassinations. Eastman describes the new and difficult era: "When the storm was over, these husky warriors dropped back perforce into the apathetic and uninteresting agency life. Many succumbed to disease caused by the sudden change to indoor and sedentary conditions, together with scanty and unwholesome food—ill-prepared bread and rancid bacon. There was no game to be had, and the conditions for farming were discouraging on the dry plains of the West. Sickness and depression were the rule rather than the exception." Unlike Black Elk, Eastman does not begin bemoaning the decline and fall of the Great Sioux Nation. Instead, as testimony to the people's resilience and perseverance, Eastman accounts for some of the ways in which the Lakota adapted and began to succeed in their new circumstances, apparently despite the Indian Bureau's negligence. Aside, then, from mentioning the move that some former warriors made into the ranks of the Indian police, Eastman points out that a substantial proportion of the child population was attending school, "in fact, nearly all the younger generation speak English and read it to some extent."[22]

The Lakota had even become rather adept at navigating the modern political world, a result of regularly dealing with the federal government on the reservation as well as a large number becoming U.S. citizens, complete with allotted lands: "In South Dakota there are new counties officered and controlled by Sioux voters." Unfortunately, the Lakota had also adapted many of the vices of modern politics, including a tendency toward self-interest: "Whereas in the old days they would gladly serve the people without pay, they have now an eye to personal advantage, and this is not strange. Much still remains to be done for their health, and they are in need of the very best religious and socializing influences, also of fuller opportunities for the higher education of such as are able to profit by it. But it is much that a large proportion are industrious, self-supporting and entirely loyal."[23]

Eastman's article is followed by a surprising piece reprinted from the *Daily Star* of Lincoln, Nebraska, titled "The Truth of the Wounded Knee Massacre." An editor's note claims, "This remarkable interview with Dr. Melvin R. Gilmore sheds some new light on the awful tragedy at Wounded Knee, Dec. 29, 1890. For the first time actual statements by an Indian survivor are given light."[24]

Later, in a section titled "Men and Women Whose Lives Count for the Red Man's Cause," both Eastman and his daughter Irene are featured. In the case of Irene, who goes by the stage name Taluta, the segment extols her accomplishments as a classically trained singer whose talent is appreciated far and wide: "With the spirit of both parents she is enabled to sing an interpretation of the strange melodies of Indian life as few singers ever will." Then, a segment on Eastman celebrates him as "the greatest Sioux of the century," who earned this distinction for the work he has done at bridging the gap between the old ways, the reservation, and mainstream American society. Eastman, "filled with the lore and philosophy of his people . . . also sees the necessity of pointing out to his race the ways of the modern world in which all men of today must live." The piece highlights some of the events in Eastman's illustrious life, as recounted in the recently published *From the Deep Woods to Civilization*.[25]

Amazingly, in the following issue, Arthur Parker acknowledged that the special on the Sioux "made a considerable impression," which was far from universally positive. Some readers had reacted with "unmixed horror," accusing Parker of becoming the "rankest Bolshevikist"; others "took up the cudgel and warned us of our error"; in addition, some feared that "we would be accused of Apacheism and ruin our good name and hinder our cause." Without boasting, Parker responds to his critics by mentioning that the criticisms of the Indian Office articulated in the Sioux issue were not only well founded but also clearly resolvable, such that they had been taken up by some with the power to make a difference: "Much that we endeavored to accomplish has been done."[26]

In the 1919 winter issue of the *American Indian Magazine,* by then edited by Gertrude Bonnin (Zitkala-Sa), Eastman was featured on the cover and his presidency of the Society of American Indians announced. Defining Eastman's presidential agenda were two articles:

"The Indian's Plea for Freedom" and "A Review of the Indian Citizenship Bills." The first item is an impassioned argument that the industrialized nations, particularly those that were engaged in the recently concluded Great War, had driven the world further than ever from the ideals that supposedly lay at these civilizations' intellectual and spiritual foundations: "The world is tired, sick, and exhausted by a war which has brought home to us the realization that our boasted progress is after all mainly industrial and commercial," and "The intellectual development connected with it has been largely heartless and soulless."[27]

Having said this, Eastman sees the world, including the United States, in a special situation in which it can make genuine progress at bringing justice and democracy to the world's people, not the least of whom are American Indians: "All we ask is full citizenship." Eastman reminds his reader that many of the traits and ideals that characterize America were originally possessed by Indian people. More importantly, Indian people still exemplify these values: "The friendship, toleration, dignity and sincerity characteristic of the American Indians have never been violated by them, and is their bequest to the nation." Eastman asserts that the probity of American Indians—and, by implication, the perfidy of Anglo-Americans—is demonstrated by the treaty tradition of the two nations. Whereas Indians had by and large lived up to their side of the agreements, the Americans had been remiss in their obligations to the nation's aborigines, personified by the Indian Bureau, which still dominated the daily lives of thousands on the reservations. Even the returned soldier had to contend with the bureau's paternalism, as Eastman states with added emphasis: *"It is not the fault of the people in the way; not perhaps the fault of any particular administration that a soldier returning from the Marne or Chateau Thierry should still find his money and land held by the Indian Bureau. When he asks for freedom, they answer him: 'Can you propose anything better than the present system?' He replies: 'Is there anything better today than American citizenship?'"*[28]

Eastman thus makes an argument that many in the sai, including Gertrude Bonnin, Arthur Parker, and Carlos Montezuma, were making on behalf of the countless disenfranchised Indians who fought for freedom and democracy abroad but could not enjoy these rights at home. Bonnin, in particular, during her tenure as editor of the *American Indian Magazine,* worked hard at advocating for Indian citizenship. Similar to

Eastman, Bonnin argued for granting Indians citizenship on the basis that they had earned the right through their sacrifices in the Great War, often volunteering to enlist in the various branches of the military. In a 1921 pamphlet titled "Americanize the First American," Bonnin asks, "Where are those bright-eyed, black-haired urchins of the out-of-doors? Where are those children whose fathers won so much acclaim for bravery in the World War now closed?" Years after the inaugural meeting of the Society of American Indians, not to mention generations after the 1887 Dawes Act was passed, the Indian children for whom Bonnin laments were still on the reservations, suffering from a prolonged wardship and the consequences of a lack of citizen's rights. What Bonnin described in 1921 was certainly true when Eastman complained about the Indian Bureau's authoritarianism. Bonnin states,

> Suffice it to say that by a system of solitary isolation from the world the Indians are virtually prisoners of war in America. Treaties with our Government made in good faith by our ancestors are still unfulfilled, while the Indians have never broken a single promise they pledged to the American people. American citizenship is withheld from some three-fourths of the Indians of the United States. On their reservations they are held subservient to political appointees upon whom our American Congress confers discretionary powers. These are unlovely facts, but they are history. Living conditions on the reservations are growing worse. In the fast approach of winter I dread to think of the want and misery the Sioux will suffer on the Pine Ridge Reservation.[29]

In *My People the Sioux,* Luther Standing Bear concludes his moving and highly engaging life story with a chapter titled "American Citizenship." After getting a taste of a wider world due to his performance experience with Buffalo Bill's Wild West Show, Standing Bear concludes that the reservation is no place for him. However, he does not forsake the reservation for his own selfish interests but, rather, because he thought "I might be able to do more for my own race off the reservation than to remain there under the iron rule of the white agent." Unfortunately, leaving the reservation at the time—Standing Bear recalls it was around 1907—was far from a casual decision. In order to leave, Standing Bear, like any other Indian under the Burke Act, had to be judged "competent" before he could assume control over his own affairs, enabling him to sell his allotment and use the money to relocate. "Several educated Indians and some half-breeds," Standing Bear recalls, "had tried to get fee patents for their lands, and were refused. Even a highly educated Omaha Indian named Tom Sloane, who was a practicing attorney, was turned down by the Government." Needless to say, Standing Bear did not hesitate to express his outrage against the inequities Indian people faced from a government that often failed to respect Indian rights even after many Indians were willing to make the ultimate sacrifice on behalf of the United States:

> When they started to draft the Indian boys, who were not even American citizens, I wrote a strong letter to the old chiefs, advising that the boys demand their citizenship if they were to be expected to go abroad and fight for Uncle Sam. Even my own brother, Ellis Standing Bear, wrote me that he had to go in the next draft. He was greatly worried as to who would care for the children he had adopted, as he and his wife were childless.
>
> One of my own sons was rejected in the draft because he was tubercular. He has since passed away. Our tribe, the Sioux, is the largest in the United States to-day, and during the World War more than *eight thousand* of our boys went across. We certainly feel that we have done our duty to the land that really belonged to our fathers, and is the land of our birth. It is ours, and we are always ready to protect it against any enemy.[30]

It is fair to say that the issue of citizenship was not without some redress at the federal level. For those concerned, as Eastman analyzes in "A Review of the Indian Citizenship Bills," there had already been some forward movement in the pursuit of becoming fully enfranchised Americans. Since its inception, the SAI collectively sought the granting of universal citizenship to American Indians as a way of alleviating the perennial problems caused by the reservation system. In fact, a common belief was that much of the "Indian problem" stemmed from the politically ambiguous status of Indians in American society. Consequently, the "transition period" in which Indians found themselves was transitional not only in the sense that Indians were subject to the process of "civilization" but also in that the foundations on which Indians traditionally understood themselves and their place in the world prior to the reservation system were in a state of flux.

According to Parker in a 1914 SAI quarterly editorial, with respect to the legal status of Indians, whereas in the 1850s through the early 1880s legalists could still clearly determine who was an Indian, once the Dawes Act was passed the waters became murky. Suddenly, being of "Indian blood" was not enough. Parker points out,

> In Oklahoma, mixed-bloods are given certain rights not enjoyed by full-bloods, but all Indians of Oklahoma are potential citizens. Indians having allotments in Nebraska are citizens. Citizen Indians resident in Illinois are without restrictions of any sort as Indians; in Wisconsin they are wards of the Nation. Indians in Maine are wards of the State; in New York they are wards of the State and the Nation. In some states allottees are citizens while others are not. One fact is significant: *No series of grades has ever been established that in a uniform way will lift the Indian from a state of pure wardship up to complete citizenship*, with all rights, duties, and responsibilities of such [emphasis in original].

The three bills Eastman reviews still retain some of the former ambiguities, however. Commenting on bills introduced individually by Senator Charles Curtis (R-Kansas) and Congressmen Carl T. Hayden (D-Arizona) and Charles D. Carter (D-Oklahoma), Eastman finds value and fault in each. Of particular concern to Eastman is enabling competent Indians to control their own property free from Indian Bureau intervention. After all, this provision was common in many treaties Indians signed with their American counterparts, as Eastman observes in a previous article: "Now every treaty with the Indians in recent times has included provision for the education of their children, and it was understood that in due time the affairs of their people should be turned over to them, and that as fast as they became able to comply with the usual requirements, they should be admitted to citizenship." Certainly, a variation on this theme existed in the 1851 treaty that was much on Eastman's mind during his lobbying days in Washington, DC. In fact, Article 4 of the 1851 treaty stipulates, "For educational purposes, the sum of six thousand dollars, ($6,000)," which was in addition to the establishment of "manual-labor schools." However, Indians who are obviously incapable of handling their own affairs in Eastman's opinion ought to be remanded to the state or to "a minor division of the Indian Bureau left in existence for that purpose, the Bureau being otherwise abolished."[31]

Finally, Eastman wrote two disparate pieces for the 1919 summer issue of the *American Indian Magazine:* "Justice for the Sioux" and "The American Eagle: An Indian Symbol." Both articles are preceded by Gertrude Bonnin's account of the "Indian Citizenship Campaign." Eastman, the "Indian philosopher and lecturer," was graciously welcomed everywhere he went. The exception, though, occurred when, accompanied by Carlos Montezuma and Father Phillip B. Gordon, Eastman attempted to take his message of Indian citizenship to the Ho-Chunk reservation in Wisconsin—unnamed in Zitkala-Sa's editorial—which the Indian Bureau prohibited from happening. To which, Zitkala-Sa inveighs,

> Indian Bureau autocracy forbade these educated, leading Indian men to hold any meeting on the Indian reservation! Though the riffraff of the white people from the four corners of the earth may enter Indian lands and homestead them, thus permitting daily contact with the very scum of other races, the educated, refined, and patriotic Indian, teaching the highest ideals of democracy is forbidden to meet with his own race, even for a day!
>
> This is not the democracy for which our soldiers fought and died!
>
> This is race discrimination and akin to the rule of might of the old-world powers![32]

This then sets the tone for what follows.

In "Justice for the Sioux," which appears after an article blatantly titled "ABOLISH THE INDIAN BUREAU," Eastman resumes the caustic critique of the U.S. government's treatment of the Lakota that appeared in the 1917 special issue on the Sioux. Specifically, the article addresses the Lakotas' ongoing interest in reclaiming the Black Hills. However, as with many other issues, the Indian Bureau stood in the way of the Lakota gaining a hearing in either the court of claims or Congress. Eastman laments, "The day that our government got the Indians' consent to reservation life, that day the Bureau assumed paternal supervision of their affairs. Then and there we lost our freedom, our personal rights, and the privileges which had been ours for untold ages." As Zitkala-Sa corroborates, the Indians "are in America, but their environment is radically different from that surrounding other [Americans]." A consequence of the Lakotas' declining status is seen in the way the federal government regarded its treaties with the Great Sioux Nation increasingly less over the years, as if there were a statute of limitations on keeping one's word. All the more astounding is the fact that many of the political and legal impediments to "Indian progress" come from an irrepressible assumption at all levels of Anglo-American society that Indians are "wild," which is to say, unsuitable for civilized life.[33]

Even when whites try to be sympathetic, they can make things difficult for Indian people, such as when the Indian Bureau attempts to "protect" Indians from "unscrupulous lawyers" by making it policy that the bureau will take charge of picking their attorneys. The Indian Bureau, consequently, refuses to acknowledge any legal representation that Indian leaders may choose to advocate for their interests, which is not only condescending but also a problem when the attorney chosen was retained for the purpose of pursuing the Indians' interests against the Indian Bureau itself. The latter is the predicament that the Lakota face with respect to the Black Hills—their adversary is the bureau—a classic case of the fox guarding the henhouse. In fact, the Lakota—and other tribes—could not "meet and discuss their own business, unless the Secretary of the Interior through the Commissioner of Indian Affairs gives his permission." Is it any wonder, then, that Indian nations like the Lakota seem perpetually trapped in the same dire straits? The federal government's idea for resolving the Black Hills issue was, aside from ignoring it, offering the Lakota money, which the people refused. The government in turn offered to relocate the Lakota to Indian Territory, which the people also refused. Finally, under duress, "246 chiefs" signed an agreement allowing the Americans to lease land for the purpose of prospecting for gold: "This is called the 'Black Hills agreement' of 1877." To the Lakotas' distress, the "Black Hills are held to this day on the grounds of that lease." Eastman concludes, "This is, in brief, the history of the case. It is time we should have justice shown us. Our boys fought shoulder to shoulder with your boys. Fellow-countrymen, will you look into our cause? We ask nothing unreasonable—only the freedom and the privileges for which your boy and mine have fought." Bonnin adds in a footnote that Eastman's own son was one of the approximately ten thousand Indian soldiers who fought for the United States in the Great War.[34]

In "The American Eagle: An Indian Symbol," which was reprinted from a 1919 issue of the Daughters of the American Revolution magazine, Eastman provides a piece that could easily have appeared in *Indian Scout Talks,* his primer for the young outdoorsman. It is also an example of the kind of bridge work that Eastman excelled at when addressing what he must have imagined was a mixed Indian and white audience. Rather than scold Anglo-Americans for appropriating an Indian symbol, the eagle, Eastman attempts to enlighten his white reader about the eagle's original meaning, as defined by the Dakota. In turn, Eastman demonstrates to his Indian reader that traditional knowledge has a place in modern America, thereby ennobling both communities. "I cannot but think," Eastman asserts, "that the American spirit has been nobly developed under the symbolic guidance of the eagle. I ask for the original and highest interpretation of our national emblem, as standing not for irresponsible power backed by violence, but for clear vision and honorable service."[35]

Not long after these publications, the SAI held its annual meeting in Minneapolis, Minnesota, during October 2–4, 1919, just shy of its eighth anniversary. As mentioned earlier, Eastman had become the organization's president, ending his long-term efforts at remaining largely aloof from the factionalism and dissension that had often characterized SAI meetings. The two most important and divisive issues were the SAI's stances on the Indian Bureau and the emergent Native American Church. With respect to the Indian Bureau, there was an ongoing debate over whether to call for its immediate abolition, which Carlos Montezuma advocated, or to promote a more gradual dissolution, as supported by Arthur Parker. Adding to the mix of opinions was Charles Daganett, one of the SAI's founding members and a senior employee of the Indian Bureau. Daganett argued that the SAI ought to take great consideration for Indians serving in the bureau. When controversy arose with his nomination for second vice president of the SAI, Daganett stated on his own behalf, "In the first place I am in the government service. I will now tell you that I am not looking for any office. If the Society declares themselves against Indians in the Indian Service by declaring against an officer who is in that service, it is going to drive a good many Indians from the Society and cause them to lose interest. There are hundreds of progressive honest men and women in that service who are loyal to their race first of all."[36]

At the other end of the spectrum was Carlos Montezuma, who attended the 1912 meeting in Columbus at which Daganett received his nomination from John M. Oskison, an Oklahoma Cherokee and editor of *Collier's Magazine*. With regard to the SAI's agenda, Montezuma is important because of his influence on Eastman. Despite their vastly different personalities, Eastman and Montezuma became fast friends. They were united, perhaps, by their common criticism of federal bureaucracy—what Montezuma called "bureauism." Equally important was their dismay over the rise in popularity of "peyotism," which included proponents in the SAI's rank and file. Together with Zitkala-Sa, Arthur Parker, and other Christian Indians, they lobbied hard to repress what they thought of as a "menace" to the Indian community.

At the same time, Montezuma must be regarded as his own person. To begin with, he was a staunch proponent of assimilation who published periodic pieces in the SAI's quarterly journal in which he launched one invective after another against the Indian Bureau. Montezuma's problem with the SAI right from the start was the affiliation some members, namely Sherman Coolidge, wanted to maintain with the Indian Bureau. In other words, Montezuma feared that the SAI was prone to become a mere wing of the bureau, particularly if SAI leadership positions were filled with bureau employees. Unsurprisingly, Montezuma boycotted the SAI's inaugural 1911 meeting because he heard that the organization would be bureau-friendly. However, Montezuma showed up for the 1912 meeting in Denver, without explanation. Nonetheless, once Montezuma got off on the wrong foot with the SAI, his love-hate relationship continued for the rest of his life. Indeed, because of his "fiery" disposition, Hertzberg felt compelled to describe him as being "by temperament and conviction a factionalist." This attitude may be the reason Montezuma did not see eye to eye with Arthur Parker, to mention but one focus of his wrath. Parker took it upon himself to play the role of peacemaker among the warring factions in the SAI, making a valiant effort at the 1916 meeting in Lawrence, Kansas. Consequently, Parker's attempts at brokering a compromise were often read by Montezuma as bids to simply appease the Indian Bureau, which he could not tolerate.[37]

Montezuma's ambivalence toward the SAI reached its climax on September 30, 1915, when he delivered his seminal address, "Let My People Go," during the annual meeting in Lawrence, Kansas. The speech was basically Montezuma's declaration of independence from the status quo. Not only was he fed up with the Indian Bureau and its authoritarian tactics; after four years of meetings, he also was fed up with the SAI's inertia. Both entities, in Montezuma's opinion, were equally inept at bringing about positive change. In "Let My People Go," he let loose all of his evangelical fervor for convincing the SAI that the Indian Bureau must be terminated.

After belittling the SAI for doing nothing more than meeting and discussing things for the full duration of its existence, Montezuma reminds his audience of the example Richard Pratt set when he went against the tide of popular opinion, which thought that Indians were incorrigible savages, and began offering them an education. Montezuma calls upon the SAI and the Indians it represents to follow in Pratt's footsteps and take a stand against the status quo. "Looking from all points of the compass," Montezuma declares, "there is only one object for this Society of Indians to work for, namely—'Freedom for our people.'" On this point, Montezuma credits Pratt with giving him the idea that the Indian Bureau ought to be abolished, quoting at length from an address Pratt delivered before the 1904 Baptist Minister's Meeting in New York City. In the quote, Pratt expresses the opinion that Indians would have been better off if the bureau never existed in the first place, as all it does is hold them back. It does this, moreover, because its livelihood depends upon Indians "needing" it. In other words, the bureau is nothing more than a parasite, and a very insidious one at that.[38]

In Montezuma's appraisal of the situation, the Indian Bureau's worst offense, even worse than its shameless grafting of Indian resources, is the way it maintains psychological oppression over the people: "It is a psychological fact that by everlastingly harping and pointing that 'you are an Indian,' that 'you are a ward,' that 'you are a child and must be protected,' that 'you have property and we must be your real estate agent,' that 'you must not do anything without your superintendent's approval,' that 'you are not ready to live as a free man' it is a scientific fact that after awhile you will actually believe that it is all true." What Montezuma recognized, one could argue, is that the reservation system was creating in Indians what Robert K. Thomas would later call "internal colonization." This result is obviously the complete opposite of "preparing" them for civilization.[39]

But it was not just the reservation Indian who was prone to becoming a "captive mind," as Czeslaw Milosz might have said. Montezuma asserts that many educated Indians, who may even be members of the SAI, have become victims of this mindset as well. Certainly, there are many among the Indian's white friends who think this way, even when they are trying to be sincerely helpful. Montezuma recounts writing to a friend for his opinion about his plan to resign from the Indian Service and return to Chicago to start a medical practice there. The friend writes back to suggest that Montezuma think twice about doing so. "If you come to Chicago," the friend wrote, "I am afraid you will not make a success here because there will be prejudice against you, even though you may be the best physician—you are an Indian."[40]

Montezuma's reaction was one of righteous indignation. But rather than give up in despair, he decided to return to Chicago anyway and fight prejudice. "To fight," Montezuma proclaimed, "is to forget ourselves as Indians in the world. To think of oneself as different from the mass is not healthy." And by "not healthy," Montezuma is referring to the deleterious effects of thinking of oneself as less than, as unprepared for and therefore unworthy of so-called civilization. Montezuma's remarks are not without precedent. William Apess reflected on the word *Indian* in *A Son of the Forest:*

> I thought it disgraceful to be called an Indian; it was considered as a slur upon an oppressed and scattered nation, and I have often been led to inquire where the whites received this word, which they so often threw as an opprobrious epithet at the sons of the forest. I could not find it in the Bible and therefore concluded that it was a word imported for the special purpose of degrading us. At other times I thought it was derived from the term *in-gen-uity.* But the proper term which ought to be applied to our nation, to distinguish it from the rest of the human family, is that of *"Natives"*—and I humbly conceive that the natives of this country are the only people under heaven who have a just title to the name, inasmuch as we are the only people who retain the original complexion of our father Adam.

Indian as an invective is a consequence of being held prisoner in the "two-world" mentality. The proposition that such a world, or worlds, exists has less to do with the recognition that Indian and white cultures are different and more to do with the lingering sense that Indians do not belong in the wider world off the reservation. As Montezuma describes it,

> Somehow or other, the idea prevails that the Indian's sphere of action in this life and in America should be limited within the wigwam. And when an Indian boy or girl goes away to school, you hear the hounding voices saying, 'Go back, go back to your home and people!' These good people and many others seem to convey the idea that Indians are strangers in America. And strange to say, these people have the whole world for their action, and they are far away from their place of birth, and when they came the Indian was here; and of course the Indians, too, must have the whole world for their sphere of action.

Of course, since "America" was now dominated by white society rather than by Indian nations, Montezuma believed that the only way for Indians to gain that wider sphere of action was to go through the same public school system that was otherwise available to other Americans, be they native born or naturalized immigrants. As evidence that Indians can benefit from off-reservation schooling, Montezuma simply lists the most prominent Indians of the day: "Senator Owens, Congressman Carter, Ex-Senator Curtis, Dr. Eastman, the late Dr. Oronhyatekha, Mr. Parker—formerly of the Treasury,—Rev. Wright, Dr. Favill, and many others." To underscore his point, Montezuma asks derisively: "Now, where are the names of those Indians who have been educated on reservations? It is not surprising that no name can be mentioned."[41]

By the time Eastman became president of the SAI in 1919, however, he was already showing signs of sympathy for Montezuma's agenda. In *From the Deep Woods to Civilization*, Eastman recounts his appeal for Indian rights before a congressional committee. Alas, as he often does, Eastman names neither the committee nor its members, but he does lucidly recall what he said to them: "We desire to learn business methods... and we can only do this by handling our own property. You learn by experience to manage your business. How are we Indians to learn if you take from us the wisdom that is born of mistakes, and leave us to suffer the stings of robbery and deception, with no opportunity to guard against its recurrence? I know that some will misuse this privilege, and some will be defrauded, but the experiment will be worth all its costs." Eastman's remarks were met with approbation from his listeners. "Where did you go to school? Why are there not more Indians like you?" they said in that strangely condescending way that some whites had when complementing a person of color. Moreover, although Eastman made his comments nearly twenty years before publishing them in *From the Deep Woods,* emphasis in the book demonstrates growing sympathy for Montezuma's impatience with the bureaucratic bulwarks that only served to forestall Indian progress and artificially justify continued government interference into Indians' personal affairs.[42]

This is not to say that Eastman and Montezuma did not see a positive role for government vis-à-vis Indian affairs. As mentioned, Eastman and Montezuma, along with a host of others, shared a common concern about the rise of "peyotism" in the Indian community. In addition to the recurring articles disparaging peyotism as a "menace" considered as bad if not worse than the scourge of alcoholism, Eastman, Bonnin, and Joe Claymore represented the Sioux delegation that gave testimony before the House Committee on Indian Affairs, chaired by Arizona representative Carl Hayden, on February 21, 22, and 25, 1918. Other delegates included Otto Wells (Comanche), Chester Arthur (Assiniboin), Fred Lookout (Osage), Arthur Bonnicastle (Osage), and a small group from the Who's Who of early twentieth-century Indian affairs: Samuel M. Brosius (Indian Rights Association), James Mooney (Bureau of American Ethnology), Francis La Flesche (Omaha; Bureau of American Ethnology), Thomas L. Sloan (Omaha; attorney), Richard H. Pratt (founder of the Carlisle Indian School), and Charles J. Kappler (former attorney for the Osage; editor of the much-used seven-volume-long *Indian Affairs: Laws and Treaties*).[43]

For Eastman's part, he came out against the legalization of peyote use among Indians, regardless of its users' religious claims, because it is "absolutely dangerous." More specifically, because peyote use leads one to stay up all night, as was the custom of the yet-to-be-incorporated Native American Church, the impact on Indian students was significant.

"Some of the brightest boys," Eastman claimed, "that were ever educated at the Indian schools have become peyote eaters, and those men have been ruined in their character, and you can not depend on them." At the same time, Eastman was not without some insight into why peyotism had become so widespread throughout the reservation community: "It is more like what happened a few years ago during the ghost-dance craze, which, as we all know, was gotten up by irresponsible, reckless, and unprincipled people who thought that under the conditions that the Indians were suffering from something like that would go, and that they would get some benefit out of it. That is the way the ghost dance started, and it started in that quarter down there [Oklahoma]. It came from that direction, and this is exactly the same way." On the basis of being like the Ghost Dance, which originated outside of the Sioux reservations, Eastman claimed peyotism was "not an Indian idea." At least, it was alien to the Dakota customs and beliefs with which Eastman was familiar. Bonnin corroborated this preconception when she stated the following regarding the SAI's ongoing effort at getting Congress to pass a bill making peyote an illegal substance:

> Now, while peyote bills are pending in Congress, is the time for activity. It has been the experience in the past that such bills die in committee. Congress has been misinformed. Peyote has [been] represented as a sacrament in an Indian religion. "I baptize thee in the name of the Father and Son and Peyote," is the baptismal formula borrowed from the ritual of the Christian church. Twelve feathers dangling from a long staff represent the twelve apostles. This twelve apostles idea is borrowed from the white man's Bible. It is not Indian. Rituals of the church have been borrowed as a cloak to hide under, and to evade the law of morals and decency. Moreover religion is the adoration of the Maker with a rational mind. No one in the state of drunkenness, by whatsoever cause, can be in his rational mind; and he cannot practice religion.

Unfortunately for Bonnin, Eastman, and everyone else in the American Indian community who fought alongside their allies in temperance organizations against the spread of peyotism, not only did the peyote bills fail but also, unlike the "ghost dance craze," the practice neither faded away nor—thankfully—was brutally suppressed. On the contrary, the

Native American Church would surpass the SAI in both longevity and capacity to draw and retain members. With regard to the Sioux community, Vine Deloria, Jr., observed many years later in *Custer Died for Your Sins,*

> The Native American Church . . . has doubled its membership in the last few years. It appears to be the religion of the future among the Indian people. At first a southwestern-based religion, it has spread since [World War II] into a great number of northern tribes. Eventually it will replace Christianity among the Indian people.
>
> When I was growing up on the Pine Ridge reservation before and during World War II, the Native American Church was something far away and officially "bad." Few adherents to this faith could be found among the two large Sioux reservations in southern South Dakota. Today a reasonable estimate would be that some 40 percent of the people are members of the Native American Church there.[44]

Peyotism's impact on the SAI's ability to function as a viable organization was being felt even as Eastman gave testimony before Congressman Hayden's committee. As acting editor of the *American Indian Magazine,* Bonnin noted that the SAI's 1918 annual meeting in Pierre, South Dakota, was "numerically small." Thus, while the SAI and its supporters did not wane in their efforts to deter the Native American Church (NAC), they also could not recover from the ideological divide the SAI leadership created among members by dissociating themselves from a major movement within the Indian community. While peyote surely was not the only issue on the progressive Indian agenda—there were still the fights for citizenship and for better education—it was nonetheless powerful enough to knock the wind out of the SAI's sails. Given that the educated Indian community, especially those from Oklahoma and the Plains states, supplied both the SAI and the NAC with members, the SAI's rejection of the NAC movement could only spell the SAI's eventual demise. By comparing peyotism with alcoholism, Eastman, Bonnin, and others blinded themselves to the fact that the sincerity behind the NAC's growth was an organic result of the collective inability of the SAI and the Indian Bureau to resolve problems on the reservation. Unlike alcohol or the Ghost Dance, Indians turned to peyote not merely to numb their pain or to pray for the disappearance of the whites but to find meaning and purpose in what was otherwise a difficult existence—the limbo of being a modern Indian while racial barriers still kept many Natives stuck on the lower rungs of the social ladder.[45]

The factionalism surrounding peyotism did not diminish the status of the SAI's leadership in the eyes of the general public, however. Blazing across the front page of the *Minneapolis Morning Tribune* on Thursday, October 2, 1919, were the headlines "Chiefs of Tribes Convene" and "300 Indians Gather for Council in City." Accompanying the article announcing the commencement of the SAI's annual meeting in Minneapolis was a large joint portrait of Eastman and Bonnin, dressed in the mainstream attire of the times. About Eastman, the paper stated, "President of the Society of American Indians, whose eighth annual convention opens in Minneapolis today, Dr. Charles A. Eastman of Amherst, Mass., is a full-blooded Sioux. He claims Minneapolis as his home, for his great grandfather, Chief Cloudman, 150 years ago, pitched his tent on the spot where Lake Harriet pavilion is now located. Here a tablet reminds visitors of the early residence of the red men in that vicinity."[46]

Despite some of the dated language, it is hard to imagine nowadays the activities of a major American Indian organization making the front page of very many mainstream newspapers. With respect to the SAI meeting, the article begins with an anecdote about a smartly dressed Indian man, Kick-a-Hole-in-the-Sky, entering the office of the mayor's secretary. Kick-a-Hole-in-the-Sky asks for the location of the SAI's meeting, to which the secretary, obviously taken aback, responds by asking, "Are you an Indian?" To which Kick-a-Hole-in-the-Sky answers with clear vexation in his tone, "Certainly . . . I might say also that Carlisle graduates aren't in the habit of running about in war paint and feathers, much as it seems to surprise you." The article recounts the various individuals and groups convening at the St. James Hotel to register for the SAI meeting, to be held at the University of Minnesota, which, fifty years later, became home to the nation's first American Indian Studies department. The article pays special attention to Eastman, recounting some biographical elements, including references to his mother and great-grandfather, as well as mentioning his Dakota name, Ohiyesa, incorrectly translated as "pitiful laugh." The article also claims that Eastman left his medical practice in order "to chronicle the history of the

Sioux and tales of the American Indians in general" and acknowledges his impressive academic record. Also mentioned are Eastman's son, recently discharged from the navy, and his daughter Irene, who had passed away the previous spring, along with an equally brief reference to "Miss Elaine Goodale," who "was" Eastman's wife. Finally, a random list of Eastman's book publications is provided.[47]

Among the "Noted Indians Coming" are Gertrude Bonnin, the SAI's secretary and treasurer, "accompanied by her husband, half Sioux, who served in the American Expeditionary Forces with the rank of captain"; Phillip Gordon, "a Catholic priest and full-blooded Ojibway"; and Sherman Coolidge, who "is a Sioux" and "an Episcopal minister and chairman of the advisory board of the society... and is a graduate of the Seabury Divinity school, Faribault, Minn." On the agenda were various speeches to be made by the convention delegates, in addition to "addresses of welcome" from Mayor J. E. Meyers, S. J. Buck, superintendent of the Minnesota Historical Society, and others. Unsurprisingly, the general public was most anxious to see something quite "traditional," in the sense that only non-Indians can give to this term: "To the general public the most interesting feature of the convention will be the Indian pageant, 'The Conspiracy of Pontiac,' to be given for the public tomorrow night at the Auditorium. The cast will include 200 Indians, old and young, who will dance and sing in the manner and costumes of their forefathers. 'The Conspiracy of Pontiac' is the story of the French and English diplomacy as regarded the Indian in the days of Louis the Fourteenth, when the Indian girl discovered the plot against her people and saved them."[48]

Most of the general public more than likely did not know that by the time Eastman gave his opening address at the SAI's 1919 meeting in Minneapolis, the situation had changed drastically from the organization's early, heady days of optimism. This is not to say that Eastman, in particular, had lost any of his idealism. After the meeting was called to order, the delegates sang "America," with "Mr. Jones, of California, at the piano." The song was followed by "Rev. Mr. Martin," who "asked the blessing." Eastman made his sentiments perfectly clear when he expounded on the reasons why America was basically an Indian nation, at least in spirit if not in fact:

We are part of this great American Nation, and we must be some
good to the country. This country is composed of hundreds of representatives of different nations and they are all contributing materially
in its progress. What have we in this? These thoughts were coming to
me. We Indians started the whole basis of Americanism. We Indians
laid the foundation of freedom and equality and democracy long
before any white people come [*sic*] here and those who came took it
up, but they do not give us the credit—that this country is absolutely
free, to whatever race.

Obviously, Eastman's idealism is mixed with a certain level of frustration. After all, it is now twenty-nine years since he took his first government post as physician at the Pine Ridge Agency and nearly fifty years
since he entered white civilization at his father's behest. Yet the "Indian
problem" is far from being resolved. Above all else, Indians still lack
universal citizenship and the Indian Bureau still rules unchallenged.
Change has always come slowly to Indian affairs, and, if Eastman can
be said to embody any of the Christian and Dakota virtues he espoused,
he undoubtedly exhibited both patience and forgiveness. With respect
to Eastman's writing and speaking career, one could say that the Minneapolis speech marked the climax to his intellectual development. At
approximately sixty-one years of age, Eastman had earned the status of
revered elder among American Indians. So, with the wisdom that
comes with age and experience, Eastman struck a prophetic note in his
thoughts about the Indian's role in America's future, which he still saw
threatened by its rampant materialism. After, once again, admonishing
Indians to take up the ways of modern life, Eastman declares,

> I have said that the Indian will save this country. The day when an
> Indian becomes leader of this country will be the day when civiliza-
> tion may come on a more stable foundation. Not that he is going to
> take this people back to the woods and the teepees. There is some-
> thing in this civilization that threatens the very vital parts. There
> must be a guiding hand and God will take from a small people a
> man who can do that work. It has been the history of our world. The
> greatest reformers are from the smallest peoples. It is not necessary
> that that man should have an education. From Moses to Abraham
> Lincoln it has been the rule. What would be more likely than God

would choose one possessing the sturdy characteristics of our race and thrust him into civilization as its leader? Then do not go madly rushing into mud holes. Be ready to help your race, your country.[49]

The Indian may yet "save" this country. In the meantime, we must realize that when Eastman gave this speech, he had returned to the Dakota homeland. What today are the cities of Minneapolis and St. Paul remain the locus of the Dakota origin story. From this natural vantage point, Eastman could see the fate of the Indian in America. While it would be easy to look at Eastman's prophecy and dismiss it with sarcasm, we would risk overlooking what other scoffers of other prophecies have overlooked, which is that a prophecy's meaning is not limited to the fulfillment of a set of predicted events but expands into a vision in which people can see that balance has been restored to the world. And where there is vision, there is also hope.

5

Exile From *Mnisota Makoce*
Eastman and the 1862 U.S.–Dakota War

Can you charge the Indians with robbing a nation almost of their whole continent, and murdering their women and children, and then depriving the remainder of their lawful rights, that nature and God require them to have?

William Apess, *An Indian's Looking-Glass for the White Man*

Once upon a time, at least in the eyes of a Dakota child, life in southern Minnesota was simply idyllic. In his 1902 autobiography, *Indian Boyhood,* Eastman very fondly recounts life as being filled with long days of plenty and contentment. Eastman writes, "When our people lived in Minnesota, a good part of their natural subsistence was furnished by the wild rice, which grew abundantly in all of that region. Around the shores and all over some of the innumerable lakes of the 'Land of Skyblue Water' was this wild cereal found. Indeed, some of the watery fields in those days might be compared in extent and fruitfulness with the fields of wheat on Minnesota's magnificent farms today."[1]

As he recounts this episode, the youthful Eastman is joyfully oblivious to the fact that surrounding the Dakota, more of a threat than their traditional Ojibwe rivals, was an encroaching settler community whose hunger for land was growing. Whereas the Dakota would take only enough wild rice to meet their needs, the white settlers and the white businessmen and politicians who backed them wanted everything. Most bizarre of all was the way in which the Americans sought to express their land lust in very formal and legalized terms, written out in treaties that they gave the Dakota not much choice but to sign.

What is a treaty? In the simplest sense of the word, it is an agreement between two sovereign nations, each with the power and authority to carry out the stipulated terms. Or, to word the definition much more formally, as did Francis Paul Prucha in his epic treatise *American Indian*

Treaties, a treaty is "a contract between two or more states, relating to peace, alliance, commerce, or other international relations, and also, the document embodying such a contract, formally signed by plenipotentiaries appointed by the government of each state." According to Eastman in *Wigwam Evenings,* the very first treaty was made between "man and the animal people" after they battled to see who would be the hunter and who the hunted. Little Boy Man, who fought on behalf of humankind, managed to prevail because of his cunning and innovation. However, when the animals sued for peace, agreeing "to give him of their flesh for food and their skins for clothing," Little Boy Man reciprocated by promising never to kill any animals "wantonly." He further agreed that the animals may "keep their weapons to use in their own defense." Thus, balance and order was achieved. From a Dakota perspective, the "treaty" between man and the animal people is a paradigm for treaties between nations—order and balance ought to be the objective, as opposed to revenge, exploitation, and subjugation. In this sense, a treaty is a solemn oath between two peoples before the eyes of the Creator. In which case, is there ever a time when one party is justified in breaking such an arrangement? According to Eastman, before the Indians knew anything about politics and legal loopholes, it never would have occurred to them to put selfish interest ahead of the needs of the nation. They only learned of such perfidy from the British and Americans, who tore apart treaties almost as quickly as they were written.[2]

In his opening address before the 1919 annual meeting of the Society of American Indians in Minneapolis, Eastman, after years of frustration dealing with both Congress and the Indian Bureau, stated before his largely Indian audience,

> The seas have casted on our shores people from all races, and we are taking care of them from the Government fund, out of the charity fund. Millions are sent back over the seas, to the Belgians, the Armenians, the Poles and to this and that. Now, we Indians, the United States owes us something. It owes us something in a business way. We have never known charity. Everything we have was promised us in treaties—and more—and they have not given it to us. The United States can give us nothing because it owes us all. The United States made treaties with us and it has not carried out these treaties, it has

misused our treaties. These treaties were agreements, contracts, they cannot change these contracts. A treaty is the highest type of agreement . . . But the Government misuses these contracts, changes them all the time for this purpose or for that, without consulting us, dividing our lands for this and that, without consulting us. Take our money for whatever they like, and do not consult us. It has been doing this all the time.

What makes government malfeasance all the more shocking is the fact that even after Indian nations were subdued discrimination against Indians continued, perpetrated by the Indian Bureau under the pretense of preparing Indians for civilization—for which they were never quite ready, no matter what, always being left to the margins of disenfranchisement. Eastman says about his own family, "My father, a full-blooded Sioux, way back in the [eighteen-]seventies, came right out of the reservation and took up a homestead under the Homestead Law and my two brothers did the same. When the Government sold these lands, did any Bureau say, 'Shoot an arrow into the air and you will be a citizen?'" A generation later, Eastman and his peers were still fighting for their rights, including citizenship. From today's perspective, when one can take for granted that Indians are not only U.S. citizens but also regarded as the "First Americans," it may seem astounding that there was a time when this struggle was necessary. However, upon closer examination of Indian-White history, more astonishing is the fact that Indians were ever acknowledged as Americans at all. For there was a time when Americans were more likely to think in terms of eradicating, removing, and/or exterminating Indians rather than grant them the privileges of citizenship. In a very real sense, no citizenship meant that they did not even exist, except as a social problem and potential threat to society.[3]

In *The History of the Seneca Indians*, which Arthur C. Parker first published in 1926, years after the Society of American Indians had seen its heyday as an Indian rights advocacy group, not to mention two years after the Indian Citizenship Act, there is a brief section titled "Sullivan's Campaign" that sheds light on the uneasy role that Indian nations played in American history. The section in question pertains to events surrounding the Seneca Nation's involvement in the American rebellion against the British crown. Because the Seneca had the audacity to side with the British, who were more responsive to Seneca interests, such as leaving their lands in their control, the Americans under General George Washington wanted revenge. Consequently, General John Sullivan was sent on a punitive expedition "to invade Seneca Country and to destroy every form of property and food, utterly devastating the Indian country." The result Parker labeled "The Hollocaust." Where Parker got this term in 1926 is unclear; nonetheless, it is quite appropriate for the events he describes: "After an attack at Newtown (near the present Elmira), the news spread that the American troops were coming, and, as the army approached, one by one the Seneca towns were abandoned. Sullivan caused the destruction of every town and hamlet that he found, burned the food supplies and cut down orchards and growing crops. The stricken Seneca were torn by fearful emotions." Worse still, the Seneca became refugees in their own country, finding it difficult to obtain food and supplies from their British allies as the Americans cut them off. Great suffering ensued. Needless to say, the Seneca would be punished further after the Revolution was over, facing a reduction in their land base and eventually removal; fortunately, some managed to remain in what was left of their ancestral homeland in what is today upstate New York. Over the years, though, Americans would largely forget that any of the Iroquois nations even played a role in the heady days of the early republic. With respect to America's relationship with Indian nations, one can see a pattern of conquest and forgetting emerging, no matter how horrific the events incurred—at least, this was the disposition among Anglo-American historians and politicians. The Indians did not forget.[4]

At the same time, it has always been difficult for Indians to determine where they might most sensibly place their loyalties, since allying for and against the Americans seems to yield the same unfortunate results. In *From the Deep Woods to Civilization*, Eastman recounts not only a panicky response—which he tried in vain to quell—from the Indian agent toward the emergent "ghost dance craze" among the Lakota but also, during the many months following the tragedy, being harassed by the acting Indian agent for his criticism of the way the Indian Bureau treated reservations like the one at Pine Ridge. In addition, Eastman kept encountering a number of people off-reservation in cities like Chicago who regarded the Wounded Knee Massacre as an "Indian uprising" perpetrated by "hostiles." Eastman, of course, did not hesitate to tell a very different tale of a desperate Indian community assailed by a perfidious Indian agency. "I have tried," Eastman states emphatically, "to make it clear that there was no 'Indian outbreak' in 1890–91." But he could not quite communicate his personal ordeal with the massacre and the events leading to it.[5]

As a government employee, Eastman held counsel with Captain Sword and Lieutenant Thunder Bear of the Indian police, along with American Horse, an influential community leader, to "serve the United States Government" even if fighting broke out between those following the Ghost Dance and the U.S. troops whose numbers were undergoing a significant surge into the area around Pine Ridge. After the bloodshed was over, however, Eastman did not fail to acknowledge that what occurred was a "massacre" as opposed to the "battle" that the U.S. cavalry later claimed took place. "It took all of my nerve," Eastman recalls upon seeing the carnage, "to keep my composure in the face of this spectacle, and of the excitement and grief of my Indian companions, nearly every one of whom was crying aloud or singing his death song."[6]

Because Wounded Knee looms so large in the history of the American West, it could be easy for some to overlook the impact that the 1862 U.S.-Dakota War had on the author of *Indian Boyhood*. What follows is a much-needed examination of how this seminal and tragic event in Santee Dakota history continued to affect Eastman throughout his writing career. The expulsion and near-annihilation of the Dakota in Minnesota would always symbolize for Eastman just how far white Americans were willing to stray from their Christian and democratic ideals for the sake of robbing Indians of their land and heritage. While many Minnesotans, even today, grow up without any knowledge of the atrocities committed during the months between August and December 1862, in spite of childhood field trips to Fort Snelling, the Dakota have not failed to remember. Indeed, what ought to become clear after looking at Eastman's treatment of 1862 is that recalling these events from a Dakota perspective was important even when that Dakota was a progressive Republican at the turn of the twentieth century.[7]

As mentioned before, in 1917, the *American Indian Magazine* published a special issue on the Sioux, which included a short piece about "The Sioux Outbreak of 1862" by Arthur C. Parker. In the two pages of the journal devoted to this event, Parker does not hold back from chastising government officials, above all, the Indian Bureau, for creating a desperate and volatile situation at Lower Sioux. Parker states in his opening paragraph, "One of the most fearful of all 'Indian outbreaks' that ever happened in the west was the Sioux uprising in 1862, concerning which so much has been written. The causes were many and the Indians were under great provocation. The Indian Administration of the time was largely at fault because of its dilatory methods and vacillation." What Parker does not acknowledge is that as of 1917 writings about the 1862 conflict were almost exclusively by non-Indian and certainly non-Dakota authors. However, as Parker proceeds with his account he clearly becomes more outraged by the government corruption that led the Dakota to make their desperate bid for what was legally theirs in the first place—the goods and annuities stipulated in the 1851 treaty. At the climax of Parker's essay, he quotes the Reverend Stephen R. Riggs, who berates the Indian Bureau for its turpitude in handling Dakota affairs:

> The whole Indian system, as adopted, and acted upon by our government, seems to be unwise. We have, in our treaty making, assumed the various Indian tribes occupying our territories are independent nations; whereas they are wanting in all the elements of sovereignty, having no government, and consequently no power to compel the fulfilment of treaty stipulations. Besides, the Indian Department has for years been proverbially corrupt and corrupting. When one administration became famous for corruption and grew rich on Indian stealings we expected that the change in parties would bring in more honest men and a better policy. But in this we were too often disappointed. The policy and practice grew worse and worse. Thus the Dakotas had many complaints to make of wrongs, real and supposed.

Naturally, as a contemporary reader of Riggs's words, I wish that I could lecture him about the truth of Indian sovereignty, even during the difficult decades of the 1850s and 1860s, as signified by the fact that the U.S. government was still making treaties with Indian nations. However, I will refrain from launching into a diatribe against Riggs and focus instead on Parker's handling of the fifty-fifth anniversary of the so-called "outbreak."[8]

Perhaps because the Society of American Indians was in an ongoing campaign to achieve citizenship for all Indians, Parker felt that Riggs captured the precarious situation in which Indians found themselves:

in limbo between lost sovereignty and no citizenship, creating a moral vacuum in which all kinds of graft and chicanery could occur without retribution, such as happened with the Dakota. In fact, the Dakota were not only expelled from Minnesota; many of them also were hung for their alleged "crimes," namely, murder, committed during what was essentially a war. Parker at this point avoids clamoring for revenge, be it in the court system or the battlefield, and opts for a more conciliatory approach:

> The shock of the executions and of the imprisonment did much to awaken a new spirit and a new determination within the Sioux. The imprisoned Sioux learned to read and write, teaching themselves, and writing upon slates given by the missionaries. Soon they began to send letters to their friends and relatives and gradually the advantages of education dawned upon them . . .
>
> The outbreak of 1862 was the dawn of a new epoch for the Sioux; it marked the beginning of their civilization. The massacre of the Sioux at Wounded Knee thirty years later marked the crystalization of civilization within the Sioux. The Sioux have overcome many things and been lashed by many wrongs, but through it all they are emerging to a greater victory.

In other words, the Sioux and other Indian nations like them have learned how to survive and even thrive in the new world around them; however, if they succeed as, say, doctors, lawyers, and teachers, they do so in defiance of the so-called civilization that wanted to destroy them. What emerged, more specifically, with respect to what Parker meant by Sioux civilization, were individuals like Eastman who possessed the skills to remind the descendents of those settlers who overran Native homelands of the human cost of westward expansion and to enlighten them about the moral ambiguity behind their treatment of Indians.[9]

While Eastman and other Dakota deserve praise for surviving the aftermath of an exceptionally bitter conflict, thereby enabling the Dakota Nation to endure the clarion call of white inhabitants of Minnesota Territory, we should not fail to acknowledge the grave injustices inflicted against the Dakota. In addition to being forcibly removed from their homeland, the Dakota who were tried by the Americans set a disturbing precedent. Carol Chomsky observes in her article, "The United States–Dakota War Trials: A Study in Military Injustice,"

"The Dakotas were tried, not in a state or federal criminal court, but before a military commission. They were convicted, not for the crime of murder, but for killings committed in warfare. The official review was conducted, not by an appellate court, but by the President of the United States. Many wars took place between Americans and members of the Indian nations, but in no others did the United States apply criminal sanctions to punish those defeated in war." The trials were questionable at best and fraudulent at worst. What happened to the Dakota, Eastman's father Many Lightnings among them, demonstrates the effects of hysteria—in this case, among white Minnesotans—when it drives the pursuit of justice. In turn, when Indians attempt to account to their white neighbors what happened as far as they were concerned, they are treated like "sore losers" who cannot admit that their day in the sun is over and a new nation has arisen where the Dakota once stood. However, when one looks at the violations of the treaties between the Dakota and the United States, which led to the 1862 conflict, a different picture emerges.[10]

When *Indian Boyhood* appeared in 1902, published in New York by McClure, Phillips & Company, forty years after the U.S.–Dakota War, it did so with what would become an often quoted dedication from Eastman to his son, Ohiyesa II, who came too late to witness for himself "the drama of savage existence," as American Indians were no longer "natural and free," having been confined to reservations, upon which "only a sort of tableau—a fictitious copy of the past" now exists. At first glance, Eastman sounds as though he is acceding to the popular notion that Indians are a "vanishing race," as later exemplified in the 1913 book by Joseph K. Dixon. According to Eastman's biographer, Raymond Wilson, *Indian Boyhood* "depicts the idyllic existence Indians once enjoyed." While, as Wilson points out, Eastman mentions some of the harsher aspects of Dakota life, including famine, disease, and warfare, he devotes even more space "to the more gratifying aspects of his childhood, idealizing and romanticizing his past and associating it with an atmosphere of childlike simplicity." I would not argue against such a reading, given that Eastman was recalling his childhood for an equally young audience, beginning with his son. At the same time, I would warn against underestimating the significance and impact of the above-mentioned references to hardship, especially for an indigenous reader. One may see from the latter perspective an Indian writer struggling with the influx of "civilization" and the fragmentation and marginalization of the Dakota Nation. Consequently, in each of Eastman's nine books, he makes a desperate but graceful attempt to grab hold of the pieces of Dakota culture and history blown away by war, disease, and broken treaties. The result is a poignant critique of American society and politics, which have been driven as much by greed and materialism as by ideals of freedom and equality. Emerging from this critique is an image of the American Indian qua Dakota: he is the focus of what makes America unique in addition to being a barometer for future progress and reform. As the Indian goes, Eastman might have put it, so goes America. And what the Indian wanted, to word things in the language of the times, was to have his rights recognized, be they based on treaties, tribal sovereignty, or common humanity.[11]

Between 1902 and 1918, references to the 1862 conflict and its aftermath occurred in half of Eastman's books, namely *Indian Boyhood* (1902), *Old Indian Days* (1907), *The Indian To-day* (1915), *From the Deep Woods to Civilization* (1916), and *Indian Heroes and Great Chieftains* (1918). This is not to say that the absence of 1862 references in Eastman's other works meant that there was a point where he "got over" those traumatic events. Considering that the descendents of the 1862 generation are still dealing with the political and cultural consequences of that conflict today, it would be naïve—even offensive—to make such a claim about Eastman. Instead, it makes more sense to state that complementing Eastman's critique of American society and politics is his work at articulating a Dakota perspective on historical events and cultural practices that preserve the Dakota worldview. Eastman developed the Dakota, or "the Indian," perspective throughout the aforementioned works, in addition to *Red Hunters and the Animal People* (1904), *Smoky Day's Wigwam Evenings* (1909), *The Soul of the Indian* (1911), and *Indian Scout Talks* (1914). After pointing out in *The Indian To-day* that Sequoyah is the only Indian in the "nation's Hall of Fame" in Washington, DC, Eastman goes on to state, "The Indian languages, more than fifty in number, are better appreciated and more studied to-day than ever before. Half our states have Indian names, and more than that proportion of our principal lakes and rivers. These names are richly sonorous as they are packed with significance, and our grandchildren will regret it if we suffer the tongues that gave them birth to die out and be forgotten."[12]

Mention of the 1862 conflict appears for the first time in the opening section of *Indian Boyhood*, "Earliest Recollections," in a chapter titled "Early Hardships": "I was a little over four years old at the time of the 'Sioux massacre' in Minnesota. In the general turmoil, we took flight into British Columbia, and the journey is still vividly remembered by all our family."[13]

As Eastman recounts his earliest memories of 1862, he reminds us that a child's view of hardship is very different from that of an adult. For example, Eastman, still only known as Hakadah, "the pitiful last," recalls the excitement he felt at the prospect of riding in a wooden wagon, in which his family would make the long trek into Manitoba, leaving their homeland along the Minnesota River for good. A mishap occurs while Hakadah is playing on the wagon: he falls under the wagon's wheels and is nearly run over by another wagon coming up from behind. After thoroughly reproaching the wagon, the young Hakadah concludes, "I was really rejoiced that we were moving away from the people who made the wagon that had almost ended my life." Eastman then claims that he never rode in that wagon again and that he was glad when it was abandoned on the banks of the Missouri River. As the Dakota continued on their exodus, however, all was clearly not play for either Hakadah or anyone else. Eastman writes, "The summer after the 'Minnesota massacre,' General Sibley pursued our people across this river. Now the Missouri is considered one of the most treacherous rivers in the world. Even a good modern boat is not safe upon its uncertain current. We were forced to cross in buffalo-skin boats—as round as tubs!" Making the river crossing all the more difficult was the fact that the Dakota men had to fight General Sibley's troops along the way, in order to gain enough time for the refugees to escape.[14]

Upon reaching the other shore, the fleeing Dakota still faced long nights of distant marches, lack of sleep, and insufficient food. Further endangering their flight for sanctuary was the venture they had to make through "the country of hostile tribes"—more than likely Ojibwe or Mandan—which harassed them "almost daily and nightly." Even the elements tested the people's endurance, as they faced a prairie fire and a winter blizzard. But life on the run was not without some fortuitous twists of fate. After the blizzard had passed, the refugees "discovered a large herd of buffaloes almost upon" them. At last, they could enjoy "a good dinner." At this point, Eastman stops to reflect, nearly forty years after these awful events took place, saying, "I was now an exile as well as motherless; yet I was not unhappy." Speaking from that five-year-old-boy's perspective, "Our wanderings from place to place afforded us many pleasant experiences and quite as many hardships and misfortunes. There were times of plenty and times of scarcity, and we had several narrow escapes from death. In savage life, the early spring is the most trying time and almost all the famines occurred at this period of the year." In spite of the distress of being forced from their homeland, Eastman remembers this time as one in which the kinship ties were still remarkably strong. "Before going further," Ella Deloria writes in *Speaking of Indians*, "I can safely say that the ultimate aim of Dakota life . . . was quite simple: One must obey kinship rules; one must be a good relative." As Deloria explains, "Without that aim and the constant struggle to attain it, the people would no longer be Dakotas in truth. They would no longer even be human. To be a good Dakota, then, was to be humanized, civilized. And to be civilized was to keep the rules imposed by kinship for achieving civility, good manners, and a sense of responsibility toward every individual dealt with. Thus only was it possible to live communally with success; that is to say, with a minimum of friction and a maximum of good will."[15]

Because of these familial bonds, the Dakota endured the hardship of hunger with the same fortitude with which they had faced previous episodes of famine. Eastman, in fact, describes his people's stamina as something that came quite naturally to them: "During the summer, when Nature is at her best, and provides abundantly for the savage, it seems to me that no life is happier than his! Food is free—lodging free—everything free! All were alike rich in the summer, and, again, all were alike poor in the winter and early spring. However, their diseases were fewer and not so destructive as now, and the Indian's health was generally good." Far from exonerating the Americans who unjustly expelled the Dakota from their homes to undergo the ordeal of becoming war refugees, Eastman instead endorses the Dakota way of life as one with which even the greatest of hardships can be coped. "There seemed to be no special anxiety on the part of our people," Eastman recalls, "they rather looked upon all this as a matter of course, knowing that the storm would cease when the time came." Indeed, just as a Dakota would never complain about the weather, similarly will he refrain from complaining about life—both are gifts from the Creator. Or, as Luther Standing Bear describes this philosophical attitude in *Land of the Spotted Eagle,* "The hottest summer sun on a bare head brought no complaint from a Lakota, for weather in any form was never a topic of conversation. Such complaints as, 'It is too hot today,' or 'It is not warm enough,' were never heard. To complain against the weather would be denying the praise offered to the Great Mystery each morning for the day and all it held." Such a natural philosophy of life would continue to influence Eastman's subsequent references to 1862.[16]

Old Indian Days, which the McClure Company published in 1907, was a sequel to *Red Hunters and the Animal People,* which had appeared three years earlier. Whereas *Red Hunters* recounted several animal legends, largely told from a given animal's perspective, *Old Indian Days* consisted of fifteen stories about "The Warrior" and "The Woman," as the two parts of the book are named respectively. Of particular interest are the stories titled "The Chief Soldier" and "The Peace-Maker."

"The Chief Soldier" is about the 1862 conflict itself and the man, Tawasuota, "Many Hailstones," who served as Little Crow's chief soldier, or "ta ákich-ítah." In one respect, the story may be regarded as a companion piece to the one Eastman would later tell about Little Crow in *Indian Heroes and Great Chieftains.* Both stories are about the complex emotions and events leading up to the decision on the part of some of the Dakota to make war upon the American settlers in southern Minnesota.

As of the time of the story, Little Crow has signed a treaty with the United States that instigated a proliferation of log homes whose presence is encroaching upon the Dakota reservation. Tawasuota comments, "Ugh! they are taking from us our beautiful and game-teeming country!" The reservation at Lower Sioux is home to Indian agency buildings and traders' posts. Tawasuota observes across the Minnesota River a white family diligently working "from sunrise to sunset, much like the beaver family." Eastman had encountered similar families during his trek to the Santee Indian School in Nebraska, an experience, later recounted in *From the Deep Woods to Civilization,* that changed his whole attitude toward "civilization."[17]

On the evening of August 17, 1862, Tawasuota suddenly heard war whoops behind him and turned to see a column of Dakota warriors from the Rice Creek band on their way. Tawasuota presumed that an Ojibwe war party had been about, "a not uncommon incident." The government employees and traders, probably making the same assumption, remained unalarmed. As the column passed through the Wahpeton village, more warriors gathered to join them. However, the reason for the commotion is not what it appeared: "It was true that there had been a growing feeling of distrust among the Indians, because their annuities had been withheld for a long time, and the money payments had been delayed again and again. There were many in great need. The traders had given them credit to some extent (charging them four times the value of the article purchased), and had likewise induced Little Crow to sign over to them ninety-eight thousand dollars, the purchase price of that part of their reservation lying north of the Minnesota, and already occupied by the whites." Little Crow became unpopular among his own people because of this negotiation, and some became restless and threatening as a consequence. So, as Eastman portrays it, when news came that members of the Rice Creek band had killed two white families, Little Crow immediately jumped on his horse, anxious to "make their cause a general one among his people." The imminent fight between the Dakota and the whites would afford Little Crow the opportunity to regain face.[18]

As Little Crow's chief soldier, Tawasuota was asked to fire the first shot. Little Crow advised Tawasuota to make haste, lest the Indians who had cut their hair and put on the white man's clothing warned those marked for retribution. Tawasuota did as he was asked, then headed for the nearby trading post. The seasoned war chief encountered James Lynd, "one of the early traders, and a good friend to the Indians." Tawasuota approached the unsuspecting white man with determination, saying, "Friend . . . we may both meet the 'Great Mystery' to-day, but you must go first." Thus began the melee that non-Indian historians would recall as the "Dakota Uprising," the "Minnesota Massacre," and the like.[19]

Eastman highlights at this point that the Dakota were not all of one mind regarding how to handle their dilemma. Christian Indians raced around with their white brethren, dismayed but trying to save themselves and their white friends as best they could. Meanwhile, the white settlements along the Minnesota River remained unaware of what was happening. In the middle of the growing turmoil sat Tawasuota, smoking his pipe and secretly rebelling against Little Crow in his heart, for Tawasuota resented being asked to commit a cowardly deed. Many younger warriors, however, appreciated the opportunity to unleash their pent-up rage against the whites. As the carnage mounted, some older warriors joined Tawasuota: " 'Ho, nephew,' said one of them with much gravity, 'you have precipitated a dreadful calamity. This means the loss of our country, the destruction of our nation. What were you thinking of?' " The one who spoke was not only Tawasuota's uncle but also the Wahpeton chief, who signed the same treaty with Little Crow. Following the chief's rebuke came word that American troops were on their way from Fort Ridgeley. At his uncle's behest, Tawasuota went to continue the fight he had begun, only this time against the troops, who were prepared to defend themselves, unlike James Lynd.[20]

When the hostilities eventually subsided, Tawasuota went home to find his lodge empty, his wife and two sons having fled. The remainder of the story consists of Tawasuota's arduous effort to find his family. In his pursuit, he located his mother and sisters. Like his uncle, Tawasuota's mother expressed distress over what her son had done. The sisters, however, defended their brother on the basis that he could not refuse the order to attack the trader, lest he be called a coward. Yet all Tawasuota was really interested in was knowing where his wife and, especially, his two sons had gone. "She has been taken away by her own mother to Faribault," his mother tells him, "among the white people." Tawasuota's wife is from people his mother describes as "lovers of the whites. They have even accepted their religion." Tawasuota's heart sank upon hearing this news.[21]

Back among Little Crow's people, things were much different. According to Gary Clayton Anderson in his book about the "spokesman for the Sioux," "While Little Crow worked on strategy . . . his warriors implemented a cultural revitalization movement on August 18. The members of the soldiers' lodge ordered Indian farmers, mixed-bloods, and white captives to take off their white man's clothing and don Indian dress. Teepees became the only acceptable housing, and women ran about camp looking for materials with which to make them."[22]

As much as Tawasuota felt that he had to fight the whites until he died, he held an equally strong desire to see his sons one more time. Even though he accepted the reproaches of his uncle and mother, he knew in his heart that his fight was not "without cause." After all, as Eastman had already acknowledged, the whites had taken over much of the Dakotas' land, leaving the Indians to eke out a meager existence. Nonetheless, the fight began because of the impetuousness of a few and did not follow the will of the people, as led by their elders.[23]

Did Little Crow reflect on these issues? And would he care about his chief soldier's fear for his family? In Eastman's story, Little Crow is only concerned with attacking the whites further. Tawasuota's sons will have to wait, as Little Crow says, "Ugh, ugh, I shall need you tomorrow! My plan is to attack the soldiers at Fort Ridgeley with a strong force. There are not many. Then we shall attack New Ulm and other towns. We shall drive them all back into Saint Paul and Fort Snelling." Tawasuota agreed to lead the proposed attack; however, because Minnesotans across the region had become alarmed, the Dakota force's efforts proved unsuccessful. Indeed, "The feeling against all Indians was great"—and this feeling resonated for many years to come, exacerbated by the 1876 annihilation of Custer's forces. Eastman encountered it firsthand while looking for farm work during summer vacation after his first year at Beloit College. Eastman recalled one farmer saying to him, "Oho! you can not work the New Ulm game on me." For his part, Tawasuota saw only a long and very difficult war with the whites, all the more daunting because some Dakota had already agreed to surrender to the white soldiers, "thereby showing that they had not been party to the massacre nor indorsed the hasty action of the tribe." In light of this circumstance, Tawasuota decided to head to Faribault to find his sons. Along the way, he saw the occasional settler home razed to the ground, the white inhabitants lying dead. Also, now and again, "Tawasuota heard at a distance the wagons of the fugitives, loaded with women and children, while armed men walked before and behind. These caravans were usually drawn by oxen and moved slowly toward some large town." After reading *Indian Boyhood*, one can easily picture Hakadah and his family slowly making their way off the reservation into exile. Upon completing his long journey, Tawasuota reached Faribault at midnight. However, even after finding the Indian village, he knew better than to enter among them, for he knew that the whites would consider it an act of treachery on the Indians' part, if they took in a "hostile." Still, he needed to see his family.[24]

Following a restless night, Tawasuota awoke to see his wife and sons nearby. It did not take long for his wife to spot him and immediately begin wailing, saying, "Oh, take us husband, take us with you! let us all die together!" She spoke from the fear that because there was a price on Tawasuota's head "some of the half-breeds," who "loved money better than the blood of their Indian mothers," would greedily betray her husband. Tawasuota knew, though, that he must think of the safety and well-being of his sons, who now spotted their father and ran to him. Tawasuota explained to his wife that she must stay for the sake of their children. He hugged his sons with tears rolling down his cheeks and disappeared into the woods, never to be seen again. As for the two sons, one of them became in "after-years a minister of the Christian gospel, under the 'Long-Haired Praying Man,' Bishop Whipple, of Minnesota."[25]

In the story titled "The Peace-Maker," which appears in the section "The Woman," the legend is about Eyatónkawee, She-whose-Voice-is-heard-afar, who "was once victorious in a hand-to-hand combat with the enemy in the woods of Minnesota." This incident occurred during a battle between the Dakota and the Sac and Fox. Because of Eyatónkawee's very brave deed, which would be recounted often, she earned the right to intervene between any persons in her tribe having a confrontation. Only someone who had accomplished a braver feat could say anything in protest to the "peace-maker"; otherwise they were obliged to stand down when reproached.[26]

The story Eastman tells includes an episode when Eyatónkawee was middle-aged. Little Crow the elder had died, leaving his sons from his three wives to vie for the position of chief. The two sons of the wife from Wabasha plotted to murder their half-brother, Taoyateduta, His-Red-Nation, son of the wife from the Kaposia band. The two Wabasha brothers sought to carry out their misdeed at Mendota, "near what is now the thriving city of Saint Paul, then a queen of trading-posts in the

Northwest." Facilitating their dark desire to be rid of their half-brother was the purchase of two kegs of whiskey. By getting themselves and others drunk, they thought they could kill Taoyateduta and excuse it as an accident. As the drinking began, the homage to the late and elder Little Crow turned into a drunken row. Violence threatened to erupt. At this moment Eyatónkawee spoke up and used her status and power to stave off a bloody conflict among the Dakota themselves, saying, "Is it becoming in a warrior to spill the blood of his tribesmen? Are there no longer any Ojibways?" Because of Eyatónkawee's moral fortitude, she saved Taoyateduta from certain death, thereby enabling him to take his father's name and become chief.[27]

Eastman goes on to comment that in "those days" quarrels among the Dakota were often precipitated by the opponents indulging in strong drink. Eyatónkawee realized this hazard, especially after her brother was killed in a drunken brawl during "the early days of the American Fur Company." Even Indian agent Lawrence Taliaferro had a low opinion of these fur traders, characterized as "men of *mean* principles and low origin—consequently are jealous—evil disposed and great vagabonds." Because of what was happening to her community, Eyatónkawee fought against alcohol abuse as much as her status as "peace-maker" enabled her to do so. Her people took her seriously enough that many of the men who drank had to do it secretly and in moderation, lest Eyatónkawee confront them. Even as a very old woman, Eyatónkawee commanded respect, perhaps more so than ever. The customary beliefs that empowered her status were still strong, "and there was not one," Eastman asserts, "to prevent her when she struck open with a single blow of her ax the keg of whisky, and the precious liquor trickled upon the ground." With this in mind, Eastman ends his account with a dramatic statement: "So trickles under the ax of Eyatónkawee the blood of an enemy of the Sioux!"[28]

In 1915, Eastman revisited the problem of alcoholism in *The Indian To-day*, which may be described as the historic precursor to *Custer Died for Your Sins*. Despite the mundane title, Eastman engages in an impassioned and informed critique of American Indian culture, history, and politics, placing emphasis on Indian-White relations and the ramifications of various policy developments over the years to account for the status of Indian affairs as of the early twentieth century.[29]

After expounding on the moral virtues practiced by "the Indian" and the social contentment that Indians knew when they followed their old ways, Eastman segues into a section titled "First Effects of Civilization." Because, as Eastman explains, Indian societies valued the individual above all else—reflected in the lack of tribal organization or centralized government—they were left vulnerable to the corporate onslaught of civilization. Even before the Americans began arriving in the Northwest, the Europeans, represented in the fur trading interests, introduced as much vice as they did civilization to Indian communities. Above all, the scourge of alcoholism has been a great concern within the Indian community ever since the first settler brought rum onto the shores of Turtle Island. For as much accommodation of white society as some American Indian intellectuals advocated making within their respective nations, none has ever condoned making spirituous liquors a normative part of Indian life. Eastman notes, "During a long period the fur trade was an important factor in the world's commerce, and accordingly the friendship and favor of the natives were eagerly sought by the leading nations of Europe. Great use was made of whiskey and gunpowder as articles of trade. Demoralization was rapid. Many tribes were decimated and others wiped out entirely by the ravages of strong drink and disease, especially small pox and cholera." Under these trying circumstances, white missionaries entered with the presumption that they needed to "civilize" the Indians, whom the traders had corrupted in the first place.[30]

Lakota anthropologist Beatrice Medicine writes about the long-term effects of alcoholism as an integral part of Indian-White relations in her article "North American Indigenous Women and Cultural Domination": "The introduction of alcohol as a control mechanism in the early fur trade era also had perduring repercussions in early reservation placements. In general, apathy and despair seemed to reign in early reservation life. More devastating, a pattern of administered human relations ensued. With the demolition of traditional leadership patterns and the establishment of new 'chiefs' with more acquiescent orientations, patterns of paternalism were firmly established." Despite the obvious harm they were doing to Indian nations—which even many white, typically Christian, reformers recognized as problems—the Europeans, and even more so the Americans after them, persisted in their so-called civilizing efforts, such as imposing their own notion of government on the tribes.

The latter included the appointment of chiefs, whom the white governments would recognize as the only valid leaders of their respective tribes, as named in treaties and commemorated with medals, which could be handed down from father to son. Of course, this setup went against the tradition among many tribes of earning leadership through experience and distinction, as opposed to heredity or alien recognition. Unsurprisingly there were altercations, and, Eastman notes, "There were instances during the nineteenth century in the vicinity of Chicago, Prairie du Chien, Saint Paul, and Kansas City, where several brothers quarreled and were in turn murdered in drunken rows." The St. Paul incident, of course, referred to the episode recounted in Eyatónkawee's story.[31]

The catastrophe, then, that befell the Minnesota Dakota was the result of American policy, especially its imperialist ambitions for controlling commerce in the Northwest. Toward this end, the Americans, who won claim to the Northwest in the aftermath of the War of 1812, wanted to end the intertribal fighting between the Dakota and the Ojibwe. Only then could American commercial interests in the Upper Mississippi be fully exploited. This objective, however, was not attained overnight. As Eastman observes—irrespective of what the United States thought was its domain—the "Sioux Nation" extended over a vast territory that included what are today the states of Minnesota, Wisconsin, Iowa, North and South Dakota, Montana, Nebraska, and even Colorado and Wyoming. Within this great expanse, the various bands and tribes inhabited differing environments, complete with equally diverse cultures, although they spoke mutually intelligible dialects of the same language. With respect to the whites that came in over the generations, Eastman states, "[The Dakota] had been at peace with the whites ever since the early French explorers and the Jesuit priests had entered their country. They had traded for many years with the Hudson Bay and American Fur companies, and no serious difficulty had arisen, nor was any obstruction offered to the progress of civilization." In 1824, however, the United States wanted the tribes, the Dakota and the Ojibwe, to maintain a firm line between their two nations, which, as mentioned before, had the paradoxical effect of intensifying tribal warfare. The American response was to appropriate more Indian land and exert more control over the indigenous population, thereby setting the stage for the 1862 conflict.[32]

In the section of *The Indian To-day* titled "The Sioux and Their Grievances," Eastman argues that the situation deteriorated between 1824 and 1851. In 1824, all but the Inkpaduta band, named for their chief, agreed to this treaty. When American settlers established homes on their land, Inkpaduta and his people soon discovered that the game on which they depended had become depleted. Turning to the settlers for help, they were treated as pests and left to starve. Thus arose the "Spirit Lake Massacre," during which as many as forty whites were killed. The rest of the Dakota condemned the act and pursued two of Inkpaduta's sons, killing them; "The others were driven back among the wild Sioux. This was their first offence, after more than a century of contact with the whites."[33]

Eastman turns once more to the 1862 conflict and Little Crow. Perhaps after contemplating the scope of Indian history and the relentlessly disappointing story of Indian-White relations, Eastman felt compelled to state that the causes of the 1862 war "were practically the same as in many other instances, for in its broad features the history of one Indian tribe is the history of all." More specifically, Eastman outlines the events leading to the U.S.–Dakota War:

> Their hunting-grounds were taken from them, and the promised support was not forthcoming. Some of the chiefs began to "play politics" like white men, and through their signatures, secretly given, a payment of $98,000 due the tribe was made to the Indian traders. Little Crow himself was involved in this steal, and was made head chief by the whites, who wished to have some one in this position whom they could deal with. But soon the non-payment of annuities brought the Indians to the verge of starvation, and in despair they forced Little Crow to lead them in revolt. In August, 1862, they massacred the agency employees and extended their attack to the white settlers, killing many and destroying a large amount of property, before a part of the tribe fled into Canada and the rest surrendered to General Sibley.[34]

One may wonder after reading this passage where Eastman's loyalty really lies. In Eastman's complex view of Dakota history, his concern is for the well-being of the people, who have been forced by the growing pressures of "progress" and "civilization" to make not only difficult decisions but also very unfortunate ones. Eastman's opinion of Little

Crow is based on the observation that he "'played politics' like a white man," meaning that he cared more for money and power than for the good of the Dakota. Consequently, in Eastman's determination, Little Crow's decision to attack the white traders and settlers was a case of opportunism, a rash attempt to re-ingratiate himself with his tribe. Because of this analysis, Little Crow is held in a different light than Red Cloud and Sitting Bull, who also fought the Americans but did so because the American government was completely inept—perhaps indifferent—about upholding its end of the treaties made with the Teton Sioux. In particular, Red Cloud distinguished himself during the war over the Bozeman Trail, in which a campaign was waged against both immigrants and soldiers. Then, as Eastman writes, with a hint of pride, "In 1868 another treaty was made, but the great chief, Red Cloud, would not sign it until he saw forts C. F. Smith and Phil Kearney abandoned. Here is probably the only instance in American history in which a single Indian chief was able to enforce his demands and make a great government back down." Without a doubt, this was a high moment in American Indian history, when the Americans were humbled into going to the negotiating table and making peace with the Lakota, along with their Cheyenne allies, who fought bravely against the white soldiers. Although Black Elk and others would later berate Red Cloud for being a "hangs-around-the-fort" chief, such language was far from anyone's mind in the months after the 1868 treaty. This was a treaty the Lakota wanted to keep. Black Elk recalls,

> It was a happy summer and nothing was afraid, because in the Moon When the Ponies Shed (May) word came from the Wasichus that there would be peace and that they would not use the road [i.e., the Bozeman Trail] any more and that all the soldiers would go away. The soldiers did go away and their towns were torn down; and in the Moon of Falling Leaves (November), they made a treaty with Red Cloud that said our country would be ours as long as grass should grow and water flow. You can see that it is not the grass and the water that have forgotten.

What ultimately made Red Cloud a hangs-around-the-fort chief in the eyes of some was the fact that when the whites laid claim to the Black Hills, in clear violation of the 1868 treaty, the aging chief refused to

fight. For the younger generation that included Black Elk, such an attitude was unconscionable. Yet, for Eastman, who was younger still,
knowing when to stop fighting is a virtue too often overlooked, especially when emotions are running high in the other direction. Eastman,
after all, witnessed both the Santee Dakota and the Teton Lakota suffer
greatly when the Americans sought retribution for losses incurred and
the humiliation they felt when the Indians fought them. When wonder-
ing where Eastman's heart may lie, one must bear in mind that he lived
through the Dakota exile and the Wounded Knee Massacre.[35]

With respect to Sitting Bull, about whom Eastman also writes in
The Indian To-day, he of course took up the Teton Sioux cause when the
United States failed to honor the treaty that Red Cloud forced the Americans to make in 1868. Just as important, with regard to my analysis of
Eastman's writings, is that Sitting Bull supported "the cause of the Eastern Sioux in Minnesota and fought Sibley and Sully in 1862." Unfortunately, when Sitting Bull was forced to defend his homeland against
gold-seekers and the Northern Pacific Railroad, his allied support was
curtailed by the fact that "the other bands of Sioux whom he had helped
in their time of need were now all settled upon reservations." Consequently, despite achieving unequivocal victory in the 1876 "Custer
fight," Sitting Bull and his followers fled into Canada. It was "Four years
later [that] Sitting Bull was induced to come in and settle down upon the
Sioux reservation." Interestingly, perhaps because it is a painful memory,
in neither *From the Deep Woods* nor *Indian Heroes* does Eastman dwell
on Sitting Bull's assassination while being apprehended by the Indian
police. Since Eastman's book is largely aimed at a white audience,
whom he was trying to convince to support Indian causes, he was probably better off omitting this difficult episode. How could he explain such
a thing so that the whites would understand?[36]

Overlapping with the era of Little Crow, Red Cloud, and Sitting Bull
was a "new Indian policy," which the Abraham Lincoln administration
initiated. Specifically, Lincoln refused "to order the execution of three
hundred Sioux braves, whom a military court had, in less than two days,
convicted of murder and condemned to be hung, in order to satisfy the
clamor of the citizens of Minnesota." As Eastman points out, white
Minnesotans wanted revenge for persons killed and property destroyed
in the 1862 U.S.–Dakota War. However, rather than concede to their

bloodlust, Eastman scolds them with a reminder of their own history: "[Minnesotans] forgot that these Sioux had been defrauded of the finest country in the world, their home, their living, and even cheated out of the ten cents per acre agreed to be paid for millions of acres of the choicest land . . . [The Dakotas] had shown their teeth at last, after more than a century of patience and self-control." Eastman reiterates this point in *From the Deep Woods to Civilization*. In *The Indian To-day*, he underscores the great deed Lincoln achieved on behalf of the Dakota by reducing the number condemned from three hundred down to forty. Minnesotans, of course, were outraged and heaped calumny upon his name. As Carol Chomsky notes in her article on the war trials that followed the 1862 conflict, "A great public outcry arose in Minnesota in response to reports that Lincoln might not carry out the full sentence of the military commission. The Stillwater, Minnesota *Messenger* demanded extermination of the Dakota: 'DEATH TO THE BARBARIANS! is the sentiment of our people.'" Governor Alexander Ramsey appealed to Lincoln personally to reconsider his decision, only to see the number executed reduced even further to thirty-eight. In the end, "many of those whom [Lincoln] pardoned afterward became leaders of the Sioux in walking the white man's road." This number included Eastman's own father and brother, Jacob and John Eastman. Still, we cannot fail to realize that, as Chomsky points out, these war trials were carried out unjustly. More specifically, Chomsky argues her case on these bases:

> The speed of the proceedings, the nature of the evidence, and the identity of the judges all combined to preclude judicious decision making and to guarantee an unjust outcome . . . More important, the commission tried the Dakota for the wrong crimes. Based on the historical and legal views prevailing in 1862 and the years that followed, the Dakota were a sovereign nation at war with the United States, and the men who fought the war were entitled to be treated as legitimate belligerents. The Dakota, therefore, should have been tried only on charges that they violated the customary rules of warfare, not for the civilian crimes of murder, rape, and robbery.[37]

In *From the Deep Woods to Civilization*, the events of 1862 are now fifty-four years in the past yet no less significant for the roughly fifty-eight-year-old Eastman, who begins where *Indian Boyhood* left off—with his father's miraculous return. After recounting the injustice that the

Dakota suffered and which led directly to the conflict, Eastman discloses the personal toll it took on his family: "My father, who was among the fugitives in Canada, had been betrayed by a half-breed across the United States line, near what is now the city of Winnipeg. Some of the party were hanged at Fort Snelling, near St. Paul. We supposed, and, in fact, we were informed that all were hanged. This was why my uncle, in whose family I lived, had taught me never to spare a white man from the United States." Had Jacob Eastman not found his son, surely the warpath is where the fifteen-year-old Ohiyesa was headed. While Eastman's uncle and grandmother never completely reduced their distrust of white men, Jacob made a firm commitment that his son, now Charles Alexander, would adjust to the new order influencing every aspect of Dakota society. Thus, the would-be warrior became a scholar and headed to a variety of schools, beginning with the Indian day school in Flandreau that eventually led him to Dartmouth College and the Boston Medical College. At this point in my discourse, we are inevitably headed back to where we began—Eastman's return to southern Minnesota. This homecoming occurs in chapter nine, titled "Civilization as Preached and Practised," in which Eastman proclaims, "After thirty years of exile from the land of my nativity and the home of my ancestors, I came back to Minnesota in 1893." Only Eastman did not return with his band of Mdewakanton Dakota: his father and grandmother were still in Flandreau, and his uncle remained exiled in Canada. Instead, Eastman moved to St. Paul with his white wife, Elaine Goodale, and the first of their children, Dora, named after Elaine's sister.[38]

In the same way that Eastman would observe in other writings how current cities, towns, and institutions now stand where Indian nations once stood, he notes with respect to the Twin Cities, "My mother was born on the shores of Lake Harriet; my great-grandfather's village is now a part of the beautiful park system of the city of Minneapolis." Moreover, because Eastman was now a trained physician rather than a young and free Dakota boy, he was obliged to tend to his career interests. With his family in mind, Eastman took the medical examination, "as Minnesota was one of the first states to pass such a law." Despite the grueling three-day exam, Eastman distinguished himself by passing a test that half of the forty-five applicants failed. Building a private practice was an equally trying process, however, and Eastman was dismayed by the kind of temptation that came his way: "I was persistently solicited for illegal practice, and this by persons who were not only intelligent, but apparently of good social standing." Furthermore, some individuals approached Eastman for "Indian medicine and treatment," which he consistently declined to provide, as he was not trained in that type of care. This reaction does not imply that Eastman was disdainful of traditional Indian medicine. Not only was his grandmother a respected herbalist whom Eastman never failed to admire, but even as a practicing physician on the Pine Ridge Reservation he was respectful of medicine men.[39]

In spite of the tragic and disheartening experience at Pine Ridge and Wounded Knee, Eastman confesses in *From the Deep Woods* that he still believed in the "Christ ideal" he first learned from his father, which was reinforced by men he grew to admire, such as the Reverend Alfred L. Riggs, superintendent of the Santee Training School, and the Reverend Dr. John P. Williamson, Presbyterian missionary and Riggs's colleague, both of whom were early mentors to Eastman as he began his transition into his new life as an "educated" Indian. Still, the contrast between the Christian principles he was taught and the irrepressibly materialistic and selfish society he saw around him must have been jarring at times. Fortunately, in Eastman's opinion, there were men like Richard Morse, John R. Mott, Wilbur Messer, and Charles Ober, whom he regarded as "the best products of American civilization." If not for these individuals, life could have easily become despondent for Eastman. As he writes in *From the Deep Woods*, "I have said some hard things of American Christianity, but in these I referred to the nation as a whole and to the majority of its people, not to individual Christians. Had I not known some such, I should long ago have gone back to the woods." This was of course before Eastman actually did venture back into the woods at the behest of George Heye. As it was, Eastman found himself reminiscing about the Dakota way he knew growing up, including the stories and the faint early memories of Minnesota before the so-called "uprising." Thus, he began writing the "sketches" that became *Indian Boyhood*.[40]

Sixteen years after *Indian Boyhood*'s publication in 1902, Eastman released his final published book, *Indian Heroes and Great Chieftains*. U.S.

entry into the European war was thick in the air; American patriotism
abounded. Yet Eastman felt inspired to write a book consisting of historical life stories of fifteen different Indian leaders. All but three were
either Lakota or Dakota, the exceptions being Roman Nose (Cheyenne),
Chief Joseph (Nez Perce), and Hole-in-the-Day (Ojibwe). Eastman
wanted to tell these stories because, as he explains on the very first page
in his account of Red Cloud, "I should like to present some of the greatest chiefs of modern times in the light of the native character and
ideals, believing that the American people will gladly do them tardy justice." Eastman, after all, wrote in a time when it was still necessary to
convince the American public that the historical Indian figures they
thought they knew were not really the "savages" they had been made
out to be. Perhaps we still live in that time.[41]

In any case, among Eastman's portraits is one of Little Crow, whom
Eastman has already faulted more than once for hastily going to war
against the Americans in 1862. Much of the previously made criticism is
retained in *Indian Heroes and Great Chieftains;* however, Eastman adds
disclosures concerning the paradoxes of Little Crow's character. Although he is described as "an intensely ambitious man and without
physical fear," he is also credited with having learned from his mother
the virtues of silence and of listening to the Great Mystery. Little Crow
is also remembered as excelling at the "sham battles" that young
Dakota boys often played, accompanied by a favorite dog. At twelve,
Little Crow saved another boy's life after he had fallen through some
ice. Little Crow's youthful courage and compassion developed into distinguishing virtues in young adulthood. And so with clear justification
he was made chief of the Kaposia band, which once resided in what is
today West St. Paul.[42]

It may have been his youth, though, that made Little Crow suscep-
tible to the temptations provided by fur companies competing in the
area. In turn, the U.S. government acknowledged Little Crow as chief
representative of the Dakota, inviting him to Washington, DC, along
with other "chiefs," such as the Ojibwe Hole-in-the-Day, where they
enjoyed the pomp and grandeur of the American capital. "More and
more as time passed," Eastman writes, "this naturally brave and ambitious man became a prey to the selfish interests of the traders and

politicians." Like a character in a Greek tragedy, Little Crow became a victim of his own flaws. The context for this drama encompassed the worsening conditions on the Lower Sioux Agency during the middle nineteenth century. In this version of Little Crow's story, Eastman elaborates a bit further on the Americans' treaty infractions, which turn out to be much more than failing to pay annuities to the Dakota: "By treaty stipulation with the government, they were to be fed and clothed, houses were to be built for them, the men taught agriculture, and schools provided for the children. In addition to this, a trust fund of a million and a half was to be set aside for them, at five per cent interest, the interest to be paid annually per capita. They had signed the treaty under pressure, believing in these promises on the faith of a great nation." Needless to say, none of these promises were kept, and the Dakota found themselves in a state of destitution. However, when Little Crow partook in an alleged deal to get $98,000 for the northern half of their reservation, he lost the people's respect when the money went instead to the traders—his supposed friends.[43]

After mentioning that Dakota hunters murdered a white family in Acton on August 17, Eastman adds two very interesting layers of complexity to the decision to fight. First, he points out that messengers were sent to all the villages with the disturbing news, the receipt of which was followed by council meetings. At the villages of Little Crow and Little Six (or Shakopee), "the war council was red-hot," and there was much talk of taking advantage of the situation "to wipe out the white settlers and regain their freedom." Those opposed to war were not heard over the din calling for vengeance. Second, when some of the Dakota wanted to vent their wrath on the mixed-blood members of their community, blaming them as part of the problem, Eastman's father intervened to stop them: "My father, Many Lightnings, who was practically the leader of the Mankato band (for Mankato, the chief, was a weak man), fought desperately for the lives of the half-breeds and the missionaries. The chiefs had great confidence in my father, yet they would not commit themselves, since their braves were clamoring for blood." When Many Lightnings realized that war would not be averted, he and two others spoke to Little Crow, asserting to him, "If you want war, you must personally lead your men to-morrow. We will not murder women and children, but we will fight the soldiers when they come." The story glosses over the part Eastman developed more fully in "The Chief Soldier" in *Old Indian Days.* Most of the remainder of the story in *Indian Heroes and Great Chieftains* is about Little Crow's attempt to return to St. Paul, after having to flee to Canada because the Dakota failed to "wipe out" the settlers. Little Crow hoped that his white friends, including the traders and the governor of Minnesota, Alexander Ramsey, would protect him.[44]

On his return journey, Little Crow was spotted by a woodchopper named Nathan Lamson. Little Crow at the time was picking wild raspberries for a meal. However, Lamson had no idea who he was looking at; he only knew it was an Indian. Lamson fired his gun and killed Little Crow. "The body of the chief was found and identified," Eastman notes, "in part by the twice broken arm." Lamson, for his part, received a bounty check for five hundred dollars as a reward. Eastman concludes his story with the shocking statement that "this arm and his scalp may be seen to-day in the collection of the Minnesota Historical Society." Little Crow's remains were eventually repatriated in 1971, one hundred and seven years after his death.[45]

In the portrait of Tamahay that follows, Eastman pieces together the following speech, given just before the U.S.–Dakota War, from the various people who heard it with their own ears. Like the rest of the Dakota Nation, Tamahay was driven from his ancestral home after 1862, in spite of the lifelong friendly relations that he maintained with the Americans. He died two years later at Fort Pierre, South Dakota. As Eastman mentions, Tamahay was the only Dakota to side with the Americans in 1812, afterward befriending Lieutenant Zebulon M. Pike, the first American military officer to explore the upper Mississippi River and "make peace" with the Indians. Because of this friendship, Tamahay assisted Pike "in obtaining land from the Sioux upon which to build Fort Snelling" in the summer of 1819. On the eve of the 1862 conflict, Tamahay, now very old, spoke with all the authority accorded the elderly:

> What! What! is this Little Crow? is that Little Six? You, too, White Dog, are you here? I cannot see well now, but I can see with my mind's eye the stream of blood you are about to pour upon the bosom of this mother of ours [meaning the earth]. I stand before you on three legs, but the third leg has brought me wisdom [refer-

ring to the staff with which he supported himself]. I have traveled
much, I have visited among the people whom you think to defy. This
means the total surrender of our beautiful land, and the land of a
thousand lakes and streams. Methinks you are about to commit an
act like that of the porcupine, who climbs a tree, balances himself
upon a springy bough, and then gnaws off the very bough upon
which he is sitting; hence, when it gives way, he falls upon the sharp
rocks below. Behold the great Pontiac, whose grave I saw near
St. Louis; he was murdered while an exile from his country! Think
of the brave Black Hawk! Methinks his spirit is still wailing through
Wisconsin and Illinois for his lost people! I do not say you have no
cause to complain, but to resist is self-destruction. I am done.[46]

At this point, I must stop to reflect on the implications of Eastman's
treatment of the 1862 U.S.–Dakota War in all of his work cited above.
Unlike what we saw in the chapter on Dakota-Ojibwe relations, Eastman does not go through a process out of which his consciousness is
raised from prejudice to acceptance. Instead, he remains consistently
disturbed by what the American settlers did to force the Dakota into a
gravely difficult situation, obliging them to make some rather unnerving decisions. While Eastman clearly aligns himself with the side that
did not want to fight the Americans, his sympathies extend to the entire
Dakota Nation. If the United States had honored all of the articles of
the 1851 treaty, there would not have been the prospect of war in the
first place.

As a writer who remembers enduring the U.S.–Dakota War as a little
boy as well as growing up listening to his elders speak of their own experiences, Eastman feels a moral obligation to give voice to the voiceless
in his work. In *From the Deep Woods to Civilization,* Eastman states that
his "chief object has been, not to entertain, but to present the American
Indian in his true character before Americans," which included expounding on "the Indian and his true place in American history." The
true place of which Eastman speaks is more than the metaphorical
place of historical context; it is also the actual places on which Indian
nations maintained their homelands, from which they were forcibly
removed because of the avaricious nature of so-called civilization. "It
is my personal belief," Eastman declares in *The Soul of the Indian,*
"after thirty-five years' experience of it, that there is no such thing as

'Christian civilization.' I believe that Christianity and modern civilization are opposed and irreconcilable."[47]

With the above invective in mind, when Eastman recalls that his
elders, be it his mother or his grandfather, Cloud Man, not to mention
ancestors like Jingling Thunder, lived along the Minnesota River, where
St. Paul and Minneapolis stand today, he is doing more than expressing
his nostalgia. Instead, he is making an ethical and political assertion
that American Indians, such as the Dakota, possess an inalienable right
to claim an ongoing and sovereign place in modern American society.
In spite of the grave injustices the Dakota endured during the 1860s at
the hands of the American military in addition to the clarion calls of
Minnesota civilians, Eastman does not seek revenge but respect for
the Dakota and all American Indians. For only by showing due respect
for American Indians—as people, as citizens, and as Indians—can
Americans begin to compensate the indigenous inhabitants of this land
for the immense sacrifices they made for the sake of building a new
nation.

Until that happens, the bonds that might otherwise join the descendents of both the Dakota and the Americans will never take hold. With
respect to what Eastman and his generation may have to teach us about
this situation, Hertzberg draws an interesting conclusion. After observ-
ing the many ways in which Indians of the early twentieth century
faced the same problems and issues as their counterparts of the early
1970s, she goes on to explain how they—for example, Eastman—preferred to handle the many offenses they had endured from white society and government:

> They preferred not to dwell too long on historic grievances, for they
> had seen too many of their kinsmen paralyzed by so doing, recount-
> ing over and over the old injustices. Despite past brutality and present
> injury they looked to the future with hope for they, and other Amer-
> icans, had confidence in the essential promise of American life. When
> and if Americans lose that confidence, and when and if American
> life does not deserve it, then Pan-Indians, like the rest of us, will
> cling to an identity narrower, more parochial, and more hostile to
> those outside our own groups.

In the spirit of Tamahay, I am done.[48]

EPILOGUE

Return to Minnesota
Eastman's Legacy

After reflecting on Eastman's life and work for the past eight years, ever since I moved to Minneapolis in the summer of 2000 and culminating in the writing of this book, the real work of learning from Eastman's legacy has only just begun. First, I had to get over my own inhibitions about embracing Eastman's work, which entailed recognizing that I had more in common with him than I had realized. Then, I had to learn how to teach his work so that my students understood the extent to which, as Eastman claims at the conclusion of *From the Deep Woods to Civilization*, he is both an Indian and an American. Just as important, I had to come to terms with the way in which Eastman was an intellectual such that he did not turn into an ivory tower stereotype. Not only was Eastman never a college professor; he also never felt compelled to narrow his writing agenda into a particular specialization, thereby becoming an "expert" of any kind. Since the Dakota do not divide knowledge into the exclusive bodies of discourse that define western "disciplines," Eastman's epistemological paradigm reflects a different worldview, in which knowledge is contained by people in social roles that were and are meaningful to the tribe: medicine, storytelling, ceremony, hunting, warfare, vision, and dream. Each may be further expanded into differing subjects and experiences, which in turn may be combined in a variety of ways. What this means to the Indian intellectual writing about any aspect of the Indian experience, including the modern, is that specializing in the analytical sense of limiting one's focus to a particular abstract topic is impossible, or at least does not make any sense. Eastman's example is one of interweaving subject and context into a coherent whole. Just as the Indian individual does not have an identity without a tribe or relatives, so too what he or she writes about does not have any meaning without the appropriate context. What results, similar to the oral tradition, is a nonlinear discourse in which a prism of ideas, values, phenomena, and concomitant discourses appear.

At this point, I cannot help but look back to when this book first began to crystallize, which was while I taught a graduate seminar titled "Lessons in Assimilation: American Indian Intellectuals, 1890–1934." At the time, I thought I was pursuing a much more ambitious project of composing an intellectual history of the prominent American Indian writers and activists of the Progressive Era. Consequently, for the spring seminar held at the Newberry Library in Chicago, under the auspices of the D'Arcy McNickle Center for American Indian History, I assigned a range of works, not only by Eastman but also by Carlos Montezuma, Arthur C. Parker, and Zitkala-Sa. My students came from an equally diverse range of graduate programs from around the Upper Midwest. Naturally, among them were some students who were suspicious of anyone who did not maintain the same "radical" values they espoused, regardless of what "excuse" may have been mustered due to historical circumstances. Since not all that long ago I held a similarly skeptical position against any and all "progressive Indians," I thought I knew where my own students had their misgivings.

Anticipating the criticism, I set out to demonstrate the myriad ways in which Eastman, whose works inaugurated the course, was an authentically indigenous intellectual, complete with traditional knowledge that many today would envy. For starters, Eastman was fluent in the Dakota language; his acquaintance with Dakota traditions was obtained in a non-reservation life in Manitoba; and he learned of Dakota and family history from a Dakota elder, Smoky Day, who taught him in Dakota. Nonetheless, one student in particular—an Okanagan from British Columbia, who was attending Ohio State University—was adamant about forging a specific agenda against everyone he was reading in this seminar and would not take into consideration any of the often-excruciating ordeals that Eastman and his peers endured for the sake of promoting Indian rights. While I was not worried about maintaining control over my class, given that the other students were enthusiastic about examining the readings from a variety of angles, nevertheless the one student's persistence led me to turn to the only person in the American Indian Studies community whose word always goes a long way at opening eyes and ears to the truth—Vine Deloria, Jr., an emeritus but quite active professor at the University of Colorado at Boulder.[1]

When I contacted Vine, I was hoping to bring "the Dean of American Indian Studies" in for a guest visit with my students; alas he was unable to oblige because of previously made commitments. Fortunately, I did manage to persuade him to address the meaning and significance of Eastman and his generation to contemporary purveyors of American Indian Studies. He wrote in an e-mail,

> People forget that there were 4 strand barbed wire fences around the Sioux reservations until the late 1920s and that Indians had to have a pass to get off the reservation—and if a group of people went off the res they had to have an Indian policeman accompany them— in this atmosphere where everything was a police state and people were forbidden to attend social events held in a traditional manner, the few who did get outside and learned to live in white society had to act as spokespeople to the larger society that Indians were people. [Charles] Eastman and [Luther] Standing Bear were among the few who aggressively told the Indian story—their work is essential because they had both grown up in pre-reservation days and knew what life was like—not to make their story the central part of relevant literature is to miss the whole point of having an Indian Studies program.[2]

It probably goes without saying that once I distributed this message to my students, the haranguing ceased being a problem. What mattered more to me, however, was the corroboration I received from Vine that the task of analyzing Eastman's writings and advocating that he did foundational work in American Indian Studies was a worthwhile endeavor. It could be argued in many ways that there is no way of knowing where we should head as contemporary American Indian intellectuals without first coming to terms with what our predecessors went through when they made the difficult transition from pre-reservation life to a reservation system in desperate need of reform. Clara Sue Kidwell and Alan Velie openly acknowledge the debt contemporary American Indian Studies (and its variants) owes to the post-1890 generation of American Indian intellectuals. Making clear references to the key figures of the era, Kidwell and Velie begin the introduction to their book, *Native American*

Studies, with the following proclamation: "Formal Native American/ American Indian Studies programs are a relatively recent phenomenon in the academic world, and although their origins are usually associated with political activism, they have drawn from a strong American Indian intellectual tradition. In the early twentieth century, college-educated American Indians were speaking out on Indian rights issues, critiquing federal Indian policy, debating issues of American Indian identity, and seeking to preserve Indian cultures, all activities that generally characterize contemporary programs."[3]

Given the intransigence of Anglo-American society at maintaining key values that are antithetical to the "Indian philosophy," such as competition, greed, and materialism—which are in clear opposition to their espoused Christian ideals—it makes sense that integral to Eastman's agenda is an attempt to get the Indian's white brothers to Indianize themselves. During Eastman's lifetime, he saw what he thought was evidence of this sought-after indigenization process, beginning with the interest that many painters, sculptors, poets, novelists, composers, and choreographers were showing in "primitive art." More important to Eastman was the rising number of children joining the Boy Scouts and Camp Fire Girls, complemented by adult interest in the outdoors as highlighted by the creation of the National Parks system. A little later in the early twentieth century, many Americans joined secret societies or lodges—from the Free Masons to the Teepee Order of America to the Improved Order of Red Men and the like—in which innumerable American males spent their evenings conducting mock Indian rituals. At the same time, these fraternal orders were not without their "authentic Indian" connections. Hazel W. Hertzberg observes,

> One of the earliest of the fraternal Pan-Indian organizations...
> was the Tepee Order of America. It first appeared in New York City
> around 1915 as a youth group, and only gradually did it develop into
> an adult movement. Its founder was Red Fox St. James, and its first
> head chief was Charles Eastman.
>
> The Tepee Order was originally a secret organization for native-
> born Protestant young people from fifteen to thirty years of age, and
> its avowed purpose was "studying the early history of the natives of
> America, its languages, customs, and to put into practice the activities
> of Indian outdoor life." The Order was primarily for boys but there

was also to be a branch for "young ladies." Its governing board was composed of *"real American Indians* and selected Boy's Work Experts exclusively," and it was to be "directed by Indians, assisted by white men." Officers held such titles as Head Chief, Medicine Man, and Scribe. Provision was made for initiation, degrees, badges, and ceremonials which were "strictly Indian, real not imitation." Each member was to get an "Indian name," and was to wear "real" Indian dress.[4]

Naturally, it would be quite easy—not to mention necessary—to ridicule these efforts at "playing Indian." However, in so doing, we might be overlooking the importance of play as a mode of learning. While it unnerves and even infuriates me to see white kids shouting war whoops, I sometimes wonder whether or not they are merely exhibiting the puerile nature of a still very young civilization. American Indians have had the benefit of living within the environs of North America since time immemorial. Their white brothers have been here only a few centuries, and only during the past century and a half have they shown an earnest interest in learning the Indian Way. Maybe this earnestness has paid off in ways that are sometimes hard to see, especially since the fight for Indian rights is still ongoing. Nonetheless, as both Vine Deloria, Jr., and Paula Gunn Allen have observed, white Americans have slowly but surely exhibited the Indian influences that pervade the landscape, even when there do not seem to be any Indians around.

In *Custer Died for Your Sins,* Deloria is intrigued by the various ways in which hippies and the corporate world have adopted a kind of tribalism. In the case of hippies, Deloria recounts "strange beings in gaudy costumes" turning up in his office to proclaim their intellectual connection with Indians. He apparently gave them the benefit of the doubt and even thought he saw some Indian-like attitudes in their concern for the person and their abhorrence of restrictive rules and regulations. Hippies also wanted to share what little wealth they possessed in a communal setting. However, although the hippies he met "were tribally oriented," they "refused to consider customs as anything more than regulations in disguise." Without a regard for custom, Deloria argues, the hippies are without a basis for maintaining their otherwise communal values; they are simply a group of individuals with a communal attitude. In contrast, Indian tribes are based on customs and highly organized clans. Corporations, on the other hand, possess a comparable value for custom and clannishness; however, unlike the hippies, corporations are not necessarily about spreading the wealth or dispensing with regulations in any free or egalitarian sense.[5]

In *The Sacred Hoop*, Allen makes a brief but meaningful observation about the social mores of many Americans, which are different from those of their European counterparts and which she can only explain in terms of Indian influence. Allen writes,

> Third- and fourth-generation Americans indulge in growing nudity, informality in social relations, egalitarianism, and the rearing of women who value autonomy, strength, freedom, and personal dignity—and who are often derided by European, Asian, and Middle Eastern men for those qualities. Contemporary Americans value leisure almost as much as tribal people do. They find themselves increasingly unable to accept child abuse as a reasonable way to nurture. They bathe more than any other industrial people on earth—much to the scorn of their white cousins across the Atlantic, and they sometimes enjoy a good laugh even at their own expense (though they still have a less developed sense of the ridiculous than one might wish).
>
> Contemporary Americans find themselves more and more likely to adopt a "live and let live" attitude in matters of personal sexual and social styles. Two-thirds of their diet and a large share of their medications and medical treatments mirror or are directly derived from Native American sources. Indianization is not a simple concept, to be sure, and it is one that Americans often find themselves resisting; but it is a process that has taken place, regardless of American resistance to recognizing the source of many if not most of America's vaunted freedoms in our personal, family, social, and political arenas.[6]

Despite these advances in the Indianization of mainstream Americans, one thing that characterized Eastman's intellectual life has remained a perennial demand of every generation of American Indian intellectuals: the need to educate non-Indians about the fundamentals of Indian culture and history. My colleagues and I in American Indian Studies face this situation on a regular basis, in which we are compelled to explain that Indian nations are sovereign entities, complete with treaties that are still valid today, or that there are Indian people still living east of the Mississippi, or that there are reasons why not all Indians are full-bloods. At a Unitarian meeting in Excelsior, Minnesota, I even had an elderly woman ask me, "Where do the Indians get off calling themselves 'Native Americans'?" As far as she was concerned, since she was born in the United States, that made her a native American, too. As an educator, I do not mind adding to the public's knowledge of Indians. Nonetheless, in a nation that was once entirely Indian Country, it is nothing short of astounding the amount of ignorance I face regularly, even among Americans who grew up in the middle of ancient Indian homelands yet do not know what tribes once lived where their own homes now stand. Until Indian components become a standard part of every American's educational experience, the peoples, nations, and events in Indian history, a crucial part of this country's story that everyone ought to know, will remain lacunae in the collective consciousness.

Take the example of Fort Snelling. Many Dakota endured excruciating hardship there after the 1862 U.S.-Dakota War, in which the United States engaged in ethnic cleansing and turned Fort Snelling into a "concentration camp." The site is a gaping wound in the heart of the Dakota Nation, and some argue it should be demolished. But is simply tearing down the fort the right answer? If the alternative is to keep the fort in its current condition as a tourist attraction in which one can be quaintly reminded of Minnesota's frontier days, then yes, the fort should be bulldozed, along with other atrociously antiseptic monuments to American triumphalism. Yet, what may generate a sensational media moment—watching the fort demolished—will likely disappear from the American consciousness as quickly as other media moments, with nothing left but an empty site that is still not in Dakota hands. Starting a tear-down-the-fort movement runs the inevitable risk of creating a pro–Fort Snelling countermovement, a social and political backlash, where none existed before.

As those concerned wrestle with the ethical question of what to do with a historic site that bears little or no memory of the Dakota, they would be wise to keep in mind that their answer may affect not only how one's ancestors are remembered and honored but also how future generations think and feel about themselves, their community, and their neighbors. At the same time, one ought to be wary of turning Indian suffering, or its attendant symbols, into fetishes. Eastman himself would argue that what needs to change more than any proposed demolition or renovation of the fort is the manner in and extent to which all Americans learn about the history of Indian nations and their historically important relation to whites. With this goal in mind, is the answer to reform and upgrade how history is taught at the fort? What if the upgrade included, as has been suggested, a language and cultural revitalization component that would benefit the Dakota community, perhaps even the Ojibwe? While radically transforming how history is represented at the fort could go a long way in enlightening visitors from all walks of life, not to mention demonstrate respect for the sanctity of the land on which the fort stands, the impact on revitalization efforts and the general public's knowledge of history will likely be minimal at best.

And yet, a highly visible component of this mission to educate the public about the Indian's place in U.S. history would involve action taken to rectify past wrongs. We must consider ways the State of Minnesota and the U.S. federal government might own up to historic injustices and make a good-faith effort at rectifying the social decay they caused in the Dakota Nation and the moral erosion they instigated in mainstream communities like the Twin Cities due to their willful omission of Dakota, Ojibwe, and Ho-Chunk history not only from tourist attractions like Fort Snelling but more importantly from the public school curriculum. The federal government, in particular, with regard to the promises it made the Dakota Nation in the 1851 treaty, ought to provide the Dakota people substantial support for rebuilding the Dakota Nation, for revitalizing their homeland.

In the continuing fight to inform the public at large about Indian history and culture, Eastman's efforts and writings offer a worthy model. And yet this story is tinged with irony, for when it comes to the education of Indians, Americans have never been reluctant about assuming that their traditions were superior and ought to be inculcated into every Indian child for the sake of his or her "uplift" into "civilization." What is interesting about this experience, of which Eastman is a prime example, is that when Indians did concede to attending school, be it day school or boarding school, Indian school or public, they mainly sought the practical arts: learning how to manage money or taking up a trade, which sometimes included doctoring or lawyering. In other words, what Indians wanted from education was very specific and noninvasive. Even when Indians converted to Christianity, as did Eastman's family, they never spoke of education as a means for inculcating children with values and beliefs, a role better left to the parents. What they, including Eastman, wanted was to serve their community in some meaningful way. This goal was often harder to achieve than it sounds, since what one learns in school, from elementary school to graduate school, may or may not coincide with the needs of one's tribe. Most schools and programs, after all, are geared for life apart from the reservation. An American Indian Studies program alone is not enough to bridge the gap.

With respect to the relation between Indian success and education, "getting an education" was a constant rallying call for the post-1890 generation. Even more than becoming a Christian, obtaining an education was key to making a successful transition into modern mainstream America. If Indians were to truly practice self-determination in the new world in which they now lived, they needed the practical and intellectual tools with which to provide for themselves. "In the olden days," Gertrude Bonnin writes in a 1918 SAI report, "the Indian hunter went forth in search of game that the family be fed and clothed. He did not sit in his tent waiting for someone to bring him food and raiment. Neither can the Indians today wait for some one else to bring to their door the indulgence of human rights. The Indians must go forth in search of the new game,—higher education, that they may enjoy equal rights with all American citizens." Then as now, Indian communities were not short of living examples of those who had made it, attaining both an education and respect from their peers. Pointing to each other, the post-1890 intellectuals proudly thought of themselves as role models for other Indians to emulate. Eastman, in particular, was the one most often held up to others as the epitome of the Indian's inherent capacity to succeed in American society.[7]

At the same time, reservation schools were held in contempt by many critics of the time as being inadequate for serving the pressing needs of the Indian population. Francis La Flesche, Gertrude Bonnin, and Luther Standing Bear, for example, all recount the inadequacies of the boarding school system in their respective books *The Middle Five* (1900), *American Indian Stories* (1921), and *My People the Sioux* (1928).

The reasons reservation schools were not producing eminent men and women were that such schools were underfunded and poorly staffed and barely provided more than an elementary education for their students. Boarding schools, of course, were not much better, even though institutions like Carlisle, Hampton, Haskell, and the Phoenix Indian School did have their champions among SAI members. Furthermore, an unsurprisingly large proportion of the SAI membership graduated from these schools, as opposed to going to schools completely within white society, as did Carlos Montezuma.

In his speeches and the newsletter *Wassaja*, Montezuma often credited his success as both a physician and an Indian rights leader to his exposure to the mainstream schooling system. Had he stayed with his Yavapai-Apache parents, never having been abducted by a Pima raiding party and sold to the itinerant photographer Carlo Gentile, Montezuma firmly believed that his life on the reservation would have been nothing more than grinding poverty. Even Eastman, whose educational career began in the woods of Minnesota and Manitoba, followed by the all-Indian schools at Flandreau and Santee, saves his loftiest claims about the virtues of education for his college days at Beloit, Knox, Dartmouth, and Boston. Eastman underscores when recalling his educational experiences that going to school in the first place was a choice that his father and he deliberately made for themselves. The absence of any kind of white-induced coercion in Eastman's narrative does not presume acquiescence to Anglo-American superiority, as some might assert. Rather, the manner in which Eastman takes responsibility for his own choices, such as continuing to Santee when he was sorely tempted to turn back, signifies a fully competent Native intelligence at work. Ultimately, what Eastman's story demonstrates, even if we disagree with his ideas and opinions, is that Indian people are completely capable of governing their lives. Obviously, though, from the perspective of many in the Indian Bureau, academia, and the philanthropic community, an independent Indian mind is something to fear. As Eastman states in *The Indian To-day*, "Who can say that civilization is beyond the reach of the untutored primitive man in a single generation? It did not take my father two thousand years, or ten years, to grasp its essential features; and although he never went to school a day in his life, he lived a broad-minded and self-respecting citizen. It took me about fifteen years to enter it on the plane of a professional man, and I have stayed with it ever since."[8]

In the opening chapter of *From the Deep Woods*, Eastman recounts his father's desire for his son to go to school based on his—perhaps reluctant—admiration of Anglo-American civilization. In response to his son's confusion over the white way of doing things, including their perplexing practice of reserving only one day for the Great Spirit, Jacob Eastman states, "But here is a race which has learned to weigh and measure everything, time and labor and the results of labor, and has learned to accumulate and preserve both wealth and the records of experience for future generations. You yourself know and use some of the wonderful inventions of the white man, such as guns and gunpowder, knives and hatchets, garments of every description, and there are thousands of other things both beautiful and useful." However, consistent with the Dakota perspective that the sacred and the ordinary are one, Jacob goes on to account for the white man's remarkable civilization as due to the power of the sacred being that guides and protects the whites: "Above all, they have their Great Teacher, whom they call Jesus, and he taught them to pass on their wisdom and knowledge to all other races." Eastman later observes the tendency of Anglo-Americans to want to spread their religion to everyone else but to save very little of it for themselves. However, this insight came only after decades of interacting with white society, initiated by Eastman's drive for higher education. Still, it would be unfair to suggest that Eastman and his father were thoroughly naïve about their reasons for undertaking white civilization.[9]

Not only was Eastman reticent about going to school; his uncle and especially his grandmother were skeptical about the benefits of supplanting their Dakota ways with those of the whites. After a difficult first day of school in Flandreau, Uncheedah empathizes with her grandson, saying emphatically to her son Jacob, "I never fully believed in these new manners! The Great Mystery cannot make a mistake. I say it is against our religion to change the customs that have been practiced by our people ages back—so far back that no one can remember it. Many of the school children have died, you have told me. It is not strange. You have offended Him, because you have made these children change the ways he has given us." Consistent with Dakota morals, Jacob does not openly disagree with his mother. He merely emphasizes the urgency of adapting to white society as a matter of their survival and future well-being: "We have entered upon this life, and there is no going back. Besides, one would be like a hobbled pony without learning to live like those among whom we must live." In the final analysis, regardless of the proportion of willingness versus coercion, the old ways are gone and the Dakota do not have very many choices about how to handle their circumstances. They can either fight the Americans, as they did in 1862, which resulted in death, imprisonment, and exile, or they can try to adapt to the world that now engulfs them. After nearly being hung for participating in the 1862 conflict, in addition to his eleven years in a Davenport, Iowa, prison, Jacob Eastman clearly does not have any fight left in him—only the will to survive. Therefore, he chooses to adapt.[10]

Eastman's story then makes clear, as he goes from the Santee Indian School in Flandreau, South Dakota, to the Boston University Medical College, that it is eminently possible for an American Indian, raised in traditional Dakota culture, to succeed in the Anglo-American world. To beat them at their own game, so to speak. This is not to say that the U.S. federal government was uninterested in "civilizing" Indians through education; rather, what Eastman emphasizes in the way he tells his story is that there is a way of indigenizing the process, which first demands the difficult task of learning the ways of a new culture. Initially, as the young Eastman tried to think of what he was doing in terms of the traditional male pursuits of hunting and warfare, he once moaned after being given some books to study: "I would have preferred one of grandmother's evening stories, or my uncle's account of his day's experiences in the chase." As for reading the likes of *Pilgrim's Progress*, "I thought it was the dullest hunting I had ever known!" However, there are two points at which Eastman recalls being inspired to learn more, in spite of the language and cultural barriers. The first occurs while he was still at Santee, where the Reverend Drs. Alfred L. Riggs and John P. Williamson served as kind and thoughtful mentors, whose encouragements kept Eastman on the path to which his father had directed him. We must simultaneously bear in mind that Eastman was getting his education at a time when the Americans were violating the 1868 Fort Laramie Treaty because of their lust for gold, land, and resources, causing significant strife across the Great Sioux Nation. Consequently, while

Eastman is critical of the Lakotas' decision to fight the Americans, he is aware that if any people are warlike it is the Americans, not the Indians. What Eastman, as a member of the Sioux Nation, wanted to do, contrary to prevailing stereotypes, was continue going to school: "I studied harder than most of the boys. Missionaries were poor, and the Government policy of education for the Indian had not then been developed. The white man in general had no use for the Indian. Sitting Bull and the Northern Cheyennes were still fighting in Wyoming and Montana, so that the outlook was not bright for me to pursue my studies among the whites, yet it was now my secret dream and ambition."[11]

Eastman's dream became a reality when he went to Beloit College in the fall of 1876. Even though Beloit was several hundred miles away from the site of Custer's resounding defeat, this physical distance did not preclude Eastman from being chided for his Sioux heritage. Teased and stared at for being "Sitting Bull's nephew," Eastman did not respond with anger but by turning the other cheek. He even recounts becoming good friends with the young men who initially taunted him. Indeed, integral to Eastman's story of getting an education in the classroom is an equally compelling story of learning about white society, its misconceptions about Indians, and ways for addressing this lack of knowledge or understanding. Throughout this process, Eastman gained an Ivy League education at the same time that he earned the respect and friendship of his classmates. While still a student at Dartmouth College, Eastman fondly recalled his relationship with the faculty and students: "I was treated with the greatest kindness by the president and faculty, and often encouraged to ask questions and express my own ideas. My uncle's observations in natural history, for which he had a positive genius, the Indian standpoint in sociology and political economy, these were the subject of some protracted discussions in the class room. This became so well understood, that some of my classmates who had failed to prepare their recitations would induce me to take up the time by advancing a native theory or first hand observation." Given what must have been a very congenial nature, Eastman was fortunate to have met an impressive range of influential people, some of whom he would turn to for support as he pursued his various careers, from medical doctor to political lobbyist. During the narrative on his undergraduate career, Eastman mentions at two points a list of names that illustrate the key connections he made.

At Knox College, Eastman names as his "stanch friends" S. S. McClure, John S. Phillips, Edgar A. Bancroft, Merritt Pinckney, and Henry Thomas Rainey. Then, at Dartmouth, he names, not as friends but as persons with whom he met and spoke, Matthew Arnold, Ralph Waldo Emerson, Henry Wadsworth Longfellow, and Francis Parkman. Eastman concludes his story of student life in the Northeast by mentioning his acquaintance with Herbert Welsh and Professor C. C. Painter of the Indian Rights Association, in addition to Bishops Henry B. Whipple and William H. Hare. Although Eastman does not recount his conversations with any of these men, he does state with enthusiasm, "I became convinced that the Indians had some real friends and this gave me much encouragement."[12]

Eastman's story does not end here, and things certainly did not remain as cheerful and optimistic as they seemed in Boston. For Eastman was headed to the Pine Ridge Agency during the late fall of 1890. There, of course, Eastman would learn firsthand what conditions were really like on the reservation, not to mention the inadequacies (to put it mildly) of the Indian Bureau. Eastman even had to relearn how to relate with Indian people. More specifically, Eastman had to adjust to the fact that he was no longer the youthful Ohiyesa, but a medical doctor in his early thirties. Consequently, just as whites would stare at him for the simple reason that he was an exotic attraction, so too would the Lakota stare at him, and just as hard, as they had never seen a "white doctor" who was also an Indian. But similar to his experience back east, Eastman eventually earned the respect of the people he now served. Speaking their language—or, at least, the Santee Dakota dialect—and showing an abundant familiarity with Sioux tradition, in addition to working hard for the welfare of the people, Eastman gained the trust of his patients and their community, in time becoming a sought-after voice of wisdom.[13]

Notes

Notes to Preface

1. Charles Alexander Eastman, *From the Deep Woods to Civilization* (1916; Lincoln, NE: Bison Books, 1977), 36.

2. Eastman, *From the Deep Woods,* 54–55.

3. Eastman, *From the Deep Woods,* 62,137.

4. Eastman, *From the Deep Woods,* 26.

5. Samson Occom, "A Sermon Preached at the Execution of Moses Paul, An Indian," *The Collected Writings of Samson Occom, Mohegan: Leadership and Literature in Eighteenth-Century Native America,* ed. Joanna Brooks (London: Oxford University Press, 2006), 177.

Notes to Chapter 1

1. Arthur C. Parker, ed., "Men and Women Whose Lives Count for the Red Man's Cause," *American Indian Magazine* 5.4 (Winter 1917): 270. Scott L. Pratt, *Native Pragmatism: Rethinking the Roots of American Philosophy* (Bloomington: Indiana University Press, 2002), does a commendable job of drawing out the historic connection between the work of Peirce, James, Dewey, and Native thinkers, as expressed by Native authors and an assortment of anthropological treatises coming out during the Progressive Era.

2. Most notably, McKenzie performed this analysis in *The Indian in Relation to the White Population of the United States,* which was his doctoral thesis presented to the Graduate School of the University of Pennsylvania and which McKenzie self-published in Columbus, Ohio, in 1908 while serving on the faculty at the Ohio State University. Raymond Wilson, *Ohiyesa: Charles Eastman, Santee Sioux* (Urbana: University of Illinois Press, 1983, 1999), xi.

3. Wilson, *Ohiyesa,* xi.

4. Vine Deloria, Jr., *God Is Red: A Native View of Religion* (Golden, CO: Fulcrum Publishing, 1994), 84–85. I do not, however, recall the fifth book named beyond the fact that it was a non-Sioux title. Also, the person who asked for Vine's five favorite books was a Dakota graduate student in American Studies, Kim Rossina.

5. Robert Allen Warrior, *Tribal Secrets: Recovering American Intellectual Traditions* (Minneapolis: University of Minnesota Press, 1994), 8. Drew Lopenzina, "'Good Indian': Charles Eastman and the Warrior as Civil Servant," *American Indian Quarterly* 27.3-4 (Summer & Fall 2003): 727.

6. The validity of this statement about time spent in Minnesota is limited to the modern boundaries of the state. With respect to the traditional boundaries of the homeland of the Sioux—Dakota, Lakota, and Nakota—we can claim in this context that Eastman did spend a significant amount of time throughout its expanses, which, as Eastman demonstrates, "occupied a vast territory, and in the middle of the nineteenth century they still held the southern half of Minnesota, a portion of Wisconsin and Iowa, all of the Dakotas, part of Montana, and nearly half of Nebraska"; see Charles A. Eastman, *The Indian To-day: The Past and Future of the First American* (New York: Doubleday, Page & Company, 1915), 26.

7. Eastman, *From the Deep Woods*, 139. The articles that appeared prior to *Indian Boyhood* were "Recollections of the Wild Life," *St. Nicholas: An Illustrated Magazine for Young Folks* 21 (December 1893–May 1894).

8. Deloria, *Indians in Unexpected Places*, 16.

9. These are the four components, at least, as outlined for me when I attended Dr. Thomas's last semester in American Indian Studies at the University of Arizona in spring of 1991 before he passed away that summer. For a slightly different variation on the Peoplehood Paradigm, see Tom Holm, et al., "Peoplehood: A Model for the Extension of Sovereignty in American Indian Studies," *American Indian Quarterly* 18.1 (2003): 7-24. It is worth noting that Dr. Holm was one of Dr. Thomas's longtime colleagues in Tucson, as well as another professor of mine.

10. Frederick E. Hoxie, "Exploring a Cultural Borderland: Native American Journeys of Discovery in the Early Twentieth Century," *Journal of American History* (Dec. 1992): 970. Donald Keene, *Modern Japanese Diaries: The Japanese at Home and Abroad as Revealed Through Their Diaries* (New York: Henry Holt and Company, 1995).

11. Eastman, *From the Deep Woods*, 31-32. Luther Standing Bear, *My People the Sioux* (Lincoln, NE: Bison Books, 1975), 124. Luther Standing Bear, *Land of the Spotted Eagle* (Lincoln, NE: Bison Books, 1978), 252-53.

12. Warrior, *Tribal Secrets*, 6-7, 8. Nicholas Black Elk, *Black Elk Speaks, as told through John G. Neihardt (Flaming Rainbow)* (Lincoln: Bison Books, 2000), 207.

13. Eastman, *From the Deep Woods*, 112, 114.

14. Robert Allen Warrior, *The People and the Word: Reading Native Nonfiction* (Minneapolis: University of Minnesota Press, 2005), 116. Gerald Vizenor, *Manifest Manners: Narratives on Postindian Survivance* (Lincoln, NE: Bison Books, 1999), 47, 50, 51.

15. Vizenor, *Manifest Manners*, 48-49, 51.

16. Charles A. Eastman, *Indian Boyhood* (1902; New York: Dover Books, 1971), 17-18.

17. Eastman, *Indian Boyhood*, 19.

18. Eastman, *Indian Boyhood*, 99.

19. Eastman, *Indian Boyhood*, 43-44, 49.

20. Eastman, *Indian Boyhood*, 247. Standing Bear, *My People the Sioux*, 190.

21. Eastman, *From the Deep Woods*, 3.

22. Eastman, *From the Deep Woods*, 8-9. Eastman, *Indian Boyhood*, 246.

23. Eastman, *From the Deep Woods*, 69. William Apess, "Eulogy on King Philip, as Pronounced at the Odeon, in Federal Street, Boston," in *A Son of the Forest and Other Writings*, ed. Barry O'Connell (Amherst: University of Massachusetts Press, 1997), 135. Francis Paul Prucha, *American Indian Treaties: The History of a Political Anomaly* (Berkeley: University of California Press, 1994), 156-207. Eastman, *The Indian To-day*, 20.

24. Eastman, *From the Deep Woods*, 65. Gerald Vizenor, *Fugitive Poses: Native American Indian Scenes of Absence and Presence* (Lincoln: University of Nebraska Press, 1998), 18.

25. Philip J. Deloria, *Playing Indian* (New Haven, CT: Yale University Press, 1998), 123. Vine Deloria, Jr., *Custer Died for Your Sins: An Indian Manifesto* (Norman: University of Oklahoma Press, 1988), 1.

26. Deloria, *Playing Indian*, 123-24. Eastman, *From the Deep Woods*, 195.

27. Carly Eastman Beane, "Charles Eastman: Activist for the Dakota *Wicoh'an*" (paper submitted to Dr. David Martínez, American Indian Intellectuals course, University of Minnesota, 2006).

Notes to Chapter 2

1. Charles A. Eastman, *Red Hunters and the Animal People* (New York: Harper & Brothers, 1904), v.

2. Zitkala-Sa, *Old Indian Legends* (Lincoln, NE: Bison Books, 1985), v, vi. Eastman, *Red Hunters*, vii. Arthur C. Parker, *Seneca*

Myths and Folk Tales (Lincoln, NE: Bison Books, 1989), xxiv.

3. Samuel W. Pond, *Dakota Life in the Upper Midwest* (St. Paul: Minnesota Historical Society Press, 2002), 6, 10–11, 63, 90, 173. I am using the most recent edition of Pond's classic study of the Santee Dakota.

4. Charles A. Eastman, *Indian Scout Craft and Lore* (1914; New York: Dover Publications, Inc., 1974), 176–77. Standing Bear, *Land of the Spotted Eagle*, 13, 15–17. Education was a starkly different story at the Carlisle Indian School, which was run by the notorious Richard Pratt and where, as Standing Bear recalls, "punishment" and "humiliation" were the driving forces. School was more about "staying in line" than "learning."

5. Frederick E. Hoxie, ed., *Talking Back to Civilization: Indian Voices from the Progressive Era* (Boston, MA: Bedford, 2001), viii.

6. See Pond, *Dakota Life*, 81, and James R. Walker, *Lakota Society* (Lincoln, NE: Bison Books, 1992), 13–18. Roy W. Meyer, *History of the Santee Sioux: United States Indian Policy on Trial* (Lincoln: University of Nebraska Press, 1993), ix.

7. Zitkala-Sa, *Old Indian Legends*, vi.

8. I use the orthography James R. Walker did when he originally recorded the Lakota for his fieldwork, beginning in the latter nineteenth century. It is easier to read than the diacritics Ella Deloria actually used in *Dakota Texts*. Ella Deloria, *Dakota Texts* (Lincoln, NE: Bison Books, 2006), xxv.

9. Deloria, *Dakota Texts*, xxvi. Standing Bear, *Land of the Spotted Eagle*, 27.

10. Eastman, *Red Hunters*, vii–viii. Charles A. Eastman, *The Soul of the Indian: An Interpretation* (1911; Lincoln, NE: Bison Books, 1980), ix–x. Standing Bear, *Land of the Spotted Eagle*, 27.

11. Eastman, *Red Hunters*, vii, 225. The Pequot intellectual William Apess said something similar when he wrote in 1831, "But to my experience—and the reader knows full well that experience is the best schoolmaster, for what we have experienced, that we know, and all the world cannot possibly beat it out of us"; see *A Son of the Forest*, 8–9.

12. Eastman, *Red Hunters*, 123–42.

13. Eastman, *Red Hunters*, 37–38.

14. Eastman, *Red Hunters*, 89, 94–95, 97–98.

15. Eastman, *Red Hunters*, 100–101. Eastman, *Indian Boyhood*, 215.

16. Eastman, *Red Hunters*, 102–3, 104–5. Eastman, *Indian Scout Craft and Lore*, 1–2.

17. Proof of this "protection" is seen in the fact that Eastman never succumbs to either alcoholism or materialism.

One of the recurring features of contemporary Eastman scholarship is debating the extent to which Elaine "coauthored" Eastman's books. This is mostly based on Eastman's admission in *From the Deep Woods*, "The present [book] is the eighth that I have done, always with the devoted cooperation of my wife. Although but one book, 'Wigwam Evenings,' bears both our names, we have worked together, she in the little leisure remaining to the mother of six children, and I in the intervals of lecturing and other employment." Some have taken this to mean that Elaine deserved coauthoring credit. However, such dilemmas may be as frustrating as trying to separate Socrates from Plato or, more appropriately here, Black Elk from Neihardt. In light of my own analyses of Eastman's writings, I have no doubt that these are rightfully labeled as Eastman's own books. There are simply too many stories, experiences, and insights that could only have come from someone living the life of an Indian in America. In a recent book on Elaine Goodale Eastman, the author states, "Elaine was the one who actually put the words on paper—*the only words the publishers would ever see*" (emphasis added). This is a little hard to believe, considering that Eastman clearly claims to be the author of the "sketches" that became *Indian Boyhood*. While it is likely the case that Elaine facilitated her husband's efforts at communicating with an Anglo-American audience—which is still an arduous task for many a Native author—there is no reason to assume that we are dealing with anything but works by a Dakota author. See Eastman, *From the Deep Woods*, 185–86, and Theodore D. Sargent, *The Life of Elaine Goodale Eastman* (Lincoln: University of Nebraska Press, 2005), 86–91.

18. Eastman, *Indian Boyhood*, 116–17.

19. Eastman, *Indian Boyhood*, 101–5.

20. Eastman, *Indian Boyhood*, 105, 106–7.

21. Eastman, *Indian Boyhood*, 107–8.

22. Eastman, *Indian Boyhood*, 126–27. Although ohunkakan refer to the myths that comprise the Creation story, insofar as ohunkakan rely on faith for their being regarded as true, the colloquial use of the term emphasizes the amazement on behalf of the listener. Ella Deloria (*Dakota Texts*) explains, "When someone wishes to express incredulity, he says *ohu'kaka s'e*—How like an *ohu'kaka!* When a person is talking nonsense, bragging or making wild promises, the people say, *ise'he'huka'kahe lo'!*—That one is merely telling an *ohu'kaka*; don't mind him! These statements indicate, I think, the light in which such tales are regarded. They are intended to amuse and entertain, but not to be believed" (ix). This is especially true of the kind of stories Deloria collected for *Dakota Texts* and categorized as ohunkakan, which were limited to trickster stories about Iktomi, Double-Face, and Coyote. Deloria also includes one Stone Boy story that is comparable to the one Eastman recalls Smoky Day telling him. Aside from being entertaining, such stories provide valuable life lessons that are even more important than whether or not one can prove that a particular story really happened. See Eastman, *The Soul of the Indian*, 121, 122–30. Eastman, of course, like other Indian intellectuals of the time, actually sought U.S. citizenship for all Indians, which they did not have universally in 1911. One might naturally think that citizenship and decolonization are incompatible and would certainly be correct to the extent that citizenship means surrendering some or all of one's sovereign status. However, what Eastman clearly has in common with today's decolonization movement is the desire to free Indian people from any and all forms of oppression, which surely characterized the Indian Bureau and its autocratic approach to the "Indian problem." Eastman wanted to give Indians the freedom and power to solve their own problems—without government dependency.

Waziyatawin Angela Wilson, *Remember This! Dakota Decolonization and the Eli Taylor Narratives* (Lincoln: University of Nebraska Press, 2005), 15.

23. Eastman, *Indian Boyhood*, 109–13.

24. Eastman, *Indian Boyhood*, 113–15.

25. Eastman, *Indian Boyhood*, 115–16. The paramount concern for kinship ties, even in the most distressful times, is a value possessed by not only mythic characters but also historical figures, as demonstrated in the stories Eastman told of Little Crow and Tawasuota in *Old Indian Days* (Lincoln: University of Nebraska Press, 1991) and *Indian Heroes and Great Chieftains* (Lincoln, NE: Bison Books, 1991).

26. Eastman, *Indian Boyhood*, 116–17.

27. Pond, *Dakota Life*, 81–82.

28. Eastman, *The Soul of the Indian*, 119–20.

29. Deloria, *God Is Red*, 85.

30. Eastman, *From the Deep Woods*, 71. Eastman, *The Soul of the Indian*, 4–5.

31. (Waziyatawin) Angela Cavender Wilson, "Grandmother to Granddaughter: Generations of Oral History in a Dakota Family," *Natives and Academics: Researching and Writing about American Indians*, ed. Devon A. Mihesuah (Lincoln: University of Nebraska Press, 1998), 28–29.

According to Anna Lee Stensland in "Charles Alexander Eastman: Sioux Storyteller and Historian," *American Indian Quarterly* 3.3 (Autumn 1977), allowing for innovation is one of the three things that problematizes Eastman's writings. More specifically, Stensland observes that Eastman was "an Indian-thinking author writing for white readers," a consequence of which is that he was not conscientious about separating "historical fact from legend." In turn, Eastman sometimes also failed "to separate the historical incidents and stories told in the tribe from his own created short stories" (199).

32. Janine Pease Pretty On Top, "Introduction," *Light on the Indian World: The Essential Writings of Charles Eastman (Ohiyesa)* (Bloomington, IN: World Wisdom, 2002), xv-xvi.

33. Pretty On Top, *Light on the Indian World*, 101-2.

34. Pretty On Top, *Light on the Indian World*, 103-6.

35. Pretty On Top, *Light on the Indian World*, 106-8. Uncheedah's alleged paroxysm of empathy for her grandson is read by David J. Carlson in a rather curious way. Carlson states, "The chapter then shifts to a surprising, speculative digression (clearly outside of the autobiographical mode) in which the narrator imagines Hakadah's grandmother nearly relenting in her insistence that the boy sacrifice his beloved pet. (This odd addition to the autobiographical narrative seems addressed primarily to some members of Eastman's middle-class audience, who may have found the entire scene distasteful)," "'Indian for a While': Charles Eastman's *Indian Boyhood* and the Discourse of Allotment," *American Indian Quarterly* 25.4 (Fall 2001): 611. Considering that one of Eastman's major concerns as both a writer and an activist is dealing with Indian stereotypes, Carlson fails to entertain the idea that Eastman wanted to demonstrate that Indians were capable of a range of emotions, as opposed to simply being wooden and stoic all of the time. In chapter eleven, "The Laughing Philosopher," Eastman addresses the latter stereotype more directly by showing the reader that humor is an important facet of Indian cultures: *Indian Boyhood*, 108-10.

36. Eastman, *Indian Boyhood*, 110-12. Carlson states, perhaps a bit too cynically, "At this moment, the narrative collapses beneath a final irony, for the reader knows that Hakadah will become the physician Charles Eastman and not a great Santee warrior," "Indian for a While," 611. Considering that a "warrior" was defined as much by being brave in the face of adversity as by actually fighting in a physical confrontation, Carlson's criticism comes across as more than a bit ethnocentric. Just because Eastman did not take to the warpath against either the Ojibwe or the U.S. Army did not mean that Eastman was not a "great Santee warrior" in other ways. As Carlson should have recalled, when Eastman goes to the Santee Normal School, as recounted in *From the Deep Woods to Civilization*, his father convinced him to go in the first place by favorably comparing the path to school with the warpath.

37. James R. Walker, *Lakota Belief and Ritual* (Lincoln, NE: Bison Books, 1991), 77. Walker holds the distinction of taking over as the government physician at the Pine Ridge Agency in 1896, not long after Eastman left for political reasons. Stensland, "Sioux Storyteller," 207.

38. Carlson, "Indian for a While," 611. It may seem apparent at this point that there is a peculiar bias against Eastman at the *American Indian Quarterly*.

39. Eastman, *Indian Boyhood*, 53, for quote "his principal occupation", 95-96. We have to always remember that Eastman is not a holy man, like Black Elk, George Sword, or Lame Deer. Eastman has to talk about sa-

cred things in a different way, one that is suitable to his knowledge of and position to sacred things.

Notes to Chapter 3

1. Eastman, *The Indian To-day*, 26.

2. William W. Warren, *History of the Ojibway People* (St. Paul: Minnesota Historical Society Press, 1984), 176.

3. Warren, *History of the Ojibway People*, 176–78.

4. Charles J. Kappler, *Indian Affairs: Laws and Treaties, Volume II* (Washington, DC: Government Printing Office, 1904), 250. Eastman, *The Indian To-day*, 27.

5. Meyer, *History of the Santee Sioux*, 40. Kappler, *Indian Affairs*, 250–53.

6. George Copway, *The Traditional History and Characteristic Sketches of the Ojibway Nation* (Honolulu, HI: University Press of the Pacific, 2002), 58, 59.

7. Eastman, *Indian Boyhood*, 6.

8. Copway, *Traditional History*, 56–57.

9. Eastman, *Indian Boyhood*, 103, 104.

10. Eastman, *Indian Boyhood*, 106.

11. Eastman, *Indian Boyhood*, 56, 93.

12. Eastman, *Indian Boyhood*, 24–25, 29.

13. Eastman, *Indian Boyhood*, 29. Katherine Elizabeth Beane, "Being Christian and Native: The Impact of Religion on My Family" (paper submitted to Dr. David Martínez, American Indian Intellectuals course, University of Minnesota, 2006).

14. Eastman, *Indian Boyhood*, 22–24.

15. Eastman, *Old Indian Days*, 19.

16. Eastman, *The Soul of the Indian*, 158–60, 167–70.

17. Eastman, *Indian Scout Craft and Lore*, 23–24.

18. Eastman, *The Indian To-day*, 13.

19. Eastman, *The Indian To-day*, 14–15.

20. Eastman, *The Indian To-day*, 15–16.

21. Eastman, *The Indian To-day*, 107–8. For a contemporary account of the historic problems at White Earth, see Melissa L. Meyer, *The White Earth Tragedy: Ethnicity and Dispossession at a Minnesota Anishinaabe*
Reservation (Lincoln, NE: Bison Books, 1994).

22. Eastman, *The Indian To-day*, 46.

23. Eastman, *The Indian To-day*, 46–48.

24. Eastman, *The Indian To-day*, 173–74.

25. Eastman, *From the Deep Woods*, 41–42, 142.

26. Eastman, *From the Deep Woods*, 166–67. Wilson, *Ohiyesa*, 150. Wilson discovered the Pennsylvania connection in *Dartmouth Alumni Magazine* (Dec. 1910), Baker Library, Dartmouth College, Hanover, NH. I am very grateful to Dr. Robert W. Preucel, Associate Curator of the American Section of the University of Pennsylvania Museum of Archaeology and Anthropology, who, in collaboration with museum archivist Alex Pezzati, uncovered this vital bit of information about Heye for me. Author unknown, *Museum Journal* 1.1 (1910): 11–12; this particular citation came to me courtesy of Dr. Patricia Nietfeld.

27. Eastman, *From the Deep Woods*, 168.

28. Eastman, *From the Deep Woods*, 171–73.

29. Eastman, *From the Deep Woods*, 177–78.

30. Eastman, *From the Deep Woods*, 178, 180, 181.

31. Eastman, *From the Deep Woods*, 170–71. For a contemporary treatment of this event, see Gerald Vizenor, *Bear Island: The War at Sugar Point* (Minneapolis: University of Minnesota Press, 2006).

32. Eastman, *Indian Heroes*, 226.

33. Eastman, *Indian Heroes*, 226–27.

34. Eastman, *Indian Heroes*, 228.

35. Eastman, *Indian Heroes*, 229–30.

36. Eastman, *Indian Heroes*, 230–33.

37. Eastman, *Indian Heroes*, 235–36.

38. Eastman, *Indian Heroes*, 236–38.

39. Eastman, *Indian Heroes*, 238–40.

40. Eastman, *Indian Heroes*, 240, 241.

Notes to Chapter 4

1. Hazel W. Hertzberg, *The Search for an American Indian Identity: Modern Pan-Indian Movements* (Syracuse, NY: Syracuse University Press, 1971), 298.

2. Lucy Maddox, *Citizen Indians: Native American Intellectuals, Race and Reform* (Ithaca, NY: Cornell University Press, 2005), 132.

3. Eastman, *The Indian To-day*, 130-31. Francis Paul Prucha, *The Great Father: The United States Government and the American Indians* (Lincoln: University of Nebraska Press, 1986), 263-79. Standing Bear, *My People the Sioux*, 242. Wilson, *Ohiyesa*, 106-16.

4. Eastman, *From the Deep Woods*, 57-58, 189. Eastman, *The Soul of the Indian*, 39.

5. Eastman, *From the Deep Woods*, 195.

6. For a look at other historically important pan-Indian organizations, see Steven J. Crum, "Almost Invisible: The Brotherhood of North American Indians (1911) and the League of North American Indians (1935)," *Wicazo Sa* 21.1 (Spring 2006): 43-59. For a very different take on the origin of the Society of American Indians, see David Anthony Tyeeme Clark, "Fayette Avery McKenzie Was Not the Father, Nor Was Arthur Caswell Parker 'Most Important': Complicating the Origins of the Society of American Indians," in *Representing Indians: Indigenous Fugitives and the Society of American Indians in the Making of Common Culture* (PhD diss., Department of American Studies, University of Kansas, 2004), 67-95. Eastman, *The Indian To-day*, 131. Hertzberg, *American Indian Identity*, 36.

7. Hertzberg, *American Indian Identity*, 38. Eastman, *From the Deep Woods*, 92, 98-99, 125.

8. Eastman, *From the Deep Woods*, 142-50.

9. Eastman, *From the Deep Woods*, 152-53, 157. Wilson, *Ohiyesa*, 92-104.

10. Eastman, *From the Deep Woods*, 163-65. *U.S. Statutes at Large* (Washington, DC: Government Printing Office), 24:388-91, 34: 182-83.

11. The Society of American Indians, "Constitution," *Quarterly Journal of the Society of American Indians* 1.2 (April-June 1913): 223.

12. Eastman, *The Indian To-day*, 132-33. Arthur C. Parker, "Editorial Comment," *Quarterly Journal of the Society of American Indians* 1.1 (April 15, 1913): 3. Eastman, *From the Deep Woods*, 1, 59-60. For an analysis of Eastman as public servant, see Lopenzina, "Good Indian," 727-57. Hertzberg, *American Indian Identity*, 239-84.

13. Parker, "Editorial Comment" (1913), 6, 8. Dennison Wheelock, "Not an Indian Problem but a Problem of Race Separation," *Quarterly Journal of the Society of American Indians* 1.4 (October-December 1913): 371.

14. Arthur C. Parker, "The Menace of the Fraudulent Wild West Show," *Quarterly Journal of the Society of American Indians* 2.3 (July-September 1914): 175.

15. Parker, "Menace of Wild West Show," 175. Luther Standing Bear recalls the difficult task he faced at keeping the Indian performers sober during Buffalo Bill's European tour, *My People the Sioux*, 248-67. Chauncey Yellow Robe, "The Menace of the Wild West Show," *Quarterly Journal of the Society of American Indians* 2.3 (July-September 1914): 225.

16. Charles A. Eastman, "The Indian's Gift to the Nation," *Quarterly Journal of the Society of American Indians* 3.1 (January-March 1915): 20-21.

17. Eastman, "Indian's Gift to the Nation," 22-23. As is well known, Sequoyah developed a syllabary, not an alphabet.

18. Eastman, "Indian's Gift to the Nation," 17, 23.

19. Charles A. Eastman, "The Indian's Health Problem," *American Indian Magazine* 4.2 (April-June 1916): 139.

20. Eastman, "The Indian's Health Problem," 142, 144-45. Intermarriage between Indians and whites was once even regulated by law, as it was in 1888; see *U.S. Statutes at Large*, 25:392. For an excellent analysis of the complications behind the racial categories of "mixed-blood," "full-blood," and "Indian," see Eva Marie Garroutte, *Real Indians: Identity and the Survival of Native America* (Berkeley: University of California Press, 2003).

21. Charles A. Eastman, "The Sioux of Yesterday and Today," *American Indian Magazine* 5.4 (Winter 1917): 234–35.

22. Eastman, "Sioux of Yesterday," 238.

23. Eastman, "Sioux of Yesterday," 239.

24. *Lincoln (NE) Daily Star,* "The Truth of the Wounded Knee Massacre," *American Indian Magazine* 5.4 (Winter 1917): 240–52.

25. Parker, ed., "Men and Women Whose Lives Count," 263–64, 269.

26. Arthur C. Parker, "In the Editorial Sanctum," *American Indian Magazine* 6.1 (Spring 1918): 41.

27. Charles A. Eastman, "The Indian's Plea for Freedom," *American Indian Magazine* 6.4 (Winter 1919): 163.

28. Eastman, "Indian's Plea for Freedom," 163, 164.

29. Zitkala-Sa, *American Indian Stories, Legends, and Other Writings,* ed. Cathy N. Davidson and Ada Norris (New York: Penguin Books, 2003), 244.

30. Standing Bear, *My People the Sioux,* 278, 279, 285–86.

31. Arthur C. Parker, "The American Indian—What Is He?" *Quarterly Journal of the Society of American Indians* 2.2 (April–June 1914): 110. Eastman, "Indian's Plea for Freedom," 164. Kappler, *Indian Affairs,* 591. Charles A. Eastman, "A Review of the Indian Citizenship Bills," *American Indian Magazine* 6.4 (Winter 1919): 182–83.

32. Wilson, *Ohiyesa,* 161–62. Zitkala-Sa, "Editorial Comment (Summer 1919)," *American Indian Stories,* 206.

33. Charles A. Eastman, "Justice for the Sioux," *American Indian Magazine* 7.2 (Summer 1919): 79. Zitkala-Sa, *American Indian Stories,* 244. For an analysis of what such a racist presumption has done to federal Indian law and policy, see Robert A. Williams, Jr., *Like a Loaded Weapon: The Rehnquist Court, Indian Rights, and the Legal History of Racism in America* (Minneapolis: University of Minnesota Press, 2005).

34. Eastman, "Justice for the Sioux," 80–81.

35. Charles A. Eastman, "The American Eagle: An Indian Symbol," *American Indian Magazine* 7.2 (Summer 1919): 91–92.

36. "Afternoon Session, October 5, 1.45 P.M.," *Quarterly Journal of the Society of American Indians* 1.2 (April–June 1913): 220.

37. Hertzberg, *American Indian Identity,* 44. For a very thoughtful and insightful analysis of Parker's leadership role in the Society of American Indians, see Joy Porter, *To Be Indian: The Life of Iroquois-Seneca Arthur Caswell Parker* (Norman: University of Oklahoma Press, 2001), 91–142.

38. Carlos Montezuma, "Let My People Go," pamphlet, 1915. During October 1972 in Minneapolis, Minnesota, the American Indian Movement promulgated the "Trail of Broken Treaties 20-Point Position Paper," in which point number 14 called for the abolition of the Bureau of Indian Affairs by 1976 (see http://www.aimovement.org/archives/index.html); Vine Deloria, Jr., stated in 1974, "The last refuge of those who would continue to keep the tribes in a condition of dependence vis-à-vis the U.S. is the argument that the Indians have neither the education nor the sophistication to manage their own affairs and shape their destiny. One finds this mentality for the most part throughout the Bureau of Indian Affairs administrative apparatus, which controls the lives of Indians in such excruciating detail. These people, of course, have a heavy vested interest in the preservation of the tutelary parent-child concept of the B.I.A.-Indian relationship": *Behind the Trail of Broken Treaties: An Indian Declaration of Independence* (Austin: University of Texas Press, 1985), 174–75.

39. Montezuma, "Let My People Go." Robert K. Thomas, "Colonialism: Classic and Internal," *New University Thought* 4 (1966–67): 39–43.

40. Montezuma, "Let My People Go."

41. Montezuma, "Let My People Go." Apess, *A Son of the Forest,* 10. Apess's refer-

ence to Adam only makes sense, as Barry O'Connell explains in a footnote, upon "Apess's belief that Native Americans were one of the Ten Lost Tribes of Israel. As such, they were 'Semites,' and thus their complexions were more like Adam's than those of Gentile Euro-Americans," 10n4.

42. Eastman, *From the Deep Woods*, 159. According to Raymond Wilson, the committee in question was the House Subcommittee on Indian Affairs: *Ohiyesa*, 104n21.

43. Francis La Flesche, among other things, is well known for having co-authored with Alice Fletcher *The Omaha Tribe*, for which he is credited as an insider to Omaha society. However, as Robin Ridington observes, some "say that La Flesche was not an Omaha because his father was adopted rather than born into the Elk clan, thus making Francis only an adopted member of the tribe." Instead, they regard him as Osage. Ridington, with the corroboration of Dennis Hastings, an Omaha elder, maintains his Omaha identity, stating, "Because Omaha clan membership passes through the father's line, the fact that his mother was a full-blooded Omaha would not have any bearing on his clan." See Ridington and Dennis Hastings, *Blessing for a Long Time: The Sacred Pole of the Omaha Tribe* (Lincoln, NE: Bison Books, 1997), xxiii.

44. Hertzberg, *American Indian Identity*, 263. Zitkala-Sa, "The Menace of Peyote," *American Indian Stories*, 240. The Hayden bill was passed; however, it was not enacted into law; see Hertzberg, *American Indian Identity*, 271. Deloria, *Custer Died for Your Sins*, 113.

45. Gertrude Bonnin, "Editorial Comment," *American Indian Magazine* 6.3 (July–September 1918): 113.

46. *Minneapolis Morning Tribune*, October 2, 1919, 1.

47. By contrast with today, in the case of local papers in the Twin Cities, such as the *Star Tribune*, the modern descendent of the *Minneapolis Morning Tribune*, the tendency is to cover recurring news pertaining to crime and poverty. For example, the way in which the urban Indian community of Little Earth, which resides in the heart of the Phillips neighborhood of Minneapolis, has been treated by the *Star Tribune* during the years 1996-2006 is symptomatic of a national trend in journalism regarding American Indians. Lora Pabst, later a reporter for the *Star Tribune*, wrote in a research paper she did while still a student at the University of Minnesota: "According to *Star Tribune* archives, there have been 19 articles written about crimes committed at Little Earth since 1998. The articles focus on major crimes, mostly homicide. While the stories themselves do not bear any racist tirades about how violent Native Americans are, they are still damaging to the community. Many of the statements made in the articles are true, but it is the context which they fall in that presents the problem. Since most of the crime stories written about Little Earth are major crimes, they receive more media attention and are displayed more prominently in newspapers. This is standard practice in journalism; murders usually receive more attention than robberies or smaller crimes. But the problem with this is that the average reader who picks up the *Star Tribune* will only see the section cover crime story with a big headline. When they are confronted with these stories, over time they will develop an idea of what happens at Little Earth. This issue affects many minority communities. It is especially damaging to the Native American community because there is so little written about them that when flashy crime stories come out, that is all the public seems to remember."

48. *Minneapolis Morning Tribune*, October 2, 1919, 1.

49. Charles A. Eastman, "Opening Address," *American Indian Magazine* 7.3 (Fall 1919): 145-46, 148.

Notes to Chapter 5

1. Eastman, *Indian Boyhood*, 200. "Land of Sky-blue Water" is Eastman's translation of the traditional name for the Dakota homeland, *Mnisota Makoce*, which is currently translated alternately as "Land Where the Waters Reflect the Skies," "Where the Cloudy Waters Reflect the Skies," and "Where the Waters Reflect the Heavens." For a very long time this book bore the lyrical title *From the Land of Sky-Blue Waters: Charles Eastman and the World of the American Indian*, which I presented to a variety of audiences, including several Dakotas, who always responded quite favorably to it. Unfortunately, as I began revising the manuscript, readers of a certain age and disposition insisted on recalling a peculiar television advertisement for Hamm's Beer. Not being from the very specific demographic that bore this memory, I had to look up the commercial in question on http:// youtube.com, where I watched a happy cartoon of a bear dance to a tune that was published in 1909 by Nelle Richmond Eberhart, who wrote the lyrics, and Charles Wakefield Cadman, who wrote the music. Their song was ominously titled "From the Land of Sky-Blue Water," which appeared in a book titled *Four American Indian Songs* (Boston, MA: White-Smith, 1909). However, during the so-called "golden age" of television, Hamm's Brewery appropriated the song and turned it into a jingle, which sang, set to a stereotypical tom-tom beat, "From the Land of Sky-Blue Waters/From the land of pines, lofty balsams/Comes the beer refreshing/Hamm's the beer refreshing." My intention with the original title of my book was to reappropriate what had been stolen from Eastman and the Dakota into America's alcoholic imagination. For better or worse, the inebriated nostalgia of some forced me to have second thoughts about the title, hence the change.

2. Prucha, *American Indian Treaties*, 24. Charles A. Eastman and Elaine Goodale Eastman, *Wigwam Evenings: Sioux Folk Tales Retold* (1909; Lincoln, NE: Bison Books, 1990), 146.

3. Eastman, "Opening Address," 149-50.

4. Arthur C. Parker, *The History of the Seneca Indians* (Port Washington, NY: Ira J. Friedman, Inc., 1967), 126-27. With respect to Parker's choice of words, namely *holocaust*, what may seem unexpected was not without further precedent. See Standing Bear, *Land of the Spotted Eagle*, 175, in which he summarizes the overwhelming tendency for destructiveness from white civilization: "With a sword, the white leader urged his warriors into conflict; cannon ball mowed down our women and children; the wicked gun brought the last buffalo to its knees; the bayonet pierced the side of our beloved Crazy Horse; dynamite desecrated nature by destroying the marvelous dams of the patient beaver, and in one holocaust two hundred Indian martyrs died at the stake; and whiskey—it is an avalanche still on its way." A footnote states that the "holocaust" in question refers to the burning of Pueblo Indians by the Spanish.

5. Eastman, *From the Deep Woods*, 117.

6. Eastman, *From the Deep Woods*, 112.

7. Even in Waziyatawin Angela Wilson's much-heralded *In the Footsteps of Our Ancestors*, Eastman barely merits a single mention by one of the contributors, Gabrielle Wynde Tateyuskanskan. See Wilson, *In the Footsteps of Our Ancestors: The Dakota Commemorative Marches of the 21st Century* (St. Paul, MN: Living Justice Press, 2006), 170.

8. Arthur C. Parker, "The Sioux Outbreak of 1862," *American Indian Magazine* 5.4 (Winter 1917): 228, 229.

9. Parker, "Sioux Outbreak of 1862," 229.

10. Carol Chomsky, "The United States-Dakota Wars Trials: A Study in Military Injustice," *Stanford Law Review* 43.1 (November 1990): 14.

11. Eastman, *Indian Boyhood*. Wilson, *Ohiyesa*, 132.

12. For recent work done on the Dakota

experience during the 1862 U.S.-Dakota War, see Wilson, *Remember This!* and Wilson, *In the Footsteps of Our Ancestors.* Eastman, *The Indian To-day,* 176-77.

13. Eastman, *Indian Boyhood,* 11.

14. Eastman, *Indian Boyhood,* 11-12. Henry H. Sibley, fur trader, legislator, and businessman, was also the first governor of Minnesota, serving from May 24, 1858, to January 2, 1860. For more on his role in the 1862 conflict, see Meyer, *History of the Santee Sioux,* 109-32; see also Gary Clayton Anderson, *Little Crow: Spokesman for the Sioux* (St. Paul: Minnesota Historical Society Press, 1986), 153-76.

15. Eastman, *Indian Boyhood,* 13-14. Eastman expands upon the Dakota concept of kinship in chapter two, "The Family Altar," in *The Soul of the Indian,* 27-50. Ella Deloria, *Speaking of Indians* (Lincoln, NE: Bison Books, 1998), 25.

16. Eastman, *Indian Boyhood,* 15,16. Standing Bear, *Land of the Spotted Eagle,* 48.

17. See "Treaty with the Sioux—Mdewakanton and Wahpakoota bands, 1851," in Kappler, *Indian Affairs,* 591-93. Eastman, *Old Indian Days,* 115,116. Eastman, *From the Deep Woods,* 35-39.

18. Eastman, *Old Indian Days,* 117-18.

19. Eastman, *Old Indian Days,* 120. James Lynd worked for Andrew Myrick, one of the more important traders in the area, who infamously responded to the Dakotas' complaints about their dire situation on the reservation, "So far as I am concerned, if they are hungry, let them eat grass"; see Meyer, *History of the Santee Sioux,* 116. Eastman's account is markedly different from the one recounted, surprisingly, in a much later source. Gary Clayton Anderson states, "At a signal, the warriors raised their motley array of rifles and shotguns and opened an indiscriminate fire, many weapons being discharged into each trade house. James W. Lynd, a clerk, fell first... Moments before, the warrior who killed him was heard muttering in an excited fashion: 'Now I will kill

the dog who wouldn't give me credit'"; see Anderson, *Little Crow,* 135.

20. For a full account of the Christian Dakota experience, see Elden Lawrence, *The Peace Seekers: Indian Christians and the Dakota Conflict* (Sioux Falls, SD: Pine Hill Press, 2005). Eastman, *Old Indian Days,* 122.

21. Eastman, *Old Indian Days,* 126-27.

22. Anderson, *Little Crow,* 143.

23. Eastman, *Old Indian Days,* 127.

24. Eastman, *Old Indian Days,* 128,129,130. Eastman, *From the Deep Woods,* 56-57.

25. Eastman, *Old Indian Days,* 131-33.

26. Eastman, *Old Indian Days,* 219.

27. Eastman, *Old Indian Days,* 222-24.

28. Eastman, *Old Indian Days,* 224-28. Meyer, *History of the Santee Sioux,* 42.

29. See Deloria, *Custer Died for Your Sins.*

30. Eastman, *The Indian To-day,* 10-11.

31. Beatrice Medicine, "North American Indigenous Women and Cultural Domination," in *Learning to Be an Anthropologist and Remaining "Native": Selected Writings* (Urbana: University of Illinois Press, 2001), 155. Eastman, *The Indian To-day,* 15-16.

32. See Meyer, *History of the Santee Sioux,* 24-47. Eastman, *The Indian To-day,* 26-27. See Article 2, "The Treaty with the Sioux, Etc.,1825," in Kappler, *Indian Affairs,* 250-51.

33. See Meyer, *History of the Santee Sioux,* 97-101. Eastman, *The Indian To-day,* 27-28.

34. Eastman, *The Indian To-day,* 28-29.

35. Eastman, *The Indian To-day,* 29-30. Black Elk, *Black Elk Speaks,* 15.

36. Eastman, *The Indian To-day,* 30-31.

37. For a fuller account of this era of federal Indian policy, see Prucha, *The Great Father,* 152-66. Eastman, *The Indian To-day,* 49-50. Chomsky, "The United States-Dakota War Trials," 14-15, 29.

38. Eastman, *From the Deep Woods,* 3,136.

39. Eastman, *From the Deep Woods,* 122-23, 136-38. For the comparison I mention here, see 52,62,65,74.

40. Eastman, *From the Deep Woods,* 151-52.

41. Eastman, *Indian Heroes,* 1.

42. Eastman, *Indian Heroes,* 44-45.

43. Eastman, *Indian Heroes*, 46-50. See Kappler, *Indian Affairs*, 591-93.

44. Eastman, *Indian Heroes*, 52-53.

45. Anderson, *Little Crow*, 167, 181. Eastman, *Indian Heroes*, 53-55.

46. Eastman, *Indian Heroes*, 61-62, 66-67. See also Meyer, *History of the Santee Sioux*, 35.

47. Eastman, *From the Deep Woods*, 187. Eastman, *The Soul of the Indian*, 24.

48. Hertzberg, *American Indian Identity*, 324.

Notes to Epilogue

1. Vine Deloria, Jr., passed away on November 13, 2005. He was seventy-two.

2. Vine Deloria, Jr., e-mail message to author, February 12, 2004.

3. Clara Sue Kidwell and Alan Velie, *Native American Studies* (Lincoln: University of Nebraska Press, 2005), 1. I spoke with Clara Sue at length about the manuscript form of *Native American Studies*, which she asked me to read while we were both on leave at the Newberry Library in Chicago, Illinois, during 2003-4. I was working on my Eastman project, while she labored over a book on Choctaw history. We often took a break together in the Newberry's lunchroom, where we ate Fritos corn chips and mulled over one another's ideas and concerns. With regard to the above book in question, Clara Sue and I spent a lengthy lunch at Papa Milano talking about what makes American Indian Studies a unique scholarly field. AIS is not a discipline but a "way of doing things." It is something more than individuals trained in mainstream disciplines who happen to be interested in Indians. AIS is ultimately grounded in indigenous ways of knowing and experiencing the world.

4. Hertzberg, *American Indian Identity*, 213-14.

5. Deloria, *Custer Died for Your Sins*, 225-42.

6. Paula Gunn Allen, *The Sacred Hoop: Recovering the Feminine in American Indian Traditions* (Boston, MA: Beacon Press, 1985), 217.

7. Gertrude Bonnin, "Secretary's Report in Brief," *American Indian Magazine* 6.3 (Autumn 1918): 124.

8. Eastman, *The Indian To-day*, 100.

9. Eastman, *From the Deep Woods*, 8.

10. Eastman, *From the Deep Woods*, 15, 24-25.

11. Eastman, *From the Deep Woods*, 44, 49.

12. Eastman, *From the Deep Woods*, 52-53, 58, 68-69, 72, 75.

13. Eastman, *From the Deep Woods*, 76.

Index

alcoholism: Beatrice Medicine on, 140; Charles Eastman on, 139-40, 169n17; compared with peyotism, 117-18

Allen, Paula Gunn, *Sacred Hoop, The,* 157-58

American Christianity, 147

"American Eagle: An Indian Symbol, The" (Eastman): on eagle's original meaning, 110; on treaties, 108

American Indian Association, 89

American Indian Magazine: "American Eagle: An Indian Symbol, The," 108, 110; on Charles Eastman, 3; Charles Eastman's contributions to, 94, 108; feature on Charles Eastman, 103-4; "Justice for the Sioux" (Eastman), 108-9; "Sioux of Yesterday and Today, The," 100-101; special issue on the Sioux, 127-28

American Indian Quarterly: analysis of Charles Eastman's intellectual agenda, 6; bias against Charles Eastman at, 171n38

American progressivism, 85

Anderson, Gary Clayton, author, 136-37

Apess, William: on importance of experience, 169n11; *Indian's Looking-Glass for the White Man, An,* 123; on "Semites," 174-75n41; *Son of the Forest, A,* 20, 113

Battle of Greasy Grass, 13; *see also* Battle of the Little Bighorn

Battle of the Little Bighorn, 101-2; *see also* Battle of Greasy Grass

Beane, Carly Eastman, descendent of John Eastman, 24

Beane, Katherine Elizabeth, descendent of John Eastman, 64-65

Bi-aus-wah, Ojibwe leader, 58

Black Elk, Nicholas, Lakota elder: on 1868 treaty, 143; on Battle of Greasy Grass, 13; quote from "Black Elk Speaks," 83

Black Hills: "Black Hills agreement of 1877," 109; Lakota interest in reclaiming, 108-9; Red Cloud and, 143-44

blood quantum, 71

Boggimogishig, Ojibwe war chief, 75, 76

Bonga, Simon, Ojibwe, 68

Bonnin, Gertrude, author: *American Indian Stories,* 161-62; *see also* Zitkala-Sa

Boy Scouts, 99

Brumble, H. David, professor, 15-16

buffalo, demise of, 34

Bureau of Indian Affairs: Carlos Montezuma and, 111-12; citizenship and, 108; control of, 13, 85-87, 104, 120; corruption of, 70-71, 91; Lakota and, 109; new generation of, 81; paternalism, 105; Society of American Indians' stance on, 110

Burke Act (1906): Luther Standing Bear and, 105-6; mixed-bloods and, 70; ramifications of, 75, 92

Camp Fire Girls, 99

Carlisle Indian School, 169n4

Carlson, David J., author, 50-51, 171n35, n36

Chomsky, Carol, professor: on Dakota Nation, 129-30; on war trials, 145

Christian idea of Brotherhood, 87

Christianity: Charles Eastman on American, 147, 152; Charles Eastman converts to, xiv; Charles Eastman on "Indian Religion" and, 45; Christian idea of Brotherhood, 87; influence of, 98;

Dakota Philosopher was designed by Will Powers at the Minnesota Historical Society Press and set in type by Allan Johnson at Phoenix Type, Appleton, Minnesota. The text type is Clifford, designed by Akira Kobayashi. The display type is Sumner Stone's Magma. Printed by Sheridan Books, Ann Arbor.

www.ingramcontent.com/pod-product-compliance
Lightning Source LLC
Jackson TN
JSHW020019141224
75386JS00025B/601